BEWARE OF AHL-BIDA

By Gregory Heary

Everyone knows the danger of sins but the most dangerous category of sins is bida or religious innovation, invention or heresy. Most sins are easy to identify but bida is disguised and misrepresented as guidance despite prophets labeling it as misguidance. Every form of Kufr or disbelief and Shirk or polytheism is a various type of bida. Whereas every type of bida is a major sin and some can result in unknowing apostasy whereby the person becomes a disbeliever without even intending it. This is because the methodology of bida is rooted in opposition to following prophetic teachings, with most done in the alleged name of goodness and guidance. The reason God sent prophets again and again to the world is not because creatures sinned but it was to eradicate the bida they had invented. Creatures will always sin and the door of repentance will remain open until their death or until specific signs of the Day of Judgment will come. Yet bida poisons the planet corrupting creeds and deeds. So never imagine God sent prophets merely to get people to stop sins alone. The primary mission of the prophets was to eradicate bida and eliminate false religious ideas and practices. Every single false religion is merely a form of bida by which creatures seek to worship through unlegislated illegal non-prophetically prescribed means. One danger of bida is that because it typically doesn't inspire guilt in its practitioners as other sins do, then they don't realize its sinfulness and persist. Some even become more addicted to bida than an ordinary sinner would be addicted to intoxicants and then they invite others to it. Then by inviting others to a religious invention which is invalid in the sight of God they are in essence calling to a different religion than the one preached by prophets. This is the very definition of combatting prophets and God and becoming an enemy of God and his prophets. An inviter to bida is an ally and soldier of the devil and most of them have no idea until they are dead that they were upon such an evil path.

Now there are two ways to explain bida. One way is to detail every single mistaken belief, speech or action known to mankind throughout all of history that is without prophetic origin.

This is not possible to do and even if it were done people would make more stuff up in the future making such a listing incomplete. The best way to explain bida is as the prophets of God did which is to say everything that has to do with religion that doesn't come with a divine prophetic stamp of approval or precedent is a bida. This is a much more effective easier method because as long as a person learns what the way to worship God is from the prophetic teachings then when they come across a bida, no matter what it is, they will be confused with the novelty and inquire for evidence just in case they were ignorant of a prophetic teaching. When no authentic prophetic evidence is presentable then it is known that this matter is one of heresy and it doesn't matter what type of heretical idea or practice it is, they all can be identified with this simple method.

Doing something the prophets didn't teach and opposing them for something else implies that you know better than God who taught the prophets. When it comes to any worship, or anything to do with religion, if it cannot be proven that the prophet did it or his companions, then it can't be accepted as a valid way to worship. Despite good intentions it's impossible to get closer to God doing something that God has not legislated or instructed to do.

- Good intention + Good action = Good deed
- Bad intention + Bad action = Bad deed
- Bad intention + Good action = Bad deed
- Good intention + Bad action = Bad deed

Everything one does must have a good sincere intention for the sake of Allah alone and the good action in our era is defined as that which is in accordance with the teachings of Allah's final prophet Muhammad peace be upon him. The test for bida in our era is to simply ask whether this idea, saying, or deed is proven to be taught by the prophet Muhammad? If not then it's undoubtedly an illegal religious invention.

So you don't have to be a learned scholar to recognize most bida. Although sometimes a scholar is needed to clarify because the people of bida cleverly use false evidence that may seem semi-legitimate in order to legitimize their ways rather than correctly abandoning them as they are commanded to do. For bida is linked in such a way to the prophetic religion as to seem nearly justified but upon scholastic examination it is utterly illegitimate despite how pious and good it may seem to the less informed. Yet typically a bida is easily recognizable if one scholastically approaches religion and religious life with the prophetic criteria regarding obedience and following nobody at all except for the prophet of their era. Bida as a rival religion seeks fuel in the form of followers since everybody always desires nearness to their deity. Whereas worship itself has a placebo effect that is pleasurable and addictive even if it is completely wrong and evil. People will always desire nearness to God through whatever they learn and who they learn religion from will drastically impact their personal beliefs, speech and practices. Since no prophets are on earth today the matter is dangerous because we have to learn from others in order to learn anything. Otherwise we'd be making ourselves into our own prophet as philosophers do by making stuff up as we go along. The sincere are eager to learn how to worship and many people are sincere in this desire. However ignorant sincerity leads to the sin of bida because lack of prophetic knowledge combined with an impatient desire to worship means usually people are willing to learn from whoever will teach them regardless of whether their teachers are upon the prophetic faith and methodology or not. Most people learn their first information about religion from their family. And many never bother to learn anything other than what their family taught them. So whether their family is right or wrong they gamble their entire afterlife based on what they were taught first. Then due to their prejudicial love for family they assume God must also feel the same way as they do, however God does not have such prejudicial emotions of unjust affection. Following your family faith is an accursed methodology even if by incident they happen to be correct because the blind-following of family, otherwise known as tribalism is an impermissible methodology. God sent prophets to teach us, not our families. If your family isn't following the prophetic teaching in one or another aspect it is a duty to follow the prophet in that regard and abandon the bida or sin of the family. The problem for many is that people fall in love with family more than they do with prophets so they are content with their religion being a family heirloom that dooms them because they feel that God must love their family because otherwise they wouldn't. Put simply God doesn't care what you think or feel about others when determining whether to love or hate them. Your opinion doesn't influence God at all. History is full of examples where prophetic teachings disrupted families and even family members of prophets themselves were doomed despite being family. Why were some family members of prophets damned to go to hell despite being blood relatives to prophets? Because of bida. So know that bida will doom you no matter who you are. God hates bida and its false rival prophets more than anything else. Whereas companionship comes with contagiousness of the ideas, manners and habits of your companion. Hence someone is typically always upon the religion of their friends or communal social circle. This brings us to the topic of this book. Being wary of the people of bida, known as Ahl-Bida though they label themselves otherwise.

God has commanded combatting bida, and essentially every creature who is upon other than what the genuine prophets authentically taught is upon bida. Yet there are two types of such people. One is someone who knows it and the other is someone who doesn't know it. Either way both are dangerous and contagious similar to how anyone infected with a plague virus can contaminate you whether they are aware of their illness or not. Those who know it are the worser type because they are without sincerity while the sincere fool is no less dangerous.

There are two different main categories of bida. There is a type that amounts to disbelief in the prophetic religion of Islam and a type of bida which does not amount to disbelief. The major type of bida can make one a disbeliever without the person knowing or intending to do so, while regarding the minor type of bida it doesn't automatically translate to disbelief if fallen into.

Despite open disbelief in the prophetic religion being a major crime and cause of sadness and destruction, that is far less of a threat to the prophetic religion than bida is. For disbelief will never triumph over the prophetic teachings, this is guaranteed. Yet bida sneaks into the prophetic nation without warning because of its hidden deceptive seemingly noble characteristics. Whereas the opposition and enmity a person of bida will display is far greater than the opposition and enmity a regular disbeliever or sinner will display for the prophetic faith and its followers. A sincere disbeliever will have the simple attitude of, we believe different things so someone is wrong, lets find out who and the fool must change or else. Whereas the innovator will come with slogans of goodness to dress up the teachings of the devil all the while making you think they are doing something good. All falsehood in a sense operates this way, by dressing up their devilishness, but when someone who believes in a legitimate prophet encounters a practitioner of bida that person is teaching them falsehood in the name of their prophet. Thereby this is worse than being a false prophet of a false religion because in actuality the proponents of bida are attributing falsehood to the truth by mixing the two and confusing people. Thus this type of combat is more dangerous than a typical disbeliever who desires 100% abolishment of the prophetic faith because people are willing to fight hard to defend themselves from a 100% defeat. Yet how many people put their life on the line for a mere 1% tenet of the 100% true prophetic faith. If 1% of the religion is compromised, it's very difficult to recognize and rectify with the same sense of urgency and importance one would have against an enemy preaching total annihilation. Yet all bida is a anti-prophetic poison that kills the religion transforming the body bit by bit until it is eventually a different faith altogether. However the process is gradual and painless and oftentimes guiltless and peaceful too. Thereby in an era without much military warfare that is labeled as explicitly religious, the way religions wage war is through peaceful infiltration of innovations or heretical inventions. Why? Because the person who practices bida is worshipping in a invalid method so when the time eventually comes for physical combative forced conversions, the person of innovation will have no true connection with the Creator from which to receive divine assistance. Thereby the person will be defeated even if they live a long natural life worshipping throughout it all. If no religious wars militarily take place the goal of Satan will be accomplished regardless. The goal of Satan is to distract creatures from worshipping God correctly as the prophets taught. If Satan must settle for someone worshipping the true God but doing so incorrectly upon a form of bida which is unacceptable to God then that is a huge win in his book because all that worship will count for nothing, that is if it's not counted as sinful. Plus since the person rarely repents from worshipping incorrectly then that person will be more sinful than the person who constantly sinned and repented throughout their life because this worshipper of bida constantly sinned without repenting.

These are just some of the negatives of bida that I have mentioned. We cannot list all the negatives of bida or every type. The point being that bida is a spiritually contagious disease that can nullify your deeds without warning. The more generations that pass from the prophetic generation the more likely you will encounter a person who claims to be upon the truth but in reality is a practitioner of bida. So therefore what will you do when you meet? The correct answer is to do what the prophets taught us to do in that situation. We can learn that from the inheritors of the prophets who inherited the knowledge of the prophets, otherwise known as the Scholars of the Salaf or pious predecessors.

Personally since becoming a Muslim after decades as a Christian many people ask me how my non-Muslim family treated my conversion or how my former friends reacted, or how my previous co-religionists reacted, or how the Government reacted. Each individual person reacts differently so I cannot generalize them as a group, yet in summary I endured boycotting, slander, permanent forbiddance from any type of communication, and even death threats from those who used to be upon the same falsehood as I was prior to Islam; while others simply ignore religious dialogue altogether hiding their enmity in disguise. Yet such opposition is expected from the ignorant allies of devils for such was how the prophets themselves were always treated by their non-Muslim contemporaries. Surprisingly though the most severe harm I have ever encountered since embracing Islam has not come from disbelieving non-Muslim relatives, former friends, former co-religionists or unislamic governments. The most harm I have endured since embracing Islam has come from people claiming to be Muslim themselves yet factually far from it. In other words, the most dangerous group for Muslims, particularly new or young Muslims, is the people of bida or ignorant/hypocritical Muslims preaching and practicing unislamic creeds, sayings or deeds. I have even been horrifically spiritually abused, hospitalized twice and medically inflicted with brain damage all through peaceful non-violent means by the practitioners of bida who have persecuted me in the name of protecting Islam and Muslims. Muslim exorcists have even diagnosed that magic was done to me by an innovator, after I sincerely friendlily tried to enlighten and educate him of his heretical error. Whereas the non-Muslim hospital doctors, who disbelieve in magic, say the non-violent emotional slander, ostracization and spiritual abuse combined with legal threats and actions which I endured from the stubborn innovator and "Islamic Society" caused such extreme stress that it caused brain damage that caused hospitalization rather than magic. So, there is a difference of opinion regarding how I got twice hospitalized. Yet both opinions agree and blame my former Muslim friend of three years and tajweed teacher who is a well-respected hafiz and khatib of the local masjid I used to attend and pray with 5 times a day, 35 times a week; oftentimes with just me and him to pray together. The two-faced individual even calls himself the innovative name of Khalilullah meaning friend of God, despite acting more devilish to me than any creature I personally ever met. Yet these people think and claim they have done well in their harm because of the power of bida to blind someone to their oppression and errors. I never thought that the most single arrogant, ignorant, dangerous, anti-islamic, cruelest person who inflicted the most harm on me out of anyone I know would be someone claiming to be a scholar of the prophetic Islamic faith who has even memorized the Book of Allah and taught me how to recite it. The tale itself is one that causes people to tear and console me when its details are told in full. It even took me three years, from 2014 to 2017 to realize the extremely heretical deviance of this creature and oppose it because it was apparently hidden to me for a while and I was less knowledgeable and naive. I thought this guy was the most pious person I knew and took him as my best living friend, but when I tried correcting a minor innovation privately and then eventually discovered his major innovations that amounted to disbelief, which I privately tried to correct, you would be surprised at the deception and devilishness such a person publicly claiming to be a religious leader would resort to in order to harm and ultimately expel me from their life and the community at large in order to maintain their deviancy, reputation and position. Wolves in sheeps' fleece act more mercifully to their prey than innovators and the ignorant who mistakenly follow such prayer leaders. I have met many deviant religious leaders in my life, one Christian priest I knew committed suicide, two other people I personally met even claimed to be prophets. Yet when all is accounted for in totality those creatures who pretend to be Muslims, while very convincingly hiding other than Islam, are truly deserving of the worst place in Hell as Allah has promised and prepared for them. Why is this? Because they are more dangerous and harmful than disbelievers are to Muslims, physically, emotionally, mentally and spiritually and in every single category of harm you will find innovators top the chart of evilness. And then they never repent because they think their harm is actually a good deed for them and take pride in their evil no matter who or what comes to them as evidence to guide them aright. Then they drag sincere Muslims into their crooked path of crime all the while such people sincerely think they are pleasing their Creator. However, unlike the regular deviant disbelievers openly outside the fold of Islam these creatures actually attribute themselves to Islam and thereby attempt to transform the prophetic faith and doom masses of less knowledgeable people who are sincere but less informed.

Not only does this apply to a personal and communal level but even politically on a national scale. In recent history the actions of the Scholastically labeled Khariji criminal Osama bin Laden caused nearly the whole world to invade Afghanistan in 2001 to dethrone the non-Khariji Sunni Islamic Emirate which ruled by nearly 100% Shariah law and replace it with a secular puppet democratic regime for 20 years causing the death of millions and triggering global prejudice, discrimination and enmity for Muslims that still has not subsided to this day. Then one of the Khariji prisoners of war during that war gave false testimony about being covertly influential in Iraq so America invaded that secular nation too 2 years after invading Afghanistan, which had previously fought two wars against deviant Shiite Iran. Thereupon America installed a Shiite democracy in Iraq that then led to the Khariji Al-Qaeda/ISIS fracture during the Syrian civil war, also started by innovators of a different type. Until now instead of the innovative Shiites being restrained to Iran they expanded to Iraq, Syria, Yemen and fortified their position in Lebanon. These are entire countries full of mischief and innovation, some are even ruled by innovation on a national scale. And this mainly happened because of a mistaken leniency showed by the Islamic Emirate of Afghanistan to a Khariji innovator bin Laden due to him having fought with them against the Atheist Soviet Union when they invaded Afghanistan in 1979. Logically most Muslims would assume since he fought with us against the non-Muslim enemies then he can't be that bad or harmful to us. Although history shows time and again the deviant "Muslims" upon bida are always more dangerous to Islam and Muslims than the non-Muslim disbelievers. Even during the American withdrawal from Afghanistan the Khariji group of ISIS attacked the kafirs in the airport despite being under covenant with the reestablished Islamic Emirate allowing them to board planes to withdraw. The Kharijites did this because they didn't want the kafir soldiers to leave and instead hoped that attacking them before they left for good would trigger the withdrawal to be reversed and the war would reignite so they might have a chance to fight more and try getting political power themselves. Likewise the medieval Crusades were triggered due to Shiite attacks on Christians mixed with lies from kuffar and the Mongol sacking of Baghdad was another plot of Shiite innovators. Innovators historically always incite the non-Muslims against us and then usually in one form or the other join them in their fight against Orthodox Fundamental prophetic Islam. The examples abound where whenever Islam suffered it was due to a chain reaction started by an innovator and leniency shown to the innovator by those unaware of their danger. So never take the masked motivations or claims of innovators at face value because if they are already known for opposing the prophetic guidance then they are not upon a path of goodness regardless of what they say they are up to. Afterall the civil war amongst the Sahabah occurred due to nothing other than the instigation of innovators against Uthman which led to his assassination, which was followed by the assassination of Ali by the Khawarij. Likewise no people other than Ahl-Bida has inflicted more harm on the Scholars of the Muslim nation nor the Muslims themselves. The mischief of innovation and innovators is unrivaled. Hence one must battle bida in a balanced way between extremes. Because there are ways to combat bida that go overzealous and ways that are negligent, both of which extremes are innovated methods of dealing with innovation. The balanced way is the prophetic path of justice as taught by the Sahabah and Salaf and those who follow them in creed, speech and deed.

The harm which was destined for me in my encounter with self-styled Sunni Muslims who in reality were innovators, led me to learn valuable lessons and strive to know what the students of the prophet Muhammad advised regarding how to interact with people of bida when one comes across the test of such a severe trial. While I probably did not need to share my own personal experience as much, I felt it important to stress the irreparable life-changing damage and soul dooming damage that an innovator and innovation can cause. Some may question if I was correct and rightly guided why did I suffer at the behest of a deviant? This is something Allah knows is a trial to distinguish the wicked from the good and test people, but personally I think it is because of my sins and most weightily the fact that I myself resorted to a innovated way of resolving the issue that only compounded the problem. So thus knowing something is an innovation while important for one's safety is not enough for total protection and victory in this world and the next. This is because if you combat a religious innovation with another religious innovation neither of which are taught by prophets, then you are similar to magicians who fight other magicians with magic. I met such a person who while tearfully repenting from magic told me they would henceforth only use magic to attack magicians. They failed to grasp that magic is forbidden sinful disbelief and evil only results in evil even if one intends good. Whereas Prophet Muhammad has condemned every bida as misguidance and every misguidance/bida as being doomed to the hellfire. Thus even if you think it is good, know that all bida is sinful and leads to hellfire and destruction of the religious affairs and the goodness of the world. So, I combatted a devil in human skin who was clearly in error farther from the truth than I was, but because of the innovative method I forbade evil in I got allegedly permanent brain damage that results in potentially life-lasting health changes which result in a harder life mixed with painful memories. Many evils are combatted with lesser evils and this is well known, yet the point is that bida is the greatest category of evil and Allah will not grant success to the innovator regardless of the situation even when they are less in the wrong than their opponent. As I wrote in my book "The Kufr of Christians and Jews", which incidentally is the Aqeedah dispute between me and my former friend turned enemy, *"It is better to have knowledge you don't need than need knowledge you don't have."*

This is because if you fail to learn the relevant wisdom before you need it then when the time of your trials arrive you will be unprepared and likely to fail miserably even if your faith survives semi-unscathed. Salvation only comes through following the prophets as they taught exactly based on the authentically proven information and not what is alleged in their names or seems to be in line with their teachings, nor what is popular in any particular locale. There is what God taught his prophets to teach us and then there is everything else, which is error. You can be following much of the prophetic teachings for a long time but any amount of religious innovation in your life will have consequences that are too great to bear and will make you regret such things more than ordinary major sins. Which ironically the innovator might think they are free from major sins not realizing bida is the greatest category of sins that exist.

Hence to promote safety from error as it pertains to bida and dealing with the people of innovation who are labeled as Ahl-Bida, I have collected Quran verses, Hadith from the Prophet Muhammad, and statements from the Sahabah and the Scholars of the Muslim nation regarding this ever increasingly relevant topic of being wary of the people of innovation or Ahl-Bida as innovated versions of Islam begin to outnumber the authentic prophetic version as time goes by, as has been prophesied.

Quranic Ayat about Ahl-Bida

Quran 1:6-7

ٱهْدِنَا ٱلصِّرَٰطَ ٱلْمُسْتَقِيمَ (٦) صِرَٰطَ ٱلَّذِينَ أَنْعَمْتَ عَلَيْهِمْ غَيْرِ ٱلْمَغْضُوبِ عَلَيْهِمْ وَلَا ٱلضَّآلِّينَ (٧)

Show us the straight path, (6) The path of those whom Thou hast favoured. Not (the path) of those who earn Thine anger nor of those who go astray. (7)

Quran 2:8-16

وَمِنَ ٱلنَّاسِ مَن يَقُولُ ءَامَنَّا بِٱللَّهِ وَبِٱلْيَوْمِ ٱلْأَخِرِ وَمَا هُم بِمُؤْمِنِينَ (٨) يُخَٰدِعُونَ ٱللَّهَ وَٱلَّذِينَ ءَامَنُوا۟ وَمَا يَخْدَعُونَ إِلَّآ أَنفُسَهُمْ وَمَا يَشْعُرُونَ (٩) فِى قُلُوبِهِم مَّرَضٌ فَزَادَهُمُ ٱللَّهُ مَرَضًا وَلَهُمْ عَذَابٌ أَلِيمٌۢ بِمَا كَانُوا۟ يَكْذِبُونَ (١٠) وَإِذَا قِيلَ لَهُمْ لَا تُفْسِدُوا۟ فِى ٱلْأَرْضِ قَالُوٓا۟ إِنَّمَا نَحْنُ مُصْلِحُونَ (١١) أَلَآ إِنَّهُمْ هُمُ ٱلْمُفْسِدُونَ وَلَٰكِن لَّا يَشْعُرُونَ (١٢) وَإِذَا قِيلَ لَهُمْ ءَامِنُوا۟ كَمَآ ءَامَنَ ٱلنَّاسُ قَالُوٓا۟ أَنُؤْمِنُ كَمَآ ءَامَنَ ٱلسُّفَهَآءُ أَلَآ إِنَّهُمْ هُمُ ٱلسُّفَهَآءُ وَلَٰكِن لَّا يَعْلَمُونَ (١٣) وَإِذَا لَقُوا۟ ٱلَّذِينَ ءَامَنُوا۟ قَالُوٓا۟ ءَامَنَّا وَإِذَا خَلَوْا۟ إِلَىٰ شَيَٰطِينِهِمْ قَالُوٓا۟ إِنَّا مَعَكُمْ إِنَّمَا نَحْنُ مُسْتَهْزِءُونَ (١٤) ٱللَّهُ يَسْتَهْزِئُ بِهِمْ وَيَمُدُّهُمْ فِى طُغْيَٰنِهِمْ يَعْمَهُونَ (١٥) أُو۟لَٰٓئِكَ ٱلَّذِينَ ٱشْتَرَوُا۟ ٱلضَّلَٰلَةَ بِٱلْهُدَىٰ فَمَا رَبِحَت تِّجَٰرَتُهُمْ وَمَا كَانُوا۟ مُهْتَدِينَ (١٦)

And of mankind, there are some (hypocrites) who say: "We believe in Allâh and the Last Day" while in fact they believe not. (8) They (think to) deceive Allâh and those who believe, while they only deceive themselves, and perceive (it) not! (9) In their hearts is a disease (of doubt and hypocrisy) and Allâh has increased their disease. A painful torment is theirs because they used to tell lies. (10) And when it is said to them: "Make not mischief on the earth," they say: "We are only peacemakers." (11) Verily! They are the ones who make mischief, but they perceive not. (12) And when it is said to them (hypocrites): "Believe as the people (followers of Muhammad, Al-Ansâr and Al-Muhajirûn) have believed," they say: "Shall we believe as the fools have believed?" Verily, they are the fools, but they know not (13) And when they meet those who believe, they say: "We believe," but when they are alone with their Shayâtin (devils - polytheists, hypocrites), they say: "Truly, we are with you; verily, we were but mocking." (14) Allâh mocks at them and gives them increase in their wrong-doings to wander blindly. (15) These are they who have purchased error for guidance, so their commerce was profitless. And they were not guided. (16)

Quran 2:26-27

۞ إِنَّ ٱللَّهَ لَا يَسْتَحْىِۦٓ أَن يَضْرِبَ مَثَلًا مَّا بَعُوضَةً فَمَا فَوْقَهَاۚ فَأَمَّا ٱلَّذِينَ ءَامَنُوا۟ فَيَعْلَمُونَ أَنَّهُ ٱلْحَقُّ مِن رَّبِّهِمْۖ وَأَمَّا ٱلَّذِينَ كَفَرُوا۟ فَيَقُولُونَ مَاذَآ أَرَادَ ٱللَّهُ بِهَٰذَا مَثَلًاۘ يُضِلُّ بِهِۦ كَثِيرًا وَيَهْدِى بِهِۦ كَثِيرًاۚ وَمَا يُضِلُّ

بِهِۦ إِلَّا ٱلْفَٰسِقِينَ (٢٦) ٱلَّذِينَ يَنقُضُونَ عَهْدَ ٱللَّهِ مِنۢ بَعْدِ مِيثَٰقِهِۦ وَيَقْطَعُونَ مَآ أَمَرَ ٱللَّهُ بِهِۦٓ أَن يُوصَلَ وَيُفْسِدُونَ فِى ٱلْأَرْضِ أُو۟لَٰٓئِكَ هُمُ ٱلْخَٰسِرُونَ (٢٧)

Verily, Allâh is not ashamed to set forth a parable even of a mosquito or so much more when it is bigger (or less when it is smaller) than it. And as for those who believe, they know that it is the Truth from their Lord, but as for those who disbelieve, they say: "What did Allâh intend by this parable?" By it He misleads many, and many He guides thereby. And He misleads thereby only those who are Al-Fâsiqûn (the rebellious, disobedient to Allâh). (26) Those who break Allâh's Covenant after ratifying it, and sever what Allâh has ordered to be joined (as regards Allâh's religion of Islâmic Monotheism, and to practise its legal laws on the earth and also as regards keeping good relations with kith and kin), and do mischief on earth, it is they who are the losers. (27)

Quran 2:58-59

وَإِذْ قُلْنَا ٱدْخُلُوا۟ هَٰذِهِ ٱلْقَرْيَةَ فَكُلُوا۟ مِنْهَا حَيْثُ شِئْتُمْ رَغَدًا وَٱدْخُلُوا۟ ٱلْبَابَ سُجَّدًا وَقُولُوا۟ حِطَّةٌ نَّغْفِرْ لَكُمْ خَطَٰيَٰكُمْ وَسَنَزِيدُ ٱلْمُحْسِنِينَ (٥٨) فَبَدَّلَ ٱلَّذِينَ ظَلَمُوا۟ قَوْلًا غَيْرَ ٱلَّذِى قِيلَ لَهُمْ فَأَنزَلْنَا عَلَى ٱلَّذِينَ ظَلَمُوا۟ رِجْزًا مِّنَ ٱلسَّمَآءِ بِمَا كَانُوا۟ يَفْسُقُونَ (٥٩)

And (remember) when We said: "Enter this town (Jerusalem) and eat bountifully therein with pleasure and delight wherever you wish, and enter the gate in prostration (or bowing with humility) and say: 'Forgive us,' and We shall forgive you your sins and shall increase (reward) for the good-doers." (58) But those who did wrong changed the word from that which had been told to them for another, so We sent upon the wrong-doers Rijzan (a punishment) from the heaven because of their rebelling against Allâh's Obedience. (59)

Quran 2:63-66

وَإِذْ أَخَذْنَا مِيثَـٰقَكُمْ وَرَفَعْنَا فَوْقَكُمُ ٱلطُّورَ خُذُوا۟ مَآ ءَاتَيْنَـٰكُم بِقُوَّةٍ وَٱذْكُرُوا۟ مَا فِيهِ لَعَلَّكُمْ تَتَّقُونَ (٦٣) ثُمَّ تَوَلَّيْتُم مِّنۢ بَعْدِ ذَٰلِكَ ۖ فَلَوْلَا فَضْلُ ٱللَّهِ عَلَيْكُمْ وَرَحْمَتُهُۥ لَكُنتُم مِّنَ ٱلْخَـٰسِرِينَ (٦٤) وَلَقَدْ عَلِمْتُمُ ٱلَّذِينَ ٱعْتَدَوْا۟ مِنكُمْ فِى ٱلسَّبْتِ فَقُلْنَا لَهُمْ كُونُوا۟ قِرَدَةً خَـٰسِـِٔينَ (٦٥) فَجَعَلْنَـٰهَا نَكَـٰلًا لِّمَا بَيْنَ يَدَيْهَا وَمَا خَلْفَهَا وَمَوْعِظَةً لِّلْمُتَّقِينَ (٦٦)

And (O Children of Israel, remember) when We took your covenant and We raised above you the Mount (saying): "Hold fast to that which We have given you, and remember that which is therein so that you may become Al-Muttaqûn (the pious). (63) Then after that you turned away. Had it not been for the Grace and Mercy of Allâh upon you, indeed you *would have been among the losers. (64) And indeed you knew those amongst you who transgressed in the matter of the Sabbath (i.e. Saturday). We said to them: "Be you monkeys, despised and rejected." (65) So We made this punishment an example to their own and to succeeding generations and a lesson to those who are Al-Muttaqûn (the pious). (66)*

Quran 2:75-79

﴿ أَفَتَطْمَعُونَ أَن يُؤْمِنُوا لَكُمْ وَقَدْ كَانَ فَرِيقٌ مِّنْهُمْ يَسْمَعُونَ كَلَٰمَ ٱللَّهِ ثُمَّ يُحَرِّفُونَهُۥ مِنۢ بَعْدِ مَا عَقَلُوهُ وَهُمْ يَعْلَمُونَ (٧٥) وَإِذَا لَقُوا۟ ٱلَّذِينَ ءَامَنُوا۟ قَالُوٓا۟ ءَامَنَّا وَإِذَا خَلَا بَعْضُهُمْ إِلَىٰ بَعْضٍ قَالُوٓا۟ أَتُحَدِّثُونَهُم بِمَا فَتَحَ ٱللَّهُ عَلَيْكُمْ لِيُحَآجُّوكُم بِهِۦ عِندَ رَبِّكُمْ ۚ أَفَلَا تَعْقِلُونَ (٧٦) أَوَلَا يَعْلَمُونَ أَنَّ ٱللَّهَ يَعْلَمُ مَا يُسِرُّونَ وَمَا يُعْلِنُونَ (٧٧) وَمِنْهُمْ أُمِّيُّونَ لَا يَعْلَمُونَ ٱلْكِتَٰبَ إِلَّآ أَمَانِىَّ وَإِنْ هُمْ إِلَّا يَظُنُّونَ (٧٨) فَوَيْلٌ لِّلَّذِينَ يَكْتُبُونَ ٱلْكِتَٰبَ بِأَيْدِيهِمْ ثُمَّ يَقُولُونَ هَٰذَا مِنْ عِندِ ٱللَّهِ لِيَشْتَرُوا۟ بِهِۦ ثَمَنًا قَلِيلًا ۖ فَوَيْلٌ لَّهُم مِّمَّا كَتَبَتْ أَيْدِيهِمْ وَوَيْلٌ لَّهُم مِّمَّا يَكْسِبُونَ (٧٩)

Do you (faithful believers) covet that they will believe in your religion inspite of the fact that a party of them (Jewish rabbis) used to hear the Word of Allâh [the Taurât (Torah)], then they used to change it knowingly after they understood it? (75) And when they (Jews) meet those who believe (Muslims), they say, "We believe", but when they meet one another in private, they say, "Shall you (Jews) tell them (Muslims) what Allâh has revealed to you [Jews, about the description and the qualities of Prophet Muhammad, that which are written in the Taurât (Torah)], that they (Muslims) may argue with you (Jews) about it before your Lord?" Have you (Jews) then no understanding? (76) Know they (Jews) not that Allâh knows what they conceal and what they reveal? (77) And there are among them (Jews) unlettered people, who know not the Book, but they trust upon false desires and they but guess. (78) Then woe to those who write the Book with their own hands and then say, "This is from Allâh," to purchase with it a little price! Woe to them for what their hands have written and woe to them for that they earn thereby. (79)

Quran 2:101

وَلَمَّا جَآءَهُمْ رَسُولٌ مِّنْ عِندِ ٱللَّهِ مُصَدِّقٌ لِّمَا مَعَهُمْ نَبَذَ فَرِيقٌ مِّنَ ٱلَّذِينَ أُوتُوا۟ ٱلْكِتَٰبَ كِتَٰبَ ٱللَّهِ وَرَآءَ ظُهُورِهِمْ كَأَنَّهُمْ لَا يَعْلَمُونَ (١٠١)

And when there came to them a Messenger from Allâh (i.e. Muhammad Peace be upon him) confirming what was with them, a party of those who were given the Scripture threw away the Book of Allâh behind their backs as if they did not know! (101)

Quran 2:118-121

وَقَالَ ٱلَّذِينَ لَا يَعْلَمُونَ لَوْلَا يُكَلِّمُنَا ٱللَّهُ أَوْ تَأْتِينَآ ءَايَةٌ ۗ كَذَٰلِكَ قَالَ ٱلَّذِينَ مِن قَبْلِهِم مِّثْلَ قَوْلِهِمْ ۘ تَشَٰبَهَتْ قُلُوبُهُمْ ۗ قَدْ بَيَّنَّا ٱلْءَايَٰتِ لِقَوْمٍ يُوقِنُونَ (١١٨) إِنَّآ أَرْسَلْنَٰكَ بِٱلْحَقِّ بَشِيرًا وَنَذِيرًا ۖ وَلَا تُسْـَٔلُ عَنْ أَصْحَٰبِ ٱلْجَحِيمِ (١١٩) وَلَن تَرْضَىٰ عَنكَ ٱلْيَهُودُ وَلَا ٱلنَّصَٰرَىٰ حَتَّىٰ تَتَّبِعَ مِلَّتَهُمْ ۗ قُلْ إِنَّ هُدَى ٱللَّهِ هُوَ ٱلْهُدَىٰ ۗ وَلَئِنِ ٱتَّبَعْتَ أَهْوَآءَهُم بَعْدَ ٱلَّذِى جَآءَكَ مِنَ ٱلْعِلْمِ ۙ مَا لَكَ مِنَ ٱللَّهِ مِن وَلِىٍّ وَلَا نَصِيرٍ (١٢٠) ٱلَّذِينَ ءَاتَيْنَٰهُمُ ٱلْكِتَٰبَ يَتْلُونَهُۥ حَقَّ تِلَاوَتِهِۦٓ أُو۟لَٰٓئِكَ يُؤْمِنُونَ بِهِۦ ۗ وَمَن يَكْفُرْ بِهِۦ فَأُو۟لَٰٓئِكَ هُمُ ٱلْخَٰسِرُونَ (١٢١)

And those who have no knowledge say: "Why does not Allâh speak to us (face to face) or why does not a sign come to us?" So said the people before them words of similar import. Their hearts are alike, We have indeed made plain the signs for people who believe with certainty. (118) Verily, We have sent you (O Muhammad) with the truth (Islâm), a bringer of glad tidings (for those who believe in what you brought, that they will enter Paradise) and a warner (for those who disbelieve in what you brought, they will enter the Hell-fire). And you will not be asked about the dwellers of the blazing Fire. (119) Never will the Jews nor the Christians be pleased with you (O Muhammad) till you follow their religion. Say: "Verily, the Guidance of Allâh (i.e. Islâmic Monotheism) that is the (only) Guidance. And if you (O Muhammad) were to follow their (Jews and

Christians) desires after what you have received of Knowledge (i.e. the Qur'ân), then you would have against Allâh neither any Walî (protector or guardian) nor any helper. (120) Those (who embraced Islâm from Banî Israel) to whom We gave the Book [the Taurât (Torah)] [or those (Muhammad's companions) to whom We have given the Book (the Qur'ân)] recite it (i.e. obey its orders and follow its teachings) as it should be recited (i.e. followed), they are the ones that believe therein. And whoso disbelieves in it (the Qur'ân), those are they who are the losers. (121)

Quran 2:137

فَإِنْ ءَامَنُواْ بِمِثْلِ مَآ ءَامَنتُم بِهِۦ فَقَدِ ٱهْتَدَواْ وَّإِن تَوَلَّوْاْ فَإِنَّمَا هُمْ فِى شِقَاقٍ فَسَيَكْفِيكَهُمُ ٱللَّهُ وَهُوَ ٱلسَّمِيعُ ٱلْعَلِيمُ (١٣٧)

So if they believe in the like of that which you believe, then they are rightly guided, but if they turn away, then they are only in opposition. So Allâh will suffice for you against them. And He is the All-Hearer, the All-Knower. (137)

Quran 2:147

ٱلْحَقُّ مِن رَّبِّكَ فَلَا تَكُونَنَّ مِنَ ٱلْمُمْتَرِينَ (١٤٧)

(This is) the truth from your Lord. So be you not one of those who doubt. (147)

Quran 2:165-170

وَمِنَ ٱلنَّاسِ مَن يَتَّخِذُ مِن دُونِ ٱللَّهِ أَندَادًا يُحِبُّونَهُمْ كَحُبِّ ٱللَّهِ ۖ وَٱلَّذِينَ ءَامَنُوٓا۟ أَشَدُّ حُبًّا لِّلَّهِ ۗ وَلَوْ يَرَى ٱلَّذِينَ ظَلَمُوٓا۟ إِذْ يَرَوْنَ ٱلْعَذَابَ أَنَّ ٱلْقُوَّةَ لِلَّهِ جَمِيعًا وَأَنَّ ٱللَّهَ شَدِيدُ ٱلْعَذَابِ (١٦٥) إِذْ تَبَرَّأَ ٱلَّذِينَ ٱتُّبِعُوا۟ مِنَ ٱلَّذِينَ ٱتَّبَعُوا۟ وَرَأَوُا۟ ٱلْعَذَابَ وَتَقَطَّعَتْ بِهِمُ ٱلْأَسْبَابُ (١٦٦) وَقَالَ ٱلَّذِينَ ٱتَّبَعُوا۟ لَوْ أَنَّ لَنَا كَرَّةً فَنَتَبَرَّأَ مِنْهُمْ كَمَا تَبَرَّءُوا۟ مِنَّا ۗ كَذَٰلِكَ يُرِيهِمُ ٱللَّهُ أَعْمَٰلَهُمْ حَسَرَٰتٍ عَلَيْهِمْ ۖ وَمَا هُم بِخَٰرِجِينَ مِنَ ٱلنَّارِ (١٦٧) يَٰٓأَيُّهَا ٱلنَّاسُ كُلُوا۟ مِمَّا فِى ٱلْأَرْضِ حَلَٰلًا طَيِّبًا وَلَا تَتَّبِعُوا۟ خُطُوَٰتِ ٱلشَّيْطَٰنِ ۚ إِنَّهُۥ لَكُمْ عَدُوٌّ مُّبِينٌ (١٦٨) إِنَّمَا يَأْمُرُكُم بِٱلسُّوٓءِ وَٱلْفَحْشَآءِ وَأَن تَقُولُوا۟ عَلَى ٱللَّهِ مَا لَا تَعْلَمُونَ (١٦٩) وَإِذَا قِيلَ لَهُمُ ٱتَّبِعُوا۟ مَآ أَنزَلَ ٱللَّهُ قَالُوا۟ بَلْ نَتَّبِعُ مَآ أَلْفَيْنَا عَلَيْهِ ءَابَآءَنَآ ۗ أَوَلَوْ كَانَ ءَابَآؤُهُمْ لَا يَعْقِلُونَ شَيْـًٔا وَلَا يَهْتَدُونَ (١٧٠)

And of mankind are some who take (for worship) others besides Allâh as rivals (to Allâh). They love them as they love Allâh. But those who believe, love Allâh more (than anything else). If only, those who do wrong could see, when they will see the torment, that all power belongs to Allâh and that Allâh is Severe in punishment. (165) When those who were followed, disown (declare themselves innocent of) those who followed (them), and they see the torment, then all their relations will be cut off from them. (166) And those who followed will say: "If only we had one more chance to return (to the worldly life), we would disown (declare ourselves as innocent from) them as they have disowned (declared themselves as innocent from) us." Thus Allâh will show them their deeds as regrets for them. And they will never get out of the Fire. (167) O mankind! Eat of that which is lawful and good on the earth, and follow not the footsteps of Shaitân (Satan). Verily, he is to you an open enemy: (168) He [Shaitân (Satan)] commands you only what is evil and Fahshâ (sinful), and that you should say against Allâh what you know not. (169) When it is said to them: "Follow what Allâh has sent down." They say: "Nay! We shall follow what we found our fathers following." (Would they do that!) even though their fathers did not understand anything nor were they guided? (170)

Quran 2:174-176

إِنَّ ٱلَّذِينَ يَكْتُمُونَ مَآ أَنزَلَ ٱللَّهُ مِنَ ٱلْكِتَٰبِ وَيَشْتَرُونَ بِهِۦ ثَمَنًا قَلِيلًا أُو۟لَٰٓئِكَ مَا يَأْكُلُونَ فِى بُطُونِهِمْ إِلَّا ٱلنَّارَ وَلَا يُكَلِّمُهُمُ ٱللَّهُ يَوْمَ ٱلْقِيَٰمَةِ وَلَا يُزَكِّيهِمْ وَلَهُمْ عَذَابٌ أَلِيمٌ (١٧٤) أُو۟لَٰٓئِكَ ٱلَّذِينَ ٱشْتَرَوُا۟ ٱلضَّلَٰلَةَ بِٱلْهُدَىٰ وَٱلْعَذَابَ بِٱلْمَغْفِرَةِ فَمَآ أَصْبَرَهُمْ عَلَى ٱلنَّارِ (١٧٥) ذَٰلِكَ بِأَنَّ ٱللَّهَ نَزَّلَ ٱلْكِتَٰبَ بِٱلْحَقِّ وَإِنَّ ٱلَّذِينَ ٱخْتَلَفُوا۟ فِى ٱلْكِتَٰبِ لَفِى شِقَاقٍۭ بَعِيدٍ (١٧٦)

Verily, those who conceal what Allâh has sent down of the Book, and purchase a small gain therewith (of worldly things), they eat into their bellies nothing but fire. Allâh will not speak to them on the Day of Resurrection, nor purify them, and theirs will be a painful torment. (174) Those are they who have purchased error at the price of Guidance, and torment at the price of Forgiveness. So how bold they are (for evil deeds which will push them) to the Fire. (175) That is because Allâh has sent down the Book (the Qur'ân) in truth. And verily, those who disputed as regards the Book are far away in opposition. (176)

Quran 2:204-208

وَمِنَ ٱلنَّاسِ مَن يُعْجِبُكَ قَوْلُهُۥ فِى ٱلْحَيَوٰةِ ٱلدُّنْيَا وَيُشْهِدُ ٱللَّهَ عَلَىٰ مَا فِى قَلْبِهِۦ وَهُوَ أَلَدُّ ٱلْخِصَامِ (٢٠٤) وَإِذَا تَوَلَّىٰ سَعَىٰ فِى ٱلْأَرْضِ لِيُفْسِدَ فِيهَا وَيُهْلِكَ ٱلْحَرْثَ وَٱلنَّسْلَ وَٱللَّهُ لَا يُحِبُّ ٱلْفَسَادَ (٢٠٥) وَإِذَا قِيلَ لَهُ ٱتَّقِ ٱللَّهَ أَخَذَتْهُ ٱلْعِزَّةُ بِٱلْإِثْمِ فَحَسْبُهُۥ جَهَنَّمُ وَلَبِئْسَ ٱلْمِهَادُ (٢٠٦) وَمِنَ ٱلنَّاسِ مَن يَشْرِى نَفْسَهُ ٱبْتِغَآءَ مَرْضَاتِ ٱللَّهِ وَٱللَّهُ رَءُوفٌۢ بِٱلْعِبَادِ (٢٠٧) يَـٰٓأَيُّهَا ٱلَّذِينَ ءَامَنُوا۟ ٱدْخُلُوا۟ فِى ٱلسِّلْمِ كَآفَّةً وَلَا تَتَّبِعُوا۟ خُطُوَٰتِ ٱلشَّيْطَـٰنِ إِنَّهُۥ لَكُمْ عَدُوٌّ مُّبِينٌ (٢٠٨)

And of mankind there is he whose speech may please you (O Muhammad), in this worldly life, and he calls Allâh to witness as to that which is in his heart, yet he is the most quarrelsome of the opponents. (204) And when he turns away (from you "O

Muhammad "), his effort in the land is to make mischief therein and to destroy the crops and the cattle, and Allâh likes not mischief. (205) And when it is said to him, "Fear Allâh", he is led by arrogance to (more) crime. So enough for him is Hell, and worst indeed is that place to rest! (206) And of mankind is he who would sell himself, seeking the Pleasure of Allâh. And Allâh is full of Kindness to (His) slaves. (207) O you who believe! Enter perfectly in Islâm (by obeying all the rules and regulations of the Islâmic religion) and follow not the footsteps of Shaitân (Satan). Verily! He is to you a plain enemy. (208)

Quran 2:211-213

سَلْ بَنِىٓ إِسْرَٰٓءِيلَ كَمْ ءَاتَيْنَٰهُم مِّنْ ءَايَةٍۭ بَيِّنَةٍۢ ۗ وَمَن يُبَدِّلْ نِعْمَةَ ٱللَّهِ مِنۢ بَعْدِ مَا جَآءَتْهُ فَإِنَّ ٱللَّهَ شَدِيدُ ٱلْعِقَابِ (٢١١) زُيِّنَ لِلَّذِينَ كَفَرُوا۟ ٱلْحَيَوٰةُ ٱلدُّنْيَا وَيَسْخَرُونَ مِنَ ٱلَّذِينَ ءَامَنُوا۟ ۘ وَٱلَّذِينَ ٱتَّقَوْا۟ فَوْقَهُمْ يَوْمَ ٱلْقِيَٰمَةِ ۗ وَٱللَّهُ يَرْزُقُ مَن يَشَآءُ بِغَيْرِ حِسَابٍۢ (٢١٢) كَانَ ٱلنَّاسُ أُمَّةًۭ وَٰحِدَةًۭ فَبَعَثَ ٱللَّهُ ٱلنَّبِيِّـۧنَ مُبَشِّرِينَ وَمُنذِرِينَ وَأَنزَلَ مَعَهُمُ ٱلْكِتَٰبَ بِٱلْحَقِّ لِيَحْكُمَ بَيْنَ ٱلنَّاسِ فِيمَا ٱخْتَلَفُوا۟ فِيهِ ۚ وَمَا ٱخْتَلَفَ فِيهِ إِلَّا ٱلَّذِينَ أُوتُوهُ مِنۢ بَعْدِ مَا جَآءَتْهُمُ ٱلْبَيِّنَٰتُ بَغْيًۢا بَيْنَهُمْ ۖ فَهَدَى ٱللَّهُ ٱلَّذِينَ ءَامَنُوا۟ لِمَا ٱخْتَلَفُوا۟ فِيهِ مِنَ ٱلْحَقِّ بِإِذْنِهِۦ ۗ وَٱللَّهُ يَهْدِى مَن يَشَآءُ إِلَىٰ صِرَٰطٍۢ مُّسْتَقِيمٍۢ (٢١٣)

Ask the Children of Israel how many clear Ayât (proofs, evidences, verses, lessons, signs, revelations, etc.) We gave them. And whoever changes Allâh's Favour after it had come to him, [e.g. renounces the

Religion of Allâh (Islâm) and accepts Kufr (disbelief),] then surely, Allâh is Severe in punishment. (211) Beautified is the life of this world for those who disbelieve, and they mock at those who believe. But those who obey Allâh's Orders and keep away from what He has forbidden, will be above them on the Day of Resurrection. And Allâh gives (of His Bounty, Blessings, Favours, Honours, on the Day of Resurrection) to whom He wills without limit. (212) Mankind were one community and Allâh sent Prophets with glad tidings and warnings, and with them He sent the Scripture in truth to judge between people in matters wherein they differed. And only those to whom (the Scripture) was given differed concerning it after clear proofs had come unto them through hatred, one to another. Then Allâh by His Leave guided those who believed to the truth of that wherein they differed. And Allâh guides whom He wills to a Straight Path. (213)

Quran 3:19-20

إِنَّ ٱلدِّينَ عِندَ ٱللَّهِ ٱلْإِسْلَٰمُ ۗ وَمَا ٱخْتَلَفَ ٱلَّذِينَ أُوتُوا۟ ٱلْكِتَٰبَ إِلَّا مِنۢ بَعْدِ مَا جَآءَهُمُ ٱلْعِلْمُ بَغْيًۢا بَيْنَهُمْ ۗ وَمَن يَكْفُرْ بِـَٔايَٰتِ ٱللَّهِ فَإِنَّ ٱللَّهَ سَرِيعُ ٱلْحِسَابِ (١٩) فَإِنْ حَآجُّوكَ فَقُلْ أَسْلَمْتُ وَجْهِىَ لِلَّهِ وَمَنِ ٱتَّبَعَنِ ۗ وَقُل لِّلَّذِينَ أُوتُوا۟ ٱلْكِتَٰبَ وَٱلْأُمِّيِّـۧنَ ءَأَسْلَمْتُمْ ۚ فَإِنْ أَسْلَمُوا۟ فَقَدِ ٱهْتَدَوا۟ ۖ وَّإِن تَوَلَّوْا۟ فَإِنَّمَا عَلَيْكَ ٱلْبَلَٰغُ ۗ وَٱللَّهُ بَصِيرٌۢ بِٱلْعِبَادِ (٢٠)

Truly, the religion with Allâh is Islâm. Those who were given the Scripture (Jews and Christians) did not differ except, out of mutual jealousy, after knowledge had come to them. And whoever disbelieves in the Ayât (proofs, evidences, verses, signs, revelations, etc.) of Allâh, then surely, Allâh is Swift in calling to account. (19) So if they dispute with you (Muhammad) say: "I have submitted myself to Allâh (in Islâm), and (so have) those who follow me." And say to those who were given the Scripture (Jews and Christians) and to those who are illiterates (Arab pagans): "Do you (also) submit yourselves (to Allâh in Islâm)?" If they do, they are rightly guided; but if they turn away, your duty is only to convey the Message; and Allâh is All-Seer of (His) slaves (20)

Quran 3:23-24

أَلَمْ تَرَ إِلَى ٱلَّذِينَ أُوتُواْ نَصِيبًا مِّنَ ٱلْكِتَٰبِ يُدْعَوْنَ إِلَىٰ كِتَٰبِ ٱللَّهِ لِيَحْكُمَ بَيْنَهُمْ ثُمَّ يَتَوَلَّىٰ فَرِيقٌ مِّنْهُمْ وَهُم مُّعْرِضُونَ (٢٣) ذَٰلِكَ بِأَنَّهُمْ قَالُواْ لَن تَمَسَّنَا ٱلنَّارُ إِلَّآ أَيَّامًا مَّعْدُودَٰتٍ وَغَرَّهُمْ فِى دِينِهِم مَّا كَانُواْ يَفْتَرُونَ (٢٤)

Have you not seen those who have been given a portion of the Scripture? They are being invited to the Book of Allâh to settle their dispute, then a party of them turn away, and they are averse. (23) This is because they say: "The Fire shall not touch us but for a number of days." And that which they used to invent regarding their religion has deceived them. (24)

Quran 3:28

لَّا يَتَّخِذِ ٱلْمُؤْمِنُونَ ٱلْكَٰفِرِينَ أَوْلِيَآءَ مِن دُونِ ٱلْمُؤْمِنِينَ ۖ وَمَن يَفْعَلْ ذَٰلِكَ فَلَيْسَ مِنَ ٱللَّهِ فِى شَىْءٍ إِلَّآ أَن تَتَّقُواْ مِنْهُمْ تُقَىٰةً ۗ وَيُحَذِّرُكُمُ ٱللَّهُ نَفْسَهُۥ ۗ وَإِلَى ٱللَّهِ ٱلْمَصِيرُ (٢٨)

Let not the believers take the disbelievers as Auliyâ (supporters, helpers) instead of the believers, and whoever does that will never be helped by Allâh in any way, except if you indeed fear a danger from them. And Allâh warns you against Himself (His Punishment), and to Allâh is the final return. (28)

Quran 3:31-32

قُلْ إِن كُنتُمْ تُحِبُّونَ ٱللَّهَ فَٱتَّبِعُونِى يُحْبِبْكُمُ ٱللَّهُ وَيَغْفِرْ لَكُمْ ذُنُوبَكُمْ ۗ وَٱللَّهُ غَفُورٌ رَّحِيمٌ (٣١) قُلْ أَطِيعُواْ ٱللَّهَ وَٱلرَّسُولَ ۖ فَإِن تَوَلَّوْاْ فَإِنَّ ٱللَّهَ لَا يُحِبُّ ٱلْكَٰفِرِينَ (٣٢)

Say (O Muhammad to mankind): "If you (really) love Allâh then follow me (i.e. accept Islâmic Monotheism, follow the Qur'ân and the Sunnah), Allâh will love you and forgive you your sins. And Allâh is Oft-Forgiving, Most Merciful." (31) Say (O

Muhammad): "Obey Allâh and the Messenger (Muhammad)." But if they turn away, then Allâh does not like the disbelievers (32)

Quran 3:63

فَإِن تَوَلَّوْاْ فَإِنَّ ٱللَّهَ عَلِيمٌۢ بِٱلْمُفْسِدِينَ (٦٣)

And if they turn away (and do not accept these true proofs and evidences), then surely, Allâh is All-Aware of those who do mischief. (63)

Quran 3:82-83

فَمَن تَوَلَّىٰ بَعْدَ ذَٰلِكَ فَأُوْلَٰٓئِكَ هُمُ ٱلْفَٰسِقُونَ (٨٢) أَفَغَيْرَ دِينِ ٱللَّهِ يَبْغُونَ وَلَهُۥٓ أَسْلَمَ مَن فِى ٱلسَّمَٰوَٰتِ وَٱلْأَرْضِ طَوْعًا وَكَرْهًا وَإِلَيْهِ يُرْجَعُونَ (٨٣)

Then whoever turns away after this, they are the Fâsiqûn (rebellious: those who turn away from Allâh's Obedience). (82) Do they seek other than the religion of Allâh (the true Islâmic Monotheism worshipping none but Allâh Alone), while to Him submitted all creatures in the heavens and the earth, willingly or unwillingly. And to Him shall they all be returned. (83)

Quran 3:85-91

وَمَن يَبْتَغِ غَيْرَ ٱلْإِسْلَٰمِ دِينًا فَلَن يُقْبَلَ مِنْهُ وَهُوَ فِى ٱلْأَخِرَةِ مِنَ ٱلْخَٰسِرِينَ (٨٥) كَيْفَ يَهْدِى ٱللَّهُ قَوْمًا كَفَرُوا۟ بَعْدَ إِيمَٰنِهِمْ وَشَهِدُوٓا۟ أَنَّ ٱلرَّسُولَ حَقٌّ وَجَآءَهُمُ ٱلْبَيِّنَٰتُ وَٱللَّهُ لَا يَهْدِى ٱلْقَوْمَ ٱلظَّٰلِمِينَ (٨٦) أُو۟لَٰٓئِكَ جَزَآؤُهُمْ أَنَّ عَلَيْهِمْ لَعْنَةَ ٱللَّهِ وَٱلْمَلَٰٓئِكَةِ وَٱلنَّاسِ أَجْمَعِينَ (٨٧) خَٰلِدِينَ فِيهَا لَا يُخَفَّفُ عَنْهُمُ ٱلْعَذَابُ وَلَا هُمْ يُنظَرُونَ (٨٨) إِلَّا ٱلَّذِينَ تَابُوا۟ مِنۢ بَعْدِ ذَٰلِكَ وَأَصْلَحُوا۟ فَإِنَّ ٱللَّهَ غَفُورٌ رَّحِيمٌ (٨٩) إِنَّ ٱلَّذِينَ كَفَرُوا۟ بَعْدَ إِيمَٰنِهِمْ ثُمَّ ٱزْدَادُوا۟ كُفْرًا لَّن تُقْبَلَ تَوْبَتُهُمْ وَأُو۟لَٰٓئِكَ هُمُ ٱلضَّآلُّونَ (٩٠) إِنَّ ٱلَّذِينَ كَفَرُوا۟ وَمَاتُوا۟ وَهُمْ كُفَّارٌ فَلَن يُقْبَلَ مِنْ أَحَدِهِم مِّلْءُ ٱلْأَرْضِ ذَهَبًا وَلَوِ ٱفْتَدَىٰ بِهِۦٓ أُو۟لَٰٓئِكَ لَهُمْ عَذَابٌ أَلِيمٌ وَمَا لَهُم مِّن نَّٰصِرِينَ (٩١)

And whoever seeks a religion other than Islâm, it will never be accepted of him, and in the Hereafter he will be one of the losers. (85) How shall Allâh guide a people who disbelieved after their belief and after they bore witness that the Messenger (Muhammad) is true and after clear proofs had come unto them? And Allâh guides not the people who are Zâlimûn (polytheists and wrong-doers). (86) They are those whose recompense is that on them (rests) the Curse of Allâh, of the angels, and of all mankind. (87) They will abide therein (Hell). Neither will their torment be lightened, nor will it be delayed or postponed (for a while). (88) Except for those who repent after that and do righteous deeds. Verily, Allâh is Oft-Forgiving, Most Merciful. (89) Verily, those who disbelieved after their Belief and then went on *increasing in their disbelief (i.e. disbelief in the Qur'ân and in Prophet Muhammad) - never will their repentance be accepted [because they repent only by their tongues and not from their hearts]. And they are those who are astray. (90) Verily, those who disbelieved, and died while they were disbelievers, the (whole) earth full of gold will not be accepted from anyone of them even if they offered it as a ransom. For them is a painful torment and they will have no helpers. (91)*

Quran 3:100-107

يَـٰٓأَيُّهَا ٱلَّذِينَ ءَامَنُوٓاْ إِن تُطِيعُواْ فَرِيقًا مِّنَ ٱلَّذِينَ أُوتُواْ ٱلۡكِتَـٰبَ يَرُدُّوكُم بَعۡدَ إِيمَـٰنِكُمۡ كَـٰفِرِينَ (١٠٠) وَكَيۡفَ تَكۡفُرُونَ وَأَنتُمۡ تُتۡلَىٰ عَلَيۡكُمۡ ءَايَـٰتُ ٱللَّهِ وَفِيكُمۡ رَسُولُهُۥ ۗ وَمَن يَعۡتَصِم بِٱللَّهِ فَقَدۡ هُدِىَ إِلَىٰ صِرَٰطٍ مُّسۡتَقِيمٍ (١٠١) يَـٰٓأَيُّهَا ٱلَّذِينَ ءَامَنُواْ ٱتَّقُواْ ٱللَّهَ حَقَّ تُقَاتِهِۦ وَلَا تَمُوتُنَّ إِلَّا وَأَنتُم مُّسۡلِمُونَ (١٠٢) وَٱعۡتَصِمُواْ بِحَبۡلِ ٱللَّهِ جَمِيعًا وَلَا تَفَرَّقُواْ ۚ وَٱذۡكُرُواْ نِعۡمَتَ ٱللَّهِ عَلَيۡكُمۡ إِذۡ كُنتُمۡ أَعۡدَآءً فَأَلَّفَ بَيۡنَ قُلُوبِكُمۡ فَأَصۡبَحۡتُم بِنِعۡمَتِهِۦٓ إِخۡوَٰنًا وَكُنتُمۡ عَلَىٰ شَفَا حُفۡرَةٍ مِّنَ ٱلنَّارِ فَأَنقَذَكُم مِّنۡهَا ۗ كَذَٰلِكَ يُبَيِّنُ ٱللَّهُ لَكُمۡ ءَايَـٰتِهِۦ لَعَلَّكُمۡ تَهۡتَدُونَ (١٠٣) وَلۡتَكُن مِّنكُمۡ أُمَّةٌ يَدۡعُونَ إِلَى ٱلۡخَيۡرِ وَيَأۡمُرُونَ بِٱلۡمَعۡرُوفِ وَيَنۡهَوۡنَ عَنِ ٱلۡمُنكَرِ ۚ وَأُوْلَـٰٓئِكَ هُمُ ٱلۡمُفۡلِحُونَ (١٠٤) وَلَا تَكُونُواْ كَٱلَّذِينَ تَفَرَّقُواْ وَٱخۡتَلَفُواْ مِنۢ بَعۡدِ مَا جَآءَهُمُ ٱلۡبَيِّنَـٰتُ ۚ وَأُوْلَـٰٓئِكَ لَهُمۡ عَذَابٌ عَظِيمٌ (١٠٥) يَوۡمَ تَبۡيَضُّ وُجُوهٌ وَتَسۡوَدُّ وُجُوهٌ ۚ فَأَمَّا ٱلَّذِينَ ٱسۡوَدَّتۡ وُجُوهُهُمۡ أَكَفَرۡتُم بَعۡدَ إِيمَـٰنِكُمۡ فَذُوقُواْ ٱلۡعَذَابَ بِمَا كُنتُمۡ تَكۡفُرُونَ (١٠٦) وَأَمَّا ٱلَّذِينَ ٱبۡيَضَّتۡ وُجُوهُهُمۡ فَفِى رَحۡمَةِ ٱللَّهِ هُمۡ فِيهَا خَـٰلِدُونَ (١٠٧)

O you who believe! If you obey a group of those who were given the Scripture (Jews and Christians), they would (indeed) render you disbelievers after you have believed! (100) And how would you disbelieve, while unto you are recited the Verses of Allâh, and among you is His Messenger (Muhammad)? And whoever holds firmly to Allâh, (i.e. follows Islâm — Allâh's Religion, and obeys all that Allâh has ordered, practically), then he is indeed guided to a Right Path. (101) O you who believe! Fear Allâh (by doing all that He has ordered and by abstaining from all that He has forbidden) as He should be feared. [Obey Him, be thankful to Him, and remember Him always], and die not except in a state of Islâm [as Muslims (with complete submission to Allâh)]. (102) And hold fast, all of you together, to the Rope of Allâh (i.e. this Qur'ân), and be not divided among yourselves, and remember Allâh's Favour on you, for you were enemies one to another but He joined your hearts together, so that, by His Grace, you became brethren (in Islâmic Faith), and you were on the brink of a pit of Fire, and He saved you from it. Thus Allâh makes His Ayât (proofs, evidences, verses, lessons, signs, revelations, etc.,) clear to you, that you may be guided. (103) Let there arise out of you a group of people inviting to all that is good (Islâm), enjoining Al-Ma'rûf (i.e. Islâmic Monotheism and all that Islâm orders one to do) and forbidding Al-Munkar (polytheism and disbelief and all that Islâm has forbidden). And it is they who are the successful. (104) And be not as those who divided and differed among themselves after the clear proofs had come to them. It is they for whom there is an awful torment. (105) On the Day (i.e. the Day of Resurrection) when some faces will become white and some faces will become black; as for those whose faces will become black (to them will be said): "Did you reject Faith after accepting it? Then taste the torment (in Hell) for rejecting Faith." (106) And for those whose faces will become white, they will be in Allâh's Mercy (Paradise), therein they shall dwell forever. (107)

Quran 3:177-179

إِنَّ ٱلَّذِينَ ٱشْتَرَوُاْ ٱلْكُفْرَ بِٱلْإِيمَـٰنِ لَن يَضُرُّواْ ٱللَّهَ شَيْـًٔا وَلَهُمْ عَذَابٌ أَلِيمٌ (١٧٧) وَلَا يَحْسَبَنَّ ٱلَّذِينَ كَفَرُوٓاْ أَنَّمَا نُمْلِى لَهُمْ خَيْرٌ لِّأَنفُسِهِمْ إِنَّمَا نُمْلِى لَهُمْ لِيَزْدَادُوٓاْ إِثْمًا وَلَهُمْ عَذَابٌ مُّهِينٌ (١٧٨) مَّا كَانَ ٱللَّهُ لِيَذَرَ ٱلْمُؤْمِنِينَ عَلَىٰ مَآ أَنتُمْ عَلَيْهِ حَتَّىٰ يَمِيزَ ٱلْخَبِيثَ مِنَ ٱلطَّيِّبِ وَمَا كَانَ ٱللَّهُ لِيُطْلِعَكُمْ عَلَى ٱلْغَيْبِ وَلَـٰكِنَّ ٱللَّهَ يَجْتَبِى مِن رُّسُلِهِۦ مَن يَشَآءُ فَـَٔامِنُواْ بِٱللَّهِ وَرُسُلِهِۦ وَإِن تُؤْمِنُواْ وَتَتَّقُواْ فَلَكُمْ أَجْرٌ عَظِيمٌ (١٧٩)

Verily, those who purchase disbelief at the price of Faith, not the least harm will they do to Allâh. For them, there is a painful torment. (177) And let not the disbelievers think that Our postponing of their punishment is good for them. We postpone the punishment only so that they may increase in sinfulness. And for them is a disgracing torment. (178) Allâh will not leave the believers in the state in which you are now, until He distinguishes the wicked from the good. Nor will Allâh disclose to you the secrets of the Ghaib (unseen), but Allâh chooses of His Messengers whom He wills. So believe in Allâh and His Messengers. And if you believe and fear Allâh, then for you there is a great reward. (179)

Quran 4:13-14

تِلْكَ حُدُودُ ٱللَّهِ وَمَن يُطِعِ ٱللَّهَ وَرَسُولَهُ يُدْخِلْهُ جَنَّـٰتٍ تَجْرِى مِن تَحْتِهَا ٱلْأَنْهَـٰرُ خَـٰلِدِينَ فِيهَا وَذَٰلِكَ ٱلْفَوْزُ ٱلْعَظِيمُ (١٣) وَمَن يَعْصِ ٱللَّهَ وَرَسُولَهُ وَيَتَعَدَّ حُدُودَهُ يُدْخِلْهُ نَارًا خَـٰلِدًا فِيهَا وَلَهُ عَذَابٌ مُّهِينٌ (١٤)

These are the limits (set by) Allâh (or ordainments as regards laws of inheritance), and whosoever obeys Allâh and His Messenger (Muhammad) will be admitted to Gardens under which rivers flow (in Paradise), to abide therein, and that will be the great success. (13) And whosoever disobeys Allâh and His Messenger (Muhammad), and transgresses His limits, He will cast him into the Fire, to abide therein; and he shall have a disgraceful torment. (14)

Quran 4:17-18

إِنَّمَا ٱلتَّوْبَةُ عَلَى ٱللَّهِ لِلَّذِينَ يَعْمَلُونَ ٱلسُّوٓءَ بِجَهَٰلَةٍ ثُمَّ يَتُوبُونَ مِن قَرِيبٍ فَأُو۟لَٰٓئِكَ يَتُوبُ ٱللَّهُ عَلَيْهِمْ وَكَانَ ٱللَّهُ عَلِيمًا حَكِيمًا (١٧) وَلَيْسَتِ ٱلتَّوْبَةُ لِلَّذِينَ يَعْمَلُونَ ٱلسَّيِّـَٔاتِ حَتَّىٰٓ إِذَا حَضَرَ أَحَدَهُمُ ٱلْمَوْتُ قَالَ إِنِّى تُبْتُ ٱلْـَٰٔنَ وَلَا ٱلَّذِينَ يَمُوتُونَ وَهُمْ كُفَّارٌ أُو۟لَٰٓئِكَ أَعْتَدْنَا لَهُمْ عَذَابًا أَلِيمًا (١٨)

Allâh accepts only the repentance of those who do evil in ignorance and foolishness and repent soon afterwards; it is they whom Allâh will forgive and Allâh is Ever All¬Knower, All¬Wise. (17) And of no effect is the repentance of those who continue to do evil deeds until death faces one of them and he says: "Now I repent;" nor of those who die while they are disbelievers. For them We have prepared a painful torment. (18)

Quran 4:27

وَٱللَّهُ يُرِيدُ أَن يَتُوبَ عَلَيْكُمْ وَيُرِيدُ ٱلَّذِينَ يَتَّبِعُونَ ٱلشَّهَوَٰتِ أَن تَمِيلُوا۟ مَيْلًا عَظِيمًا (٢٧)

Allâh wishes to accept your repentance, but those who follow their lusts, wish that you (believers) should deviate tremendously away (from the Right Path). (27)

Quran 4:60-65

أَلَمْ تَرَ إِلَى ٱلَّذِينَ يَزْعُمُونَ أَنَّهُمْ ءَامَنُواْ بِمَآ أُنزِلَ إِلَيْكَ وَمَآ أُنزِلَ مِن قَبْلِكَ يُرِيدُونَ أَن يَتَحَاكَمُوٓاْ إِلَى ٱلطَّٰغُوتِ وَقَدْ أُمِرُوٓاْ أَن يَكْفُرُواْ بِهِۦ وَيُرِيدُ ٱلشَّيْطَٰنُ أَن يُضِلَّهُمْ ضَلَٰلًۢا بَعِيدًا (٦٠) وَإِذَا قِيلَ لَهُمْ تَعَالَوْاْ إِلَىٰ مَآ أَنزَلَ ٱللَّهُ وَإِلَى ٱلرَّسُولِ رَأَيْتَ ٱلْمُنَٰفِقِينَ يَصُدُّونَ عَنكَ صُدُودًا (٦١) فَكَيْفَ إِذَآ أَصَٰبَتْهُم مُّصِيبَةٌۢ بِمَا قَدَّمَتْ أَيْدِيهِمْ ثُمَّ جَآءُوكَ يَحْلِفُونَ بِٱللَّهِ إِنْ أَرَدْنَآ إِلَّآ إِحْسَٰنًا وَتَوْفِيقًا (٦٢) أُوْلَٰٓئِكَ ٱلَّذِينَ يَعْلَمُ ٱللَّهُ مَا فِى قُلُوبِهِمْ فَأَعْرِضْ عَنْهُمْ وَعِظْهُمْ وَقُل لَّهُمْ فِىٓ أَنفُسِهِمْ قَوْلًۢا بَلِيغًا (٦٣) وَمَآ أَرْسَلْنَا مِن رَّسُولٍ إِلَّا لِيُطَاعَ بِإِذْنِ ٱللَّهِ وَلَوْ أَنَّهُمْ إِذ ظَّلَمُوٓاْ أَنفُسَهُمْ جَآءُوكَ فَٱسْتَغْفَرُواْ ٱللَّهَ وَٱسْتَغْفَرَ لَهُمُ ٱلرَّسُولُ لَوَجَدُواْ ٱللَّهَ تَوَّابًا رَّحِيمًا (٦٤) فَلَا وَرَبِّكَ لَا يُؤْمِنُونَ حَتَّىٰ يُحَكِّمُوكَ فِيمَا شَجَرَ بَيْنَهُمْ ثُمَّ لَا يَجِدُواْ فِىٓ أَنفُسِهِمْ حَرَجًا مِّمَّا قَضَيْتَ وَيُسَلِّمُواْ تَسْلِيمًا (٦٥)

Have you seen those (hyprocrites) who claim that they believe in that which has been sent down to you, and that which was sent down before you, and they wish to go for judgement (in their disputes) to the Tâghût (false judges) while they have been ordered to reject them. But Shaitân (Satan) wishes to lead them far astray. (60) And when it is said to them: "Come to what Allâh has sent down and to the Messenger (Muhammad)," you (Muhammad) see the hypocrites turn away from you (Muhammad) with aversion (61) How then, when a catastrophe befalls them because of what their hands have sent forth, they come to you swearing by Allâh, "We meant no more than goodwill and conciliation!" (62) They (hypocrites) are those of whom Allâh knows what is in their hearts; so turn aside from them (do not punish them) but admonish them, and speak to them an effective word (i.e. to believe in Allâh, worship Him, obey Him, and be afraid of Him) to reach their innerselves (63) We sent no Messenger, but to be obeyed by Allâh's Leave. If they (hypocrites), when they had been unjust to themselves, had come to you (Muhammad) and begged Allâh's Forgiveness, and the Messenger had begged forgiveness for them: indeed, they would have found Allâh All-Forgiving (One Who forgives and accepts repentance), Most Merciful. (64) But no, by your Lord, they can have no Faith, until they make you (O Muhammad) judge in all disputes between them, and find in themselves no resistance against your decisions, and accept (them) with full submission. (65)

Quran 4:80-83

مَّن يُطِعِ ٱلرَّسُولَ فَقَدْ أَطَاعَ ٱللَّهَ وَمَن تَوَلَّىٰ فَمَا أَرْسَلْنَٰكَ عَلَيْهِمْ حَفِيظًا (٨٠) وَيَقُولُونَ طَاعَةٌ فَإِذَا بَرَزُوا۟ مِنْ عِندِكَ بَيَّتَ طَآئِفَةٌ مِّنْهُمْ غَيْرَ ٱلَّذِى تَقُولُ وَٱللَّهُ يَكْتُبُ مَا يُبَيِّتُونَ فَأَعْرِضْ عَنْهُمْ وَتَوَكَّلْ عَلَى ٱللَّهِ وَكَفَىٰ بِٱللَّهِ وَكِيلًا (٨١) أَفَلَا يَتَدَبَّرُونَ ٱلْقُرْءَانَ وَلَوْ كَانَ مِنْ عِندِ غَيْرِ ٱللَّهِ لَوَجَدُوا۟

فِيهِ ٱخْتِلَٰفًا كَثِيرًا (٨٢) وَإِذَا جَآءَهُمْ أَمْرٌ مِّنَ ٱلْأَمْنِ أَوِ ٱلْخَوْفِ أَذَاعُوا۟ بِهِۦ ۖ وَلَوْ رَدُّوهُ إِلَى ٱلرَّسُولِ وَإِلَىٰٓ أُو۟لِى ٱلْأَمْرِ مِنْهُمْ لَعَلِمَهُ ٱلَّذِينَ يَسْتَنۢبِطُونَهُۥ مِنْهُمْ ۗ وَلَوْلَا فَضْلُ ٱللَّهِ عَلَيْكُمْ وَرَحْمَتُهُۥ لَٱتَّبَعْتُمُ ٱلشَّيْطَٰنَ إِلَّا قَلِيلًا (٨٣)

He who obeys the Messenger (Muhammad), has indeed obeyed Allâh, but he who turns away, then we have not sent you (O Muhammad) as a watcher over them. (80) They say: "We are obedient," but when they leave you (Muhammad), a section of them spend all night in planning other than what you say. But Allâh records their nightly (plots). So turn aside from them (do not punish them), and put your trust in Allâh. And Allâh is Ever All¬Sufficient as a Disposer of affairs. (81) Do they not then consider the Qur'ân carefully? Had it been from other than Allâh, they would surely have found therein many contradictions. (82) When there comes to them some matter touching (public) safety or fear, they make it known (among the people), if only they had referred it to the Messenger or to those charged with authority among them, the proper investigators would have understood it from them (directly). Had it not been for the Grace and Mercy of Allâh upon you, you would have followed Shaitân (Satan), save a few of you. (83)

Quran 4:85

مَّن يَشْفَعْ شَفَٰعَةً حَسَنَةً يَكُن لَّهُۥ نَصِيبٌ مِّنْهَا ۖ وَمَن يَشْفَعْ شَفَٰعَةً سَيِّئَةً يَكُن لَّهُۥ كِفْلٌ مِّنْهَا ۗ وَكَانَ ٱللَّهُ عَلَىٰ كُلِّ شَىْءٍ مُّقِيتًا (٨٥)

Whosoever intercedes for a good cause will have the reward thereof, and whosoever intercedes for an evil cause will have a share in its burden. And Allâh is Ever All-Able to do (and also an All-Witness to) everything. (85)

Quran 4:88-91

۞ فَمَا لَكُمْ فِى ٱلْمُنَٰفِقِينَ فِئَتَيْنِ وَٱللَّهُ أَرْكَسَهُم بِمَا كَسَبُوٓا۟ ۚ أَتُرِيدُونَ أَن تَهْدُوا۟ مَنْ أَضَلَّ ٱللَّهُ ۖ وَمَن يُضْلِلِ ٱللَّهُ فَلَن تَجِدَ لَهُۥ سَبِيلًا (٨٨) وَدُّوا۟ لَوْ تَكْفُرُونَ كَمَا كَفَرُوا۟ فَتَكُونُونَ سَوَآءً ۖ فَلَا تَتَّخِذُوا۟ مِنْهُمْ أَوْلِيَآءَ حَتَّىٰ يُهَاجِرُوا۟ فِى سَبِيلِ ٱللَّهِ ۚ فَإِن تَوَلَّوْا۟ فَخُذُوهُمْ وَٱقْتُلُوهُمْ حَيْثُ وَجَدتُّمُوهُمْ ۖ وَلَا تَتَّخِذُوا۟ مِنْهُمْ وَلِيًّا وَلَا نَصِيرًا (٨٩) إِلَّا ٱلَّذِينَ يَصِلُونَ إِلَىٰ قَوْمٍۭ بَيْنَكُمْ وَبَيْنَهُم مِّيثَٰقٌ أَوْ جَآءُوكُمْ حَصِرَتْ صُدُورُهُمْ أَن يُقَٰتِلُوكُمْ أَوْ يُقَٰتِلُوا۟ قَوْمَهُمْ ۚ وَلَوْ شَآءَ ٱللَّهُ لَسَلَّطَهُمْ عَلَيْكُمْ فَلَقَٰتَلُوكُمْ ۚ فَإِنِ ٱعْتَزَلُوكُمْ فَلَمْ يُقَٰتِلُوكُمْ وَأَلْقَوْا۟ إِلَيْكُمُ ٱلسَّلَمَ فَمَا جَعَلَ ٱللَّهُ لَكُمْ عَلَيْهِمْ سَبِيلًا (٩٠) سَتَجِدُونَ ءَاخَرِينَ يُرِيدُونَ أَن يَأْمَنُوكُمْ وَيَأْمَنُوا۟ قَوْمَهُمْ كُلَّ مَا رُدُّوٓا۟ إِلَى ٱلْفِتْنَةِ أُرْكِسُوا۟ فِيهَا ۚ فَإِن لَّمْ يَعْتَزِلُوكُمْ وَيُلْقُوٓا۟ إِلَيْكُمُ ٱلسَّلَمَ وَيَكُفُّوٓا۟ أَيْدِيَهُمْ فَخُذُوهُمْ وَٱقْتُلُوهُمْ حَيْثُ ثَقِفْتُمُوهُمْ ۚ وَأُو۟لَٰٓئِكُمْ جَعَلْنَا لَكُمْ عَلَيْهِمْ سُلْطَٰنًا مُّبِينًا (٩١)

Then what is the matter with you that you are divided into two parties about the hypocrites? Allâh has cast them back (to disbelief) because of what they have earned. Do you want to guide him whom Allâh *has made to go astray? And he whom Allâh has made to go astray, you will never find for him any way (of guidance). (88) They wish that you reject Faith, as they have rejected (Faith), and thus that you all become equal (like one another). So take not Auliyâ' (protectors or friends) from them, till they emigrate in the Way of Allâh (to Muhammad). But if they turn back (from Islâm), take (hold of) them and kill them wherever you find them, and take neither Auliyâ' (protectors or friends) nor helpers from them. (89) Except those who join a group, between you and whom there is a treaty (of peace), or those who approach you with their breasts restraining from fighting you as well as fighting their own people. Had Allâh willed, indeed He would have given them power over you, and they would have fought you. So if they withdraw from you, and fight not against you, and offer you peace, then Allâh has opened no way for you against them. (90) You will find others that wish to have security from you and security from their people. Every time they are sent back to temptation, they yield thereto. If they withdraw not from you, nor offer you peace, nor restrain their hands, take (hold of) them and kill them wherever you find them. In* their case, We have provided you with a clear warrant against them. (91)

Quran 4:105-113

إِنَّآ أَنزَلْنَآ إِلَيْكَ ٱلْكِتَٰبَ بِٱلْحَقِّ لِتَحْكُمَ بَيْنَ ٱلنَّاسِ بِمَآ أَرَىٰكَ ٱللَّهُ وَلَا تَكُن لِّلْخَآئِنِينَ خَصِيمًا (١٠٥) وَٱسْتَغْفِرِ ٱللَّهَ إِنَّ ٱللَّهَ كَانَ غَفُورًا رَّحِيمًا (١٠٦) وَلَا تُجَٰدِلْ عَنِ ٱلَّذِينَ يَخْتَانُونَ أَنفُسَهُمْ إِنَّ ٱللَّهَ لَا يُحِبُّ مَن كَانَ خَوَّانًا أَثِيمًا (١٠٧) يَسْتَخْفُونَ مِنَ ٱلنَّاسِ وَلَا يَسْتَخْفُونَ مِنَ ٱللَّهِ وَهُوَ مَعَهُمْ إِذْ يُبَيِّتُونَ مَا لَا يَرْضَىٰ مِنَ ٱلْقَوْلِ وَكَانَ ٱللَّهُ بِمَا يَعْمَلُونَ مُحِيطًا (١٠٨) هَٰٓأَنتُمْ هَٰٓؤُلَآءِ جَٰدَلْتُمْ عَنْهُمْ فِى ٱلْحَيَوٰةِ ٱلدُّنْيَا فَمَن يُجَٰدِلُ ٱللَّهَ عَنْهُمْ يَوْمَ ٱلْقِيَٰمَةِ أَم مَّن يَكُونُ عَلَيْهِمْ وَكِيلًا (١٠٩) وَمَن يَعْمَلْ سُوٓءًا أَوْ يَظْلِمْ نَفْسَهُۥ ثُمَّ يَسْتَغْفِرِ ٱللَّهَ يَجِدِ ٱللَّهَ غَفُورًا رَّحِيمًا (١١٠) وَمَن يَكْسِبْ إِثْمًا فَإِنَّمَا يَكْسِبُهُۥ عَلَىٰ نَفْسِهِۦ وَكَانَ ٱللَّهُ عَلِيمًا حَكِيمًا (١١١) وَمَن يَكْسِبْ خَطِيٓـَٔةً أَوْ إِثْمًا ثُمَّ يَرْمِ بِهِۦ بَرِيٓـًٔا فَقَدِ ٱحْتَمَلَ بُهْتَٰنًا وَإِثْمًا مُّبِينًا (١١٢) وَلَوْلَا فَضْلُ ٱللَّهِ عَلَيْكَ وَرَحْمَتُهُۥ لَهَمَّت طَّآئِفَةٌ مِّنْهُمْ أَن يُضِلُّوكَ وَمَا يُضِلُّونَ إِلَّآ أَنفُسَهُمْ وَمَا يَضُرُّونَكَ مِن شَىْءٍ وَأَنزَلَ ٱللَّهُ عَلَيْكَ ٱلْكِتَٰبَ وَٱلْحِكْمَةَ وَعَلَّمَكَ مَا لَمْ تَكُن تَعْلَمُ وَكَانَ فَضْلُ ٱللَّهِ عَلَيْكَ عَظِيمًا (١١٣)

Surely, We have sent down to you (O Muhammad) the Book (this Qur'ân) in truth that you might judge between men by that which Allâh has shown you (i.e. has taught you through Divine Revelation), so be not a pleader for the treacherous. (105) And seek the Forgiveness of Allâh, certainly, Allâh is Ever Oft¬Forgiving, Most Merciful (106) And argue not on behalf of those who deceive themselves. Verily,

Allâh does not like anyone who is a betrayer of his trust, and sinner. (107) They may hide (their crimes) from men, but they cannot hide (them) from Allâh, for He is with them (by His Knowledge), when they plot by night in words that He does not approve, And Allâh ever encompasses what they do. (108) Lo! You are those who have argued for them in the life of this world, but who will argue for them on the Day of Resurrection against Allâh, or who will then be their defender? (109) And whoever does evil or wrongs himself but afterwards seeks Allâh's Forgiveness, he will find Allâh Oft¬Forgiving, Most Merciful. (110) And whoever earns sin, he earns it only against himself. And Allâh is Ever All-Knowing, All-Wise. (111) And whoever earns a fault or a sin and then throws it on to someone innocent, he has indeed burdened himself with falsehood and a manifest sin. (112) Had not the Grace of Allâh and His Mercy been upon you (O Muhammad), a party of them would certainly have made a decision to mislead you, but (in fact) they mislead none except their own selves, and no harm can they do to you in the least. Allâh has sent down to you the Book (The Qur'ân), and Al¬Hikmah (Islâmic laws, knowledge of legal and illegal things i.e. the Prophet's Sunnah), and taught you that which you knew not. And Ever Great is the Grace of Allâh unto you (O Muhammad) (113)

Quran 4:115

وَمَن يُشَاقِقِ ٱلرَّسُولَ مِنۢ بَعْدِ مَا تَبَيَّنَ لَهُ ٱلْهُدَىٰ وَيَتَّبِعْ غَيْرَ سَبِيلِ ٱلْمُؤْمِنِينَ نُوَلِّهِۦ مَا تَوَلَّىٰ وَنُصْلِهِۦ جَهَنَّمَ ۖ وَسَآءَتْ مَصِيرًا (١١٥)

And whoever contradicts and opposes the Messenger (Muhammad) after the right path has been shown clearly to him, and follows other than the believers' way. We shall keep him in the path he has chosen, and burn him in Hell - what an evil destination. (115)

Quran 4:118-120

لَّعَنَهُ ٱللَّهُ ۘ وَقَالَ لَأَتَّخِذَنَّ مِنْ عِبَادِكَ نَصِيبًا مَّفْرُوضًا (١١٨) وَلَأُضِلَّنَّهُمْ وَلَأُمَنِّيَنَّهُمْ وَلَـَٔامُرَنَّهُمْ فَلَيُبَتِّكُنَّ ءَاذَانَ ٱلْأَنْعَٰمِ وَلَـَٔامُرَنَّهُمْ فَلَيُغَيِّرُنَّ خَلْقَ ٱللَّهِ ۚ وَمَن يَتَّخِذِ ٱلشَّيْطَٰنَ وَلِيًّا مِّن دُونِ ٱللَّهِ فَقَدْ خَسِرَ خُسْرَانًا مُّبِينًا (١١٩) يَعِدُهُمْ وَيُمَنِّيهِمْ ۖ وَمَا يَعِدُهُمُ ٱلشَّيْطَٰنُ إِلَّا غُرُورًا (١٢٠)

Allâh cursed him. And he [Shaitân (Satan)] said: "I will take an appointed portion of your slaves; (118) Verily, I will mislead them, and surely, I will arouse in them false desires; and certainly, I will order them to slit the ears of cattle, and indeed I will order them to change the nature created by Allâh." And whoever takes Shaitân (Satan) as a Walî (protector or helper) instead of Allâh, has surely suffered a manifest loss. (119) He [Shaitan (Satan)] makes promises to them, and arouses in them false desires; and Shaitan's (Satan) promises are nothing but deceptions. (120)

Quan 4:137-146

إِنَّ ٱلَّذِينَ ءَامَنُواْ ثُمَّ كَفَرُواْ ثُمَّ ءَامَنُواْ ثُمَّ كَفَرُواْ ثُمَّ ٱزْدَادُواْ كُفْرًا لَّمْ يَكُنِ ٱللَّهُ لِيَغْفِرَ لَهُمْ وَلَا لِيَهْدِيَهُمْ سَبِيلًۢا (١٣٧) بَشِّرِ ٱلْمُنَٰفِقِينَ بِأَنَّ لَهُمْ عَذَابًا أَلِيمًا (١٣٨) ٱلَّذِينَ يَتَّخِذُونَ ٱلْكَٰفِرِينَ أَوْلِيَآءَ مِن دُونِ ٱلْمُؤْمِنِينَ ۚ أَيَبْتَغُونَ عِندَهُمُ ٱلْعِزَّةَ فَإِنَّ ٱلْعِزَّةَ لِلَّهِ جَمِيعًا (١٣٩) وَقَدْ نَزَّلَ عَلَيْكُمْ فِى ٱلْكِتَٰبِ أَنْ إِذَا سَمِعْتُمْ ءَايَٰتِ ٱللَّهِ يُكْفَرُ بِهَا وَيُسْتَهْزَأُ بِهَا فَلَا تَقْعُدُواْ مَعَهُمْ حَتَّىٰ يَخُوضُواْ فِى حَدِيثٍ غَيْرِهِۦٓ ۚ إِنَّكُمْ إِذًا مِّثْلُهُمْ ۗ إِنَّ ٱللَّهَ جَامِعُ ٱلْمُنَٰفِقِينَ وَٱلْكَٰفِرِينَ فِى جَهَنَّمَ جَمِيعًا (١٤٠) ٱلَّذِينَ يَتَرَبَّصُونَ بِكُمْ فَإِن كَانَ لَكُمْ فَتْحٌ مِّنَ ٱللَّهِ قَالُوٓاْ أَلَمْ نَكُن مَّعَكُمْ وَإِن كَانَ لِلْكَٰفِرِينَ نَصِيبٌ قَالُوٓاْ أَلَمْ نَسْتَحْوِذْ عَلَيْكُمْ وَنَمْنَعْكُم مِّنَ ٱلْمُؤْمِنِينَ ۚ فَٱللَّهُ يَحْكُمُ بَيْنَكُمْ يَوْمَ ٱلْقِيَٰمَةِ ۗ وَلَن يَجْعَلَ ٱللَّهُ لِلْكَٰفِرِينَ عَلَى ٱلْمُؤْمِنِينَ سَبِيلًا (١٤١) إِنَّ ٱلْمُنَٰفِقِينَ يُخَٰدِعُونَ ٱللَّهَ وَهُوَ خَٰدِعُهُمْ وَإِذَا قَامُوٓاْ إِلَى ٱلصَّلَوٰةِ قَامُواْ كُسَالَىٰ يُرَآءُونَ ٱلنَّاسَ وَلَا يَذْكُرُونَ ٱللَّهَ إِلَّا قَلِيلًا (١٤٢) مُّذَبْذَبِينَ بَيْنَ ذَٰلِكَ لَآ إِلَىٰ هَٰٓؤُلَآءِ وَلَآ إِلَىٰ هَٰٓؤُلَآءِ ۚ وَمَن يُضْلِلِ ٱللَّهُ فَلَن تَجِدَ لَهُۥ سَبِيلًا (١٤٣) يَٰٓأَيُّهَا ٱلَّذِينَ ءَامَنُواْ لَا تَتَّخِذُواْ ٱلْكَٰفِرِينَ أَوْلِيَآءَ مِن دُونِ ٱلْمُؤْمِنِينَ ۚ أَتُرِيدُونَ أَن تَجْعَلُواْ لِلَّهِ عَلَيْكُمْ سُلْطَٰنًا مُّبِينًا (١٤٤) إِنَّ ٱلْمُنَٰفِقِينَ فِى ٱلدَّرْكِ ٱلْأَسْفَلِ مِنَ ٱلنَّارِ وَلَن تَجِدَ لَهُمْ نَصِيرًا (١٤٥) إِلَّا ٱلَّذِينَ تَابُواْ وَأَصْلَحُواْ وَٱعْتَصَمُواْ بِٱللَّهِ وَأَخْلَصُواْ دِينَهُمْ لِلَّهِ فَأُوْلَٰٓئِكَ مَعَ ٱلْمُؤْمِنِينَ ۖ وَسَوْفَ يُؤْتِ ٱللَّهُ ٱلْمُؤْمِنِينَ أَجْرًا عَظِيمًا (١٤٦)

Verily, those who believe, then disbelieve, then believe (again), and (again) disbelieve, and go on increasing in disbelief; Allâh will not forgive them, nor guide them on the (Right) Way (137) Give to the hypocrites the tidings that there is for them a painful torment. (138) Those who take disbelievers for Auliyâ' (protectors or helpers or friends) instead of believers, do they seek honour, power and glory with them? Verily, then to Allâh belongs all honour, power and glory. (139) And it has already been revealed to you in the Book (this Qur'ân) that when you hear the Verses of Allâh being denied and mocked at, then sit not with them, until they engage in a talk other than that; (but if you stayed with them) certainly in that case you would be like them. Surely, Allâh will collect the hypocrites and disbelievers all together in Hell, (140) Those (hypocrites) who wait and watch about you; if you gain a victory from Allâh, they say: "Were we not with you?" But if the disbelievers gain a success, they say (to them): "Did we not gain mastery over you and did we not protect you from the believers?" Allâh will judge between you (all) on the Day of Resurrection. And never will Allâh grant to the disbelievers a way (to triumph) over the believers. (141) Verily, the hypocrites seek to deceive Allâh, but it is He Who deceives them. And when they stand up for As-Salât (the prayer), they stand with laziness and to be seen of men, and they do not remember Allâh but little. (142) (They are) swaying between this and that, belonging neither to these nor to those, and he whom Allâh sends astray, you will not find for him a way (to the truth - Islâm). (143) O you who believe! Take not for Auliyâ' (protectors or helpers or friends) disbelievers instead of believers. Do you wish to offer Allâh a manifest proof against yourselves? (144) Verily, the hypocrites will be in the lowest depths (grade) of the Fire; no helper will you find for them. (145) Except those who repent (from hypocrisy), do righteous good deeds, hold fast to Allâh, and purify their religion for Allâh (by worshipping none but Allâh, and do good for Allâh's sake only, not to show off), then they will be with the believers. And Allâh will grant the believers a great reward. (146)

Quran 5:13-16

فَبِمَا نَقْضِهِم مِّيثَٰقَهُمْ لَعَنَّٰهُمْ وَجَعَلْنَا قُلُوبَهُمْ قَٰسِيَةً ۖ يُحَرِّفُونَ ٱلْكَلِمَ عَن مَّوَاضِعِهِۦ ۙ وَنَسُوا۟ حَظًّا مِّمَّا ذُكِّرُوا۟ بِهِۦ ۚ وَلَا تَزَالُ تَطَّلِعُ عَلَىٰ خَآئِنَةٍ مِّنْهُمْ إِلَّا قَلِيلًا مِّنْهُمْ ۖ فَٱعْفُ عَنْهُمْ وَٱصْفَحْ ۚ إِنَّ ٱللَّهَ يُحِبُّ ٱلْمُحْسِنِينَ (١٣) وَمِنَ ٱلَّذِينَ قَالُوٓا۟ إِنَّا نَصَٰرَىٰٓ أَخَذْنَا مِيثَٰقَهُمْ فَنَسُوا۟ حَظًّا مِّمَّا ذُكِّرُوا۟ بِهِۦ فَأَغْرَيْنَا بَيْنَهُمُ ٱلْعَدَاوَةَ وَٱلْبَغْضَآءَ إِلَىٰ يَوْمِ ٱلْقِيَٰمَةِ ۚ وَسَوْفَ يُنَبِّئُهُمُ ٱللَّهُ بِمَا

كَانُواْ يَصْنَعُونَ (١٤) يَـٰٓأَهْلَ ٱلْكِتَـٰبِ قَدْ جَآءَكُمْ رَسُولُنَا يُبَيِّنُ لَكُمْ كَثِيرًا مِّمَّا كُنتُمْ تُخْفُونَ مِنَ ٱلْكِتَـٰبِ وَيَعْفُواْ عَن كَثِيرٍ ۚ قَدْ جَآءَكُم مِّنَ ٱللَّهِ نُورٌ وَكِتَـٰبٌ مُّبِينٌ (١٥) يَهْدِى بِهِ ٱللَّهُ مَنِ ٱتَّبَعَ رِضْوَٰنَهُۥ سُبُلَ ٱلسَّلَـٰمِ وَيُخْرِجُهُم مِّنَ ٱلظُّلُمَـٰتِ إِلَى ٱلنُّورِ بِإِذْنِهِۦ وَيَهْدِيهِمْ إِلَىٰ صِرَٰطٍ مُّسْتَقِيمٍ (١٦)

So because of their breach of their covenant, We cursed them, and made their hearts grow hard. They change the words from their (right) places and have abandoned a good part of the Message that was sent to them. And you will not cease to discover deceit in them, except a few of them. But forgive them, and overlook (their misdeeds). Verily, Allâh loves Al¬Muhsinûn (good¬doers). (13) And from those who call themselves Christians, We took their covenant, but they have abandoned a good part of the Message that was sent to them. So We planted amongst them enmity and hatred till the Day of Resurrection (when they discarded Allâh's Book, disobeyed Allâh's Messengers and His Orders and transgressed beyond bounds in Allâh's disobedience), and Allâh will inform them of what they used to do. (14) O people of the Scripture (Jews and Christians)! Now has come to you Our Messenger (Muhammad) explaining to you much of that which you used to hide from the Scripture and pass over (i.e. leaving out without explaining) much. Indeed, there has come to you from Allâh a light (Prophet Muhammad) and a plain Book (this Qur'ân). (15) Wherewith Allâh guides all those who seek His Good Pleasure to ways of peace, and He brings them out of darkness by His Will unto light and guides them to a Straight Way (Islâmic Monotheism) (16)

Quran 5:33-37

إِنَّمَا جَزَٰٓؤُا۟ ٱلَّذِينَ يُحَارِبُونَ ٱللَّهَ وَرَسُولَهُۥ وَيَسْعَوْنَ فِى ٱلْأَرْضِ فَسَادًا أَن يُقَتَّلُوٓا۟ أَوْ يُصَلَّبُوٓا۟ أَوْ تُقَطَّعَ أَيْدِيهِمْ وَأَرْجُلُهُم مِّنْ خِلَٰفٍ أَوْ يُنفَوْا۟ مِنَ ٱلْأَرْضِ ۚ ذَٰلِكَ لَهُمْ خِزْىٌ فِى ٱلدُّنْيَا ۖ وَلَهُمْ فِى ٱلْءَاخِرَةِ عَذَابٌ عَظِيمٌ (٣٣) إِلَّا ٱلَّذِينَ تَابُوا۟ مِن قَبْلِ أَن تَقْدِرُوا۟ عَلَيْهِمْ ۖ فَٱعْلَمُوٓا۟ أَنَّ ٱللَّهَ غَفُورٌ رَّحِيمٌ (٣٤) يَٰٓأَيُّهَا ٱلَّذِينَ ءَامَنُوا۟ ٱتَّقُوا۟ ٱللَّهَ وَٱبْتَغُوٓا۟ إِلَيْهِ ٱلْوَسِيلَةَ وَجَٰهِدُوا۟ فِى سَبِيلِهِۦ لَعَلَّكُمْ تُفْلِحُونَ (٣٥) إِنَّ ٱلَّذِينَ كَفَرُوا۟ لَوْ أَنَّ لَهُم مَّا فِى ٱلْأَرْضِ جَمِيعًا وَمِثْلَهُۥ مَعَهُۥ لِيَفْتَدُوا۟ بِهِۦ مِنْ عَذَابِ يَوْمِ ٱلْقِيَٰمَةِ مَا تُقُبِّلَ مِنْهُمْ ۖ وَلَهُمْ عَذَابٌ أَلِيمٌ (٣٦) يُرِيدُونَ أَن يَخْرُجُوا۟ مِنَ ٱلنَّارِ وَمَا هُم بِخَٰرِجِينَ مِنْهَا ۖ وَلَهُمْ عَذَابٌ مُّقِيمٌ (٣٧)

The recompense of those who wage war against Allâh and His Messenger and do mischief in the land is only that they shall be killed or crucified or their hands and their feet be cut off from the opposite sides, or be exiled from the land. That is their disgrace in this world, and a great torment is theirs in the Hereafter. (33) Except for those who (having fled away and then) came back (as Muslims) with repentance before they fall into your power; in that case, know that Allâh is Oft-Forgiving, Most Merciful. (34) O you who believe! Do your duty to Allâh and fear Him. Seek the means of approach to Him, and strive hard in His Cause (as much as you can). So that you may be successful. (35) Verily, those who disbelieve, if they had all that is in the earth, and as much again therewith to ransom themselves thereby from the torment on the Day of Resurrection, it would never be accepted of them, and theirs would be a painful torment.(36) They will long to get out of the Fire, but never will they get out therefrom, and theirs will be a lasting torment. (37)

Quran 5:41-42

يَٰٓأَيُّهَا ٱلرَّسُولُ لَا يَحْزُنكَ ٱلَّذِينَ يُسَٰرِعُونَ فِى ٱلْكُفْرِ مِنَ ٱلَّذِينَ قَالُوٓاْ ءَامَنَّا بِأَفْوَٰهِهِمْ وَلَمْ تُؤْمِن قُلُوبُهُمْ وَمِنَ ٱلَّذِينَ هَادُواْ سَمَّٰعُونَ لِلْكَذِبِ سَمَّٰعُونَ لِقَوْمٍ ءَاخَرِينَ لَمْ يَأْتُوكَ يُحَرِّفُونَ ٱلْكَلِمَ مِنۢ بَعْدِ مَوَاضِعِهِۦ يَقُولُونَ إِنْ أُوتِيتُمْ هَٰذَا فَخُذُوهُ وَإِن لَّمْ تُؤْتَوْهُ فَٱحْذَرُواْ وَمَن يُرِدِ ٱللَّهُ فِتْنَتَهُۥ فَلَن تَمْلِكَ لَهُۥ مِنَ ٱللَّهِ شَيْـًٔا أُوْلَٰٓئِكَ ٱلَّذِينَ لَمْ يُرِدِ ٱللَّهُ أَن يُطَهِّرَ قُلُوبَهُمْ لَهُمْ فِى ٱلدُّنْيَا خِزْىٌ وَلَهُمْ فِى ٱلْءَاخِرَةِ عَذَابٌ عَظِيمٌ (٤١) سَمَّٰعُونَ لِلْكَذِبِ أَكَّٰلُونَ لِلسُّحْتِ فَإِن جَآءُوكَ فَٱحْكُم بَيْنَهُمْ أَوْ أَعْرِضْ عَنْهُمْ وَإِن تُعْرِضْ عَنْهُمْ فَلَن يَضُرُّوكَ شَيْـًٔا وَإِنْ حَكَمْتَ فَٱحْكُم بَيْنَهُم بِٱلْقِسْطِ إِنَّ ٱللَّهَ يُحِبُّ ٱلْمُقْسِطِينَ (٤٢)

O Messenger (Muhammad)! Let not those who hurry to fall into disbelief grieve you, of such who say: "We believe" *with their mouths but their hearts have no faith. And of the Jews are men who listen much and eagerly to lies - listen to others who have not come to you. They change the words from their places; they say, "If you are given this, take it, but if you are not given this, then beware!" And whomsoever Allâh wants to put in Al¬Fitnah [error, because of his rejecting the Faith], you can do nothing for him against Allâh. Those are the ones whose hearts Allâh does not want to purify (from disbelief and hypocrisy); for them there is a disgrace in this world, and in the Hereafter a great torment. (41) (They like to) listen to falsehood, to devour anything forbidden. So if they come to you (O Muhammad), either judge between them, or turn away from them. If you turn away from them, they cannot hurt you in the least. And if you judge, judge with justice between them. Verily, Allâh loves those who act justly. (42)*

Quran 5:49-57

وَأَنِ ٱحۡكُم بَيۡنَهُم بِمَآ أَنزَلَ ٱللَّهُ وَلَا تَتَّبِعۡ أَهۡوَآءَهُمۡ وَٱحۡذَرۡهُمۡ أَن يَفۡتِنُوكَ عَنۢ بَعۡضِ مَآ أَنزَلَ ٱللَّهُ إِلَيۡكَۖ فَإِن تَوَلَّوۡاْ فَٱعۡلَمۡ أَنَّمَا يُرِيدُ ٱللَّهُ أَن يُصِيبَهُم بِبَعۡضِ ذُنُوبِهِمۡۗ وَإِنَّ كَثِيرٗا مِّنَ ٱلنَّاسِ لَفَٰسِقُونَ (٤٩) أَفَحُكۡمَ ٱلۡجَٰهِلِيَّةِ يَبۡغُونَۚ وَمَنۡ أَحۡسَنُ مِنَ ٱللَّهِ حُكۡمٗا لِّقَوۡمٖ يُوقِنُونَ (٥٠) ۞ يَٰٓأَيُّهَا ٱلَّذِينَ ءَامَنُواْ لَا تَتَّخِذُواْ ٱلۡيَهُودَ وَٱلنَّصَٰرَىٰٓ أَوۡلِيَآءَۘ بَعۡضُهُمۡ أَوۡلِيَآءُ بَعۡضٖۚ وَمَن يَتَوَلَّهُم مِّنكُمۡ فَإِنَّهُۥ مِنۡهُمۡۗ إِنَّ ٱللَّهَ لَا يَهۡدِي ٱلۡقَوۡمَ ٱلظَّٰلِمِينَ (٥١) فَتَرَى

ٱلَّذِينَ فِى قُلُوبِهِم مَّرَضٌ يُسَٰرِعُونَ فِيهِمْ يَقُولُونَ نَخْشَىٰٓ أَن تُصِيبَنَا دَآئِرَةٌ ۚ فَعَسَى ٱللَّهُ أَن يَأْتِىَ بِٱلْفَتْحِ أَوْ أَمْرٍ مِّنْ عِندِهِۦ فَيُصْبِحُوا۟ عَلَىٰ مَآ أَسَرُّوا۟ فِىٓ أَنفُسِهِمْ نَٰدِمِينَ (٥٢) وَيَقُولُ ٱلَّذِينَ ءَامَنُوٓا۟ أَهَٰٓؤُلَآءِ ٱلَّذِينَ أَقْسَمُوا۟ بِٱللَّهِ جَهْدَ أَيْمَٰنِهِمْ ۙ إِنَّهُمْ لَمَعَكُمْ ۚ حَبِطَتْ أَعْمَٰلُهُمْ فَأَصْبَحُوا۟ خَٰسِرِينَ (٥٣) يَٰٓأَيُّهَا ٱلَّذِينَ ءَامَنُوا۟ مَن يَرْتَدَّ مِنكُمْ عَن دِينِهِۦ فَسَوْفَ يَأْتِى ٱللَّهُ بِقَوْمٍ يُحِبُّهُمْ وَيُحِبُّونَهُۥٓ أَذِلَّةٍ عَلَى ٱلْمُؤْمِنِينَ أَعِزَّةٍ عَلَى ٱلْكَٰفِرِينَ يُجَٰهِدُونَ فِى سَبِيلِ ٱللَّهِ وَلَا يَخَافُونَ لَوْمَةَ لَآئِمٍ ۚ ذَٰلِكَ فَضْلُ ٱللَّهِ يُؤْتِيهِ مَن يَشَآءُ ۚ وَٱللَّهُ وَٰسِعٌ عَلِيمٌ (٥٤) إِنَّمَا وَلِيُّكُمُ ٱللَّهُ وَرَسُولُهُۥ وَٱلَّذِينَ ءَامَنُوا۟ ٱلَّذِينَ يُقِيمُونَ ٱلصَّلَوٰةَ وَيُؤْتُونَ ٱلزَّكَوٰةَ وَهُمْ رَٰكِعُونَ (٥٥) وَمَن يَتَوَلَّ ٱللَّهَ وَرَسُولَهُۥ وَٱلَّذِينَ ءَامَنُوا۟ فَإِنَّ حِزْبَ ٱللَّهِ هُمُ ٱلْغَٰلِبُونَ (٥٦) يَٰٓأَيُّهَا ٱلَّذِينَ ءَامَنُوا۟ لَا تَتَّخِذُوا۟ ٱلَّذِينَ ٱتَّخَذُوا۟ دِينَكُمْ هُزُوًا وَلَعِبًا مِّنَ ٱلَّذِينَ أُوتُوا۟ ٱلْكِتَٰبَ مِن قَبْلِكُمْ وَٱلْكُفَّارَ أَوْلِيَآءَ ۚ وَٱتَّقُوا۟ ٱللَّهَ إِن كُنتُم مُّؤْمِنِينَ (٥٧)

And so judge (you O Muhammad) among them by what Allâh has revealed and follow not their vain desires, but beware of them lest they turn you (O Muhammad) far away from some of that which Allâh has sent down to you. And if they turn away, then know that Allâh's Will is to punish them for some sins of theirs. And truly, most of men are Fâsiqûn (rebellious and disobedient to Allâh). (49) Do they then seek the judgement of (the days of) Ignorance? And who is better in judgement than Allâh for a people who have firm Faith. (50) O you who believe! Take not the Jews and the Christians as Auliyâ' (friends, protectors, helpers), they are but Auliyâ' of each other. And if any amongst you takes them (as

Auliyâ'), then surely he is one of them. Verily, Allâh guides not those people who are the Zâlimûn (polytheists and wrong-doers and unjust). (51) And you see those in whose hearts there is a disease (of hypocrisy), they hurry to their friendship, saying: "We fear lest some misfortune of a disaster may befall us." Perhaps Allâh may bring a victory or a decision according to His Will. Then they will become regretful for what they have been keeping as a secret in themselves. (52) And those who believe will say: "Are these the men (hypocrites) who swore their strongest oaths by Allâh that they were with you (Muslims)?" All that they did has been in vain (because of their hypocrisy), and they have become the losers. (53) O you who believe! Whoever from among you turns back from his religion (Islâm), Allâh will bring a people whom He will love and they will love Him; humble towards the believers, stern towards the disbelievers, fighting in the Way of Allâh, and never fear of the blame of the blamers. That is the Grace of Allâh which He bestows on whom He wills. And Allâh is All-Sufficient for His creatures' needs, All-Knower. (54) Verily, your Walî (Protector or Helper) is none other than Allâh, His Messenger, and the believers, - those who perform

As-Salât (Iqâmat-as-Salât), and give Zakât, and they are Rakiun (those who bow down or submit themselves with obedience to Allâh in prayer). (55) And whosoever takes Allâh, His Messenger, and those who have believed, as Protectors, then the party of Allâh will be the victorious. (56) O you who believe! Take not as Auliyâ' (protectors and helpers) those who take your religion as a mockery and fun from among those who received the Scripture (Jews and Christians) before you, nor from among the disbelievers; and fear Allâh if you indeed are true believers. (57)

Quran 5:57-81

قُلْ يَٰٓأَهْلَ ٱلْكِتَٰبِ لَا تَغْلُوا۟ فِى دِينِكُمْ غَيْرَ ٱلْحَقِّ وَلَا تَتَّبِعُوٓا۟ أَهْوَآءَ قَوْمٍ قَدْ ضَلُّوا۟ مِن قَبْلُ وَأَضَلُّوا۟ كَثِيرًا وَضَلُّوا۟ عَن سَوَآءِ ٱلسَّبِيلِ (٧٧) لُعِنَ ٱلَّذِينَ كَفَرُوا۟ مِنۢ بَنِىٓ إِسْرَٰٓءِيلَ عَلَىٰ لِسَانِ دَاوُۥدَ وَعِيسَى ٱبْنِ مَرْيَمَ ذَٰلِكَ بِمَا عَصَوا۟ وَّكَانُوا۟ يَعْتَدُونَ (٧٨) كَانُوا۟ لَا يَتَنَاهَوْنَ عَن مُّنكَرٍ فَعَلُوهُ لَبِئْسَ مَا كَانُوا۟ يَفْعَلُونَ (٧٩) تَرَىٰ كَثِيرًا مِّنْهُمْ يَتَوَلَّوْنَ ٱلَّذِينَ كَفَرُوا۟ لَبِئْسَ مَا قَدَّمَتْ لَهُمْ أَنفُسُهُمْ أَن سَخِطَ ٱللَّهُ عَلَيْهِمْ وَفِى ٱلْعَذَابِ هُمْ خَٰلِدُونَ (٨٠) وَلَوْ كَانُوا۟ يُؤْمِنُونَ بِٱللَّهِ وَٱلنَّبِىِّ وَمَآ أُنزِلَ إِلَيْهِ مَا ٱتَّخَذُوهُمْ أَوْلِيَآءَ وَلَٰكِنَّ كَثِيرًا مِّنْهُمْ فَٰسِقُونَ (٨١)

Say (O Muhammad): "O people of the Scripture (Jews and Christians)! Exceed not the limits in your religion (by believing in something) other than the truth, and do not follow the vain desires of people who went astray before, and who misled many, and strayed (themselves) from the Right Path." (77) Those among the Children of Israel who disbelieved were cursed by the tongue of Dawûd (David) and 'Īsā (Jesus), son of Maryam (Mary). That was because they disobeyed (Allâh and the Messengers) and were ever transgressing beyond bounds. (78) They used not to forbid one another from Al-Munkar (wrong, evil-doing, sins, polytheism, disbelief) which they committed. Vile indeed was what they used to do. (79) You see many of them taking the disbelievers as their Auliyâ' (protectors and helpers). Evil indeed is that which their ownselves have sent forward before them, for that (reason) Allâh's Wrath fell upon them and in torment they will abide. (80) And had they believed in Allâh, and in the Prophet (Muhammad) and in what has been revealed to him, never would they have taken them (the disbelievers) as Auliyâ' (protectors and helpers), but many of them are the Fâsiqûn (rebellious, disobedient to Allâh). (81)

Quran 5:100

قُل لَّا يَسْتَوِى ٱلْخَبِيثُ وَٱلطَّيِّبُ وَلَوْ أَعْجَبَكَ كَثْرَةُ ٱلْخَبِيثِ فَٱتَّقُواْ ٱللَّهَ يَـٰٓأُوْلِى ٱلْأَلْبَـٰبِ لَعَلَّكُمْ تُفْلِحُونَ (١٠٠)

Say (O Muhammad): "Not equal are Al¬Khabîth (all that is evil and bad as regards things, deeds, beliefs, persons, and foods) and At-Tayyib (all that is good as regards things, deeds, beliefs, persons, and foods), even though the abundance of Al-Khabîth may please you." So fear Allâh, O men of understanding in order that you may be successful. (100)

Quran 5:104-105

وَإِذَا قِيلَ لَهُمْ تَعَالَوْاْ إِلَىٰ مَآ أَنزَلَ ٱللَّهُ وَإِلَى ٱلرَّسُولِ قَالُواْ حَسْبُنَا مَا وَجَدْنَا عَلَيْهِ ءَابَآءَنَآ أَوَلَوْ كَانَ ءَابَآؤُهُمْ لَا يَعْلَمُونَ شَيْـًٔا وَلَا يَهْتَدُونَ (١٠٤) يَـٰٓأَيُّهَا ٱلَّذِينَ ءَامَنُواْ عَلَيْكُمْ أَنفُسَكُمْ لَا يَضُرُّكُم مَّن ضَلَّ إِذَا ٱهْتَدَيْتُمْ إِلَى ٱللَّهِ مَرْجِعُكُمْ جَمِيعًا فَيُنَبِّئُكُم بِمَا كُنتُمْ تَعْمَلُونَ (١٠٥)

And when it is said to them: "Come to what Allâh has revealed and unto the Messenger (Muhammad for the verdict of that which you have made unlawful)." They say: "Enough for us is that which we found our fathers following," even though their fathers had no knowledge whatsoever and nor guidance. (104) O you who believe! Take care of your ownselves, If you follow the (right) guidance (and enjoin what is right Islâmic Monotheism and all that Islâm orders one to do) and forbid what is wrong (polytheism, disbelief and all that Islâm has forbidden) no hurt can come to you from those who are in error. The return of you all is to Allâh, then He will inform you about (all) that which you used to do. (105)

Quran 6:21-28

وَمَنْ أَظْلَمُ مِمَّنِ ٱفْتَرَىٰ عَلَى ٱللَّهِ كَذِبًا أَوْ كَذَّبَ بِـَٔايَـٰتِهِۦٓ ۗ إِنَّهُۥ لَا يُفْلِحُ ٱلظَّـٰلِمُونَ (٢١) وَيَوْمَ نَحْشُرُهُمْ جَمِيعًا ثُمَّ نَقُولُ لِلَّذِينَ أَشْرَكُوٓا۟ أَيْنَ شُرَكَآؤُكُمُ ٱلَّذِينَ كُنتُمْ تَزْعُمُونَ (٢٢) ثُمَّ لَمْ تَكُن فِتْنَتُهُمْ إِلَّآ أَن قَالُوا۟ وَٱللَّهِ رَبِّنَا مَا كُنَّا مُشْرِكِينَ (٢٣) ٱنظُرْ كَيْفَ كَذَبُوا۟ عَلَىٰٓ أَنفُسِهِمْ ۚ وَضَلَّ عَنْهُم مَّا كَانُوا۟ يَفْتَرُونَ (٢٤) وَمِنْهُم مَّن يَسْتَمِعُ إِلَيْكَ ۖ وَجَعَلْنَا عَلَىٰ قُلُوبِهِمْ أَكِنَّةً أَن يَفْقَهُوهُ وَفِىٓ ءَاذَانِهِمْ وَقْرًا ۚ وَإِن يَرَوْا۟ كُلَّ ءَايَةٍ لَّا يُؤْمِنُوا۟ بِهَا ۚ حَتَّىٰٓ إِذَا جَآءُوكَ يُجَـٰدِلُونَكَ يَقُولُ ٱلَّذِينَ كَفَرُوٓا۟ إِنْ هَـٰذَآ إِلَّآ أَسَـٰطِيرُ ٱلْأَوَّلِينَ (٢٥) وَهُمْ يَنْهَوْنَ عَنْهُ وَيَنْـَٔوْنَ عَنْهُ ۖ وَإِن يُهْلِكُونَ إِلَّآ أَنفُسَهُمْ وَمَا يَشْعُرُونَ (٢٦) وَلَوْ تَرَىٰٓ إِذْ وُقِفُوا۟ عَلَى ٱلنَّارِ فَقَالُوا۟ يَـٰلَيْتَنَا نُرَدُّ وَلَا نُكَذِّبَ بِـَٔايَـٰتِ رَبِّنَا وَنَكُونَ مِنَ ٱلْمُؤْمِنِينَ (٢٧) بَلْ بَدَا لَهُم مَّا كَانُوا۟ يُخْفُونَ مِن قَبْلُ ۖ وَلَوْ رُدُّوا۟ لَعَادُوا۟ لِمَا نُهُوا۟ عَنْهُ وَإِنَّهُمْ لَكَـٰذِبُونَ (٢٨)

And who does more wrong aggression and than he who invents a lie against Allâh or rejects His Ayât (proofs, evidences, verses, lessons, or revelations)? Verily, the Zâlimûn (polytheists and wrong-doers,) shall never be successful. (21) And on the Day when We shall gather them all together, We shall say to those who joined partners (in worship with Us): "Where are your partners (false deities) whom you used to assert (as partners in worship with Allâh)?" (22) There will then be (left) no Fitnah (excuses or *statements or arguments) for them but to say: "By Allâh, our Lord, we were not those who joined others in worship with Allâh." (23) Look! How they lie against themselves! But the (lie) which they invented will disappear from them. (24) And of them there are some who listen to you; but We have set veils on their hearts, so they understand it not, and deafness in their ears; and even if they see every one of the Ayât (proofs, evidences, verses, lessons, signs, revelations, etc.) they will not believe therein; to the point that when they come to you to argue with you, the disbelievers say: "These are nothing but tales of the men of old." (25) And they prevent others from him (from following Prophet Muhammad) and they themselves keep away from him, and (by doing so) they destroy not but their ownselves, yet they perceive (it) not. (26) If you could but see when they will be held over the (Hell) Fire! They will say: "Would that we were but sent back (to the world)! Then we would not deny the Ayât (proofs, evidences, verses, lessons, revelations, etc.) of our Lord, and we would be of the believers!" (27) Nay, it has become manifest to them what they had been concealing before. But if they were returned (to the world), they* would certainly revert to that which they were forbidden. And indeed they are liars. (28)

Quran 6:56-57

قُلْ إِنِّى نُهِيتُ أَنْ أَعْبُدَ ٱلَّذِينَ تَدْعُونَ مِن دُونِ ٱللَّهِ ۚ قُل لَّا أَتَّبِعُ أَهْوَآءَكُمْ ۙ قَدْ ضَلَلْتُ إِذًا وَمَآ أَنَا۠ مِنَ ٱلْمُهْتَدِينَ (٥٦) قُلْ إِنِّى عَلَىٰ بَيِّنَةٍ مِّن رَّبِّى وَكَذَّبْتُم بِهِ ۚ مَا عِندِى مَا تَسْتَعْجِلُونَ بِهِ ۚ إِنِ ٱلْحُكْمُ إِلَّا لِلَّهِ ۖ يَقُصُّ ٱلْحَقَّ ۖ وَهُوَ خَيْرُ ٱلْفَٰصِلِينَ (٥٧)

Say (O Muhammad): "I have been forbidden to worship those whom you invoke (worship) besides Allâh." Say: "I will not follow your vain desires. If I did, I would go astray, and I would not be one of the rightly guided." (56) Say (O Muhammad): "I am on clear proof from my Lord (Islâmic Monotheism), but you deny (the truth that has come to me from Allâh). I have not gotten what you are asking for impatiently (the torment). The decision is only for Allâh, He declares the truth, and He is the Best of judges." (57)

Quran 6:68-71

وَإِذَا رَأَيْتَ ٱلَّذِينَ يَخُوضُونَ فِىٓ ءَايَٰتِنَا فَأَعْرِضْ عَنْهُمْ حَتَّىٰ يَخُوضُوا۟ فِى حَدِيثٍ غَيْرِهِ ۚ وَإِمَّا يُنسِيَنَّكَ ٱلشَّيْطَٰنُ فَلَا تَقْعُدْ بَعْدَ ٱلذِّكْرَىٰ مَعَ ٱلْقَوْمِ ٱلظَّٰلِمِينَ (٦٨) وَمَا عَلَى ٱلَّذِينَ يَتَّقُونَ مِنْ حِسَابِهِم مِّن شَىْءٍ وَلَٰكِن ذِكْرَىٰ لَعَلَّهُمْ يَتَّقُونَ (٦٩) وَذَرِ ٱلَّذِينَ ٱتَّخَذُوا۟ دِينَهُمْ لَعِبًا وَلَهْوًا وَغَرَّتْهُمُ ٱلْحَيَوٰةُ ٱلدُّنْيَا ۚ وَذَكِّرْ بِهِۦٓ أَن تُبْسَلَ نَفْسٌۢ بِمَا كَسَبَتْ لَيْسَ لَهَا مِن دُونِ ٱللَّهِ وَلِىٌّ وَلَا شَفِيعٌ وَإِن تَعْدِلْ كُلَّ عَدْلٍ لَّا يُؤْخَذْ مِنْهَآ ۗ أُو۟لَٰٓئِكَ

ٱلَّذِينَ أُبْسِلُوا۟ بِمَا كَسَبُوا۟ لَهُمْ شَرَابٌ مِّنْ حَمِيمٍ وَعَذَابٌ أَلِيمٌۢ بِمَا كَانُوا۟ يَكْفُرُونَ (٧٠) قُلْ أَنَدْعُوا۟ مِن دُونِ ٱللَّهِ مَا لَا يَنفَعُنَا وَلَا يَضُرُّنَا وَنُرَدُّ عَلَىٰٓ أَعْقَابِنَا بَعْدَ إِذْ هَدَىٰنَا ٱللَّهُ كَٱلَّذِى ٱسْتَهْوَتْهُ ٱلشَّيَـٰطِينُ فِى ٱلْأَرْضِ حَيْرَانَ لَهُۥٓ أَصْحَـٰبٌ يَدْعُونَهُۥٓ إِلَى ٱلْهُدَى ٱئْتِنَا ۗ قُلْ إِنَّ هُدَى ٱللَّهِ هُوَ ٱلْهُدَىٰ ۖ وَأُمِرْنَا لِنُسْلِمَ لِرَبِّ ٱلْعَـٰلَمِينَ (٧١)

And when you (Muhammad) see those who engage in a false conversation about Our Verses (of the Qur'ân) by mocking at them, stay away from them till they turn to another topic. And if Shaitân (Satan) causes you to forget, then after the remembrance sit not you in the company of those people who are the Zâlimûn (polytheists and wrong-doers). (68) Those who fear Allâh, keep their duty to Him and avoid evil are not responsible for them (the disbelievers) in any case, but (their duty) is to remind them, that they may fear Allah (and refrain from mocking at the Quran). (69) And leave alone those who take their religion as play and amusement, and whom the life of this world has deceived. But remind (them) with it (the Qur'ân) lest a person be given up to destruction for that which he has earned, when he will find for himself no protector or intercessor besides Allâh, and even if he offers every ransom, it will not be accepted from him. Such are they who are given up to destruction because of that which they have earned.

For them will be a drink of boiling water and a painful torment because they used to disbelieve. (70) Say (O Muhammad): "Shall we invoke others besides Allâh (false deities), that can do us neither good nor harm, and shall we turn back on our heels after Allâh has guided us (to true Monotheism)? - like one whom the Shayâtin (devils) have made to go astray, in the land in confusion, his companions calling him to guidance (saying): 'Come to us.' " Say: "Verily, Allâh's Guidance is the only guidance, and we have been commanded to submit (ourselves) to the Lord of the 'Alamîn (mankind, jinn and all that exists); (71)

Quran 6:93-94

وَمَنْ أَظْلَمُ مِمَّنِ ٱفْتَرَىٰ عَلَى ٱللَّهِ كَذِبًا أَوْ قَالَ أُوحِيَ إِلَيَّ وَلَمْ يُوحَ إِلَيْهِ شَيْءٌ وَمَن قَالَ سَأُنزِلُ مِثْلَ مَا أَنزَلَ ٱللَّهُ وَلَوْ تَرَىٰ إِذِ ٱلظَّٰلِمُونَ فِى غَمَرَٰتِ ٱلْمَوْتِ وَٱلْمَلَٰٓئِكَةُ بَاسِطُوٓا۟ أَيْدِيهِمْ أَخْرِجُوٓا۟ أَنفُسَكُمُ ٱلْيَوْمَ تُجْزَوْنَ عَذَابَ ٱلْهُونِ بِمَا كُنتُمْ تَقُولُونَ عَلَى ٱللَّهِ غَيْرَ ٱلْحَقِّ وَكُنتُمْ عَنْ ءَايَٰتِهِۦ تَسْتَكْبِرُونَ (٩٣) وَلَقَدْ جِئْتُمُونَا فُرَٰدَىٰ كَمَا خَلَقْنَٰكُمْ أَوَّلَ مَرَّةٍ وَتَرَكْتُم مَّا خَوَّلْنَٰكُمْ وَرَآءَ ظُهُورِكُمْ وَمَا نَرَىٰ مَعَكُمْ شُفَعَآءَكُمُ ٱلَّذِينَ زَعَمْتُمْ أَنَّهُمْ فِيكُمْ شُرَكَٰٓؤُا۟ لَقَد تَّقَطَّعَ بَيْنَكُمْ وَضَلَّ عَنكُم مَّا كُنتُمْ تَزْعُمُونَ (٩٤)

And who can be more unjust than he who invents a lie against Allâh, or says: "A revelation has come to me," whereas as no revelation has come to him in anything; and who says, "I will reveal the like of what Allâh has revealed." And if you could but see when the Zâlimûn (polytheists and wrong-doers) are in the agonies of death, while the angels are stretching forth their hands (saying): "Deliver your souls! This day you shall be recompensed with the torment of degradation because of what you used to utter against Allâh other than the truth. And you used to reject His Ayât (proofs, evidences, verses, lessons, signs, revelations etc.) with disrespect!" (93) And truly you have come unto Us alone (without wealth, companions or anything else) as We created you the first time. You have left behind you all that which We had bestowed on you. We see not with you your intercessors whom you claimed to be partners with Allâh. Now all relations between you and them have been cut off, and all that you used to claim has vanished from you. (94)

Quran 6:104-106

قَدْ جَاءَكُم بَصَآئِرُ مِن رَّبِّكُمْ ۖ فَمَنْ أَبْصَرَ فَلِنَفْسِهِ ۖ وَمَنْ عَمِىَ فَعَلَيْهَا ۚ وَمَآ أَنَا۠ عَلَيْكُم بِحَفِيظٍ (١٠٤) وَكَذَٰلِكَ نُصَرِّفُ ٱلْءَايَٰتِ وَلِيَقُولُوا۟ دَرَسْتَ وَلِنُبَيِّنَهُۥ لِقَوْمٍ يَعْلَمُونَ (١٠٥) ٱتَّبِعْ مَآ أُوحِىَ إِلَيْكَ مِن رَّبِّكَ ۖ لَآ إِلَٰهَ إِلَّا هُوَ ۖ وَأَعْرِضْ عَنِ ٱلْمُشْرِكِينَ (١٠٦)

Verily, proofs have come to you from your Lord, so whosoever sees, will do so for (the good of) his ownself, and whosoever blinds himself, will do so to his own harm, and I (Muhammad) am not a watcher over you. (104) Thus We explain variously the Verses so that they (the disbelievers) may say: "You have studied (the Books of the people of the Scripture and brought this Qur'ân from that)" and that We may make the matter clear for the people who have knowledge. (105) Follow what has been revealed to you (O Muhammad) from your Lord, Lâ ilâha illa Huwa (none has the right to be worshipped but He) and turn aside from Al-Mushrikûn. (106)

Quran 6:112-117

وَكَذَٰلِكَ جَعَلْنَا لِكُلِّ نَبِيٍّ عَدُوًّا شَيَٰطِينَ ٱلْإِنسِ وَٱلْجِنِّ يُوحِى بَعْضُهُمْ إِلَىٰ بَعْضٍ زُخْرُفَ ٱلْقَوْلِ غُرُورًا ۚ وَلَوْ شَآءَ رَبُّكَ مَا فَعَلُوهُ ۖ فَذَرْهُمْ وَمَا يَفْتَرُونَ (١١٢) وَلِتَصْغَىٰٓ إِلَيْهِ أَفْـِٔدَةُ ٱلَّذِينَ لَا يُؤْمِنُونَ بِٱلْءَاخِرَةِ وَلِيَرْضَوْهُ وَلِيَقْتَرِفُوا۟ مَا هُم مُّقْتَرِفُونَ (١١٣) أَفَغَيْرَ ٱللَّهِ أَبْتَغِى حَكَمًا وَهُوَ ٱلَّذِىٓ أَنزَلَ إِلَيْكُمُ ٱلْكِتَٰبَ مُفَصَّلًا ۚ وَٱلَّذِينَ ءَاتَيْنَٰهُمُ ٱلْكِتَٰبَ يَعْلَمُونَ أَنَّهُۥ مُنَزَّلٌ مِّن رَّبِّكَ بِٱلْحَقِّ ۖ فَلَا تَكُونَنَّ مِنَ ٱلْمُمْتَرِينَ (١١٤) وَتَمَّتْ كَلِمَتُ رَبِّكَ صِدْقًا وَعَدْلًا ۚ لَّا مُبَدِّلَ لِكَلِمَٰتِهِۦ ۚ وَهُوَ ٱلسَّمِيعُ ٱلْعَلِيمُ (١١٥) وَإِن تُطِعْ أَكْثَرَ مَن فِى ٱلْأَرْضِ يُضِلُّوكَ عَن سَبِيلِ ٱللَّهِ ۚ إِن يَتَّبِعُونَ إِلَّا ٱلظَّنَّ وَإِنْ هُمْ إِلَّا يَخْرُصُونَ (١١٦) إِنَّ رَبَّكَ هُوَ أَعْلَمُ مَن يَضِلُّ عَن سَبِيلِهِۦ ۖ وَهُوَ أَعْلَمُ بِٱلْمُهْتَدِينَ (١١٧)

And so We have appointed for every Prophet enemies - Shayâtin (devils) among mankind and jinn, inspiring one another with adorned speech as a delusion (or by way of deception). If your Lord had so willed, they would not have done it, so leave them alone with their fabrications. (112) (And this is in order) that the hearts of those who disbelieve in the Hereafter may incline to such (deceit), and that they may remain pleased with it, and that they may commit what they are committing (all kinds of sins and evil deeds). (113) [Say (O Muhammad)] "Shall I seek a judge other than Allâh while it is He Who has sent down unto you the Book (the Qur'ân), explained in detail." Those unto whom We gave the Scripture [the Taurât (Torah) and the Injeel] know that it is revealed from your Lord in truth. So be not you of those who doubt. (114) And the Word of your Lord has been fulfilled in truth and in justice. None can change His Words. And He is the All¬Hearer, the All¬Knower. (115) And if you obey most of those on the earth, they will mislead you far away from Allâh's Path. They follow nothing but conjectures, and they do nothing but lie. (116) Verily, your Lord! It is He Who knows best who strays from His Way, and He knows best the rightly guided ones. (117)

Quran 6:123

وَكَذَٰلِكَ جَعَلْنَا فِى كُلِّ قَرْيَةٍ أَكَـٰبِرَ مُجْرِمِيهَا لِيَمْكُرُوا۟ فِيهَا ۖ وَمَا يَمْكُرُونَ إِلَّا بِأَنفُسِهِمْ وَمَا يَشْعُرُونَ (١٢٣)

And thus We have set up in every town great ones of its wicked people to plot therein. But they plot not except against their ownselves, and they perceive (it) not. (123)

Quran 6:148-150

سَيَقُولُ ٱلَّذِينَ أَشْرَكُوا۟ لَوْ شَاءَ ٱللَّهُ مَا أَشْرَكْنَا وَلَا ءَابَآؤُنَا وَلَا حَرَّمْنَا مِن شَىْءٍ ۚ كَذَٰلِكَ كَذَّبَ ٱلَّذِينَ مِن قَبْلِهِمْ حَتَّىٰ ذَاقُوا۟ بَأْسَنَا ۗ قُلْ هَلْ عِندَكُم مِّنْ عِلْمٍ فَتُخْرِجُوهُ لَنَآ ۖ إِن تَتَّبِعُونَ إِلَّا ٱلظَّنَّ وَإِنْ أَنتُمْ إِلَّا تَخْرُصُونَ (١٤٨) قُلْ فَلِلَّهِ ٱلْحُجَّةُ ٱلْبَـٰلِغَةُ ۖ فَلَوْ شَآءَ لَهَدَىٰكُمْ أَجْمَعِينَ (١٤٩) قُلْ هَلُمَّ شُهَدَآءَكُمُ ٱلَّذِينَ يَشْهَدُونَ أَنَّ ٱللَّهَ حَرَّمَ هَـٰذَا ۖ فَإِن شَهِدُوا۟ فَلَا تَشْهَدْ مَعَهُمْ ۚ وَلَا تَتَّبِعْ أَهْوَآءَ ٱلَّذِينَ كَذَّبُوا۟ بِـَٔايَـٰتِنَا وَٱلَّذِينَ لَا يُؤْمِنُونَ بِٱلْـَٔاخِرَةِ وَهُم بِرَبِّهِمْ يَعْدِلُونَ (١٥٠)

Those who took partners (in worship) with Allâh will say: "If Allâh had willed, we would not have taken partners (in worship) with Him, nor would our fathers, and we would not have forbidden anything (against His Will)." Likewise belied those who were before them, (they argued falsely with Allâh's Messengers), till they tasted Our Wrath. Say: "Have you any knowledge (proof) that you can produce before us? Verily, you follow nothing but guess and you do nothing but lie." (148) Say: "With Allâh is the perfect proof and argument, (i.e. the Oneness of Allâh, the sending of His Messengers and His Holy Books to mankind), had He so willed, He would indeed have guided you all." (149) Say: "Bring forward your witnesses, who can testify that Allâh has forbidden this. Then if they testify, testify not you (O Muhammad) with them. And you should not follow the vain desires of such as treat Our Ayât (proofs, evidences, verses, lessons, signs, revelations, etc.) as falsehoods, and such as believe not in the Hereafter, and they hold others as equal (in worship) with their Lord." (150)

Quran 6:159

إِنَّ ٱلَّذِينَ فَرَّقُوا۟ دِينَهُمْ وَكَانُوا۟ شِيَعًا لَّسْتَ مِنْهُمْ فِى شَىْءٍ إِنَّمَآ أَمْرُهُمْ إِلَى ٱللَّهِ ثُمَّ يُنَبِّئُهُم بِمَا كَانُوا۟ يَفْعَلُونَ (١٥٩)

Verily, those who divide their religion and break up into sects (all kinds of religious sects), you (O Muhammad) have no concern in them in the least. Their affair is only with Allâh, Who then will tell them what they used to do. (159)

Quran 7:6-9

فَلَنَسْـَٔلَنَّ ٱلَّذِينَ أُرْسِلَ إِلَيْهِمْ وَلَنَسْـَٔلَنَّ ٱلْمُرْسَلِينَ (٦) فَلَنَقُصَّنَّ عَلَيْهِم بِعِلْمٍ ۖ وَمَا كُنَّا غَآئِبِينَ (٧) وَٱلْوَزْنُ يَوْمَئِذٍ ٱلْحَقُّ ۚ فَمَن ثَقُلَتْ مَوَٰزِينُهُ ۥ فَأُو۟لَـٰٓئِكَ هُمُ ٱلْمُفْلِحُونَ (٨) وَمَنْ خَفَّتْ مَوَٰزِينُهُ ۥ فَأُو۟لَـٰٓئِكَ ٱلَّذِينَ خَسِرُوٓا۟ أَنفُسَهُم بِمَا كَانُوا۟ بِـَٔايَـٰتِنَا يَظْلِمُونَ (٩)

Then surely, We shall question those (people) to whom it (the Book) was sent and verily, We shall question the Messengers. (6) Then surely, We shall narrate unto them (their whole story) with knowledge, and indeed We were not been absent. (7) And the weighing on that day (Day of Resurrection) will be the true (weighing). So as for those whose scale (of good deeds) will be heavy, they will be the successful (by entering Paradise). (8) And as for those whose scale will be light, they are those who will lose their ownselves (by entering Hell) because they denied and rejected Our Ayât (proofs, evidences, verses, lessons, signs, revelations, etc.). (9)

Quran 7:21

وَقَاسَمَهُمَآ إِنِّى لَكُمَا لَمِنَ ٱلنَّـٰصِحِينَ (٢١)

And he [Shaitân (Satan)] swore by Allâh to them both (saying): "Verily, I am one of the sincere well-wishers for you both." (21)

Quran 7:27-28

يَٰبَنِىٓ ءَادَمَ لَا يَفْتِنَنَّكُمُ ٱلشَّيْطَٰنُ كَمَآ أَخْرَجَ أَبَوَيْكُم مِّنَ ٱلْجَنَّةِ يَنزِعُ عَنْهُمَا لِبَاسَهُمَا لِيُرِيَهُمَا سَوْءَٰتِهِمَآ إِنَّهُۥ يَرَىٰكُمْ هُوَ وَقَبِيلُهُۥ مِنْ حَيْثُ لَا تَرَوْنَهُمْ إِنَّا جَعَلْنَا ٱلشَّيَٰطِينَ أَوْلِيَآءَ لِلَّذِينَ لَا يُؤْمِنُونَ (٢٧) وَإِذَا فَعَلُواْ فَٰحِشَةً قَالُواْ وَجَدْنَا عَلَيْهَآ ءَابَآءَنَا وَٱللَّهُ أَمَرَنَا بِهَا قُلْ إِنَّ ٱللَّهَ لَا يَأْمُرُ بِٱلْفَحْشَآءِ أَتَقُولُونَ عَلَى ٱللَّهِ مَا لَا تَعْلَمُونَ (٢٨)

O Children of Adam! Let not Shaitân (Satan) deceive you, as he got your parents [Adam and Hawwa (Eve)] out of Paradise, stripping them of their raiments, to show them their private parts. Verily, he and Qabîluhu (his soldiers from the jinn or his tribe) see you from where you cannot see them. Verily, We made the Shayâtin (devils) Auliyâ' (protectors and helpers) for those who believe not. (27) And when they commit a Fâhishah (evil deed, going round the Ka'bah in naked state, and every kind of unlawful sexual intercourse), they say: "We found our fathers doing it, and Allâh has commanded it on us." Say: "Nay, Allâh never commands of Fâhishah. Do you say of Allâh what you know not? (28)

Quran 7:30

فَرِيقًا هَدَىٰ وَفَرِيقًا حَقَّ عَلَيْهِمُ ٱلضَّلَٰلَةُ إِنَّهُمُ ٱتَّخَذُواْ ٱلشَّيَٰطِينَ أَوْلِيَآءَ مِن دُونِ ٱللَّهِ وَيَحْسَبُونَ أَنَّهُم مُّهْتَدُونَ (٣٠)

A group He has guided, and a group deserved to be in error; (because) surely they took the Shayâtin (devils) as Auliyâ' (protectors and helpers) instead of Allâh, and think that they are guided. (30)

Quran 7:35-40

يَٰبَنِىٓ ءَادَمَ إِمَّا يَأْتِيَنَّكُمْ رُسُلٌ مِّنكُمْ يَقُصُّونَ عَلَيْكُمْ ءَايَٰتِى فَمَنِ ٱتَّقَىٰ وَأَصْلَحَ فَلَا خَوْفٌ عَلَيْهِمْ وَلَا هُمْ يَحْزَنُونَ (٣٥) وَٱلَّذِينَ كَذَّبُوا۟ بِـَٔايَٰتِنَا وَٱسْتَكْبَرُوا۟ عَنْهَآ أُو۟لَٰٓئِكَ أَصْحَٰبُ ٱلنَّارِ هُمْ فِيهَا خَٰلِدُونَ (٣٦) فَمَنْ أَظْلَمُ مِمَّنِ ٱفْتَرَىٰ عَلَى ٱللَّهِ كَذِبًا أَوْ كَذَّبَ بِـَٔايَٰتِهِۦٓ أُو۟لَٰٓئِكَ يَنَالُهُمْ نَصِيبُهُم مِّنَ ٱلْكِتَٰبِ حَتَّىٰٓ إِذَا جَآءَتْهُمْ رُسُلُنَا يَتَوَفَّوْنَهُمْ قَالُوٓا۟ أَيْنَ مَا كُنتُمْ تَدْعُونَ مِن دُونِ ٱللَّهِ قَالُوا۟ ضَلُّوا۟ عَنَّا وَشَهِدُوا۟ عَلَىٰٓ أَنفُسِهِمْ أَنَّهُمْ كَانُوا۟ كَٰفِرِينَ (٣٧) قَالَ ٱدْخُلُوا۟ فِىٓ أُمَمٍ قَدْ خَلَتْ مِن قَبْلِكُم مِّنَ ٱلْجِنِّ وَٱلْإِنسِ فِى ٱلنَّارِ كُلَّمَا دَخَلَتْ أُمَّةٌ لَّعَنَتْ أُخْتَهَا حَتَّىٰٓ إِذَا ٱدَّارَكُوا۟ فِيهَا جَمِيعًا قَالَتْ أُخْرَىٰهُمْ لِأُولَىٰهُمْ رَبَّنَا هَٰٓؤُلَآءِ أَضَلُّونَا فَـَٔاتِهِمْ عَذَابًا ضِعْفًا مِّنَ ٱلنَّارِ قَالَ لِكُلٍّ ضِعْفٌ وَلَٰكِن لَّا تَعْلَمُونَ (٣٨) وَقَالَتْ أُولَىٰهُمْ لِأُخْرَىٰهُمْ فَمَا كَانَ لَكُمْ عَلَيْنَا مِن فَضْلٍ فَذُوقُوا۟ ٱلْعَذَابَ بِمَا كُنتُمْ تَكْسِبُونَ (٣٩) إِنَّ ٱلَّذِينَ كَذَّبُوا۟ بِـَٔايَٰتِنَا وَٱسْتَكْبَرُوا۟ عَنْهَا لَا تُفَتَّحُ لَهُمْ أَبْوَٰبُ ٱلسَّمَآءِ وَلَا يَدْخُلُونَ ٱلْجَنَّةَ حَتَّىٰ يَلِجَ ٱلْجَمَلُ فِى سَمِّ ٱلْخِيَاطِ وَكَذَٰلِكَ نَجْزِى ٱلْمُجْرِمِينَ (٤٠)

O Children of Adam! If there come to you Messengers from amongst you, reciting to you, My Verses, then whosoever becomes pious and righteous, on them shall be no fear, nor shall they grieve (35) But those who reject Our Ayât (proofs, evidences, verses, lessons, signs, revelations,) and treat them with arrogance, they are the dwellers of the (Hell) Fire, they will abide therein forever (36) Who is more unjust than one who invents a lie against Allâh or rejects His Ayât (proofs, evidences, verses, lessons, signs, revelations)? For such their appointed portion (good things of this worldly life and their period of stay therein) will reach them from the Book (of Decrees) until, when Our Messengers (the angel of death and his assistants) come to them to take their souls, they (the angels) will say: "Where are those whom you used to invoke and worship besides Allâh," they will reply, "They have vanished and deserted us." And they will bear witness against themselves, that they were disbelievers. (37) (Allâh) will say: "Enter you in the company of nations who passed away before you, of men and jinn, into the Fire." Every time a new nation enters, it curses its sister nation (that went before), until they will be gathered all together in the Fire. The last of them will say to the first of them: "Our Lord! These misled us, so give them a double torment of the Fire." He will say: "For each one there is double (torment), but you know not." (38) The first of them will say to the last of them: "You were not better than us, so taste the torment for what you used to earn." (39) Verily, those who belie Our Ayât (proofs, evidences, verses, lessons, signs, revelations) and treat them with arrogance, for them the gates of heaven will not be opened, and they will not enter Paradise until the camel goes through the eye of the needle (which is impossible). Thus do We recompense the Mujrimûn (criminals, polytheists, and sinners). (40)

Quran 7:45-49

ٱلَّذِينَ يَصُدُّونَ عَن سَبِيلِ ٱللَّهِ وَيَبْغُونَهَا عِوَجًا وَهُم بِٱلْأَخِرَةِ كَٰفِرُونَ (٤٥) وَبَيْنَهُمَا حِجَابٌ وَعَلَى ٱلْأَعْرَافِ رِجَالٌ يَعْرِفُونَ كُلًّا بِسِيمَىٰهُمْ وَنَادَوْاْ أَصْحَٰبَ ٱلْجَنَّةِ أَن سَلَٰمٌ عَلَيْكُمْ لَمْ يَدْخُلُوهَا وَهُمْ يَطْمَعُونَ (٤٦) ۞ وَإِذَا صُرِفَتْ أَبْصَٰرُهُمْ تِلْقَآءَ أَصْحَٰبِ ٱلنَّارِ قَالُواْ رَبَّنَا لَا تَجْعَلْنَا مَعَ ٱلْقَوْمِ ٱلظَّٰلِمِينَ (٤٧) وَنَادَىٰٓ أَصْحَٰبُ ٱلْأَعْرَافِ رِجَالًا يَعْرِفُونَهُم بِسِيمَىٰهُمْ قَالُواْ مَآ أَغْنَىٰ عَنكُمْ جَمْعُكُمْ وَمَا كُنتُمْ تَسْتَكْبِرُونَ (٤٨) أَهَٰٓؤُلَآءِ ٱلَّذِينَ أَقْسَمْتُمْ لَا يَنَالُهُمُ ٱللَّهُ بِرَحْمَةٍ ٱدْخُلُواْ ٱلْجَنَّةَ لَا خَوْفٌ عَلَيْكُمْ وَلَا أَنتُمْ تَحْزَنُونَ (٤٩)

Those who hindered (men) from the Path of Allâh, and would seek to make it crooked, and they were disbelievers in the Hereafter. (45) And between them will be a (barrier) screen and on Al-A'râf (a wall with elevated places) will be men (whose good and evil deeds would be equal in scale), who would recognise all (of the Paradise and Hell people), by their marks (the dwellers of Paradise by their white faces and the dwellers of Hell by their black faces), they will call out to the dwellers of Paradise, "Salâmun 'Alaikûm" (peace be on you), and at that time they (men on Al-A'râf) will not yet have entered it (Paradise), but they will hope to enter (it) with certainty. (46) And when their eyes will be turned towards the dwellers of the Fire, they will say: "Our Lord! Place us not with the people who are Zâlimûn (polytheists and wrong-doers)." (47) And the men on Al-A'râf (the wall) will call unto the men whom they would recognise by their marks, saying: "Of what benefit to you were your great numbers (and hoards of wealth), and your arrogance (against Faith)?" (48) Are they those, of whom you swore that Allâh would never show them mercy. (Behold! It has been said to them): "Enter Paradise, no fear shall be on you, nor shall you grieve." (49)

Quran 7:56

وَلَا تُفۡسِدُواْ فِى ٱلۡأَرۡضِ بَعۡدَ إِصۡلَٰحِهَا وَٱدۡعُوهُ خَوۡفًا وَطَمَعًا إِنَّ رَحۡمَتَ ٱللَّهِ قَرِيبٌ مِّنَ ٱلۡمُحۡسِنِينَ (٥٦)

And do not do mischief on the earth, after it has been set in order, and invoke Him with fear and hope; Surely, Allâh's Mercy is (ever) near unto the good-doers. (56)

Quran 7:146-147

سَأَصۡرِفُ عَنۡ ءَايَٰتِىَ ٱلَّذِينَ يَتَكَبَّرُونَ فِى ٱلۡأَرۡضِ بِغَيۡرِ ٱلۡحَقِّ وَإِن يَرَوۡاْ كُلَّ ءَايَةٍ لَّا يُؤۡمِنُواْ بِهَا وَإِن يَرَوۡاْ سَبِيلَ ٱلرُّشۡدِ لَا يَتَّخِذُوهُ سَبِيلًا وَإِن يَرَوۡاْ سَبِيلَ ٱلۡغَىِّ يَتَّخِذُوهُ سَبِيلًا ذَٰلِكَ بِأَنَّهُمۡ كَذَّبُواْ بِـَٔايَٰتِنَا وَكَانُواْ عَنۡهَا

غَٰفِلِينَ (١٤٦) وَٱلَّذِينَ كَذَّبُواْ بِـَٔايَٰتِنَا وَلِقَآءِ ٱلْءَاخِرَةِ حَبِطَتْ أَعْمَٰلُهُمْ هَلْ يُجْزَوْنَ إِلَّا مَا كَانُواْ يَعْمَلُونَ (١٤٧)

I shall turn away from My Ayât (verses of the Qur'ân) those who behave arrogantly on the earth, without a right, and (even) if they see all the Ayât (proofs, evidences, verses, lessons, signs, revelations, etc.), they will not believe in them. And if they see the way of righteousness (monotheism, piety, and good deeds), they will not adopt it as the Way, but if they see the way of error (polytheism, crimes and evil deeds), they will adopt that way, that is because they have rejected Our Ayât (proofs, evidences, verses, lessons, signs, revelations, etc.) and were heedless (to learn a lesson) from them (146) Those who deny Our Ayât (proofs, evidences, verses, lessons, signs, revelations, etc.) and the Meeting in the Hereafter (Day of Resurrection,), vain are their deeds. Are they requited with anything except what they used to do? (147)

Quran 7:155-157

وَٱخْتَارَ مُوسَىٰ قَوْمَهُۥ سَبْعِينَ رَجُلًا لِّمِيقَٰتِنَا ۖ فَلَمَّآ أَخَذَتْهُمُ ٱلرَّجْفَةُ قَالَ رَبِّ لَوْ شِئْتَ أَهْلَكْتَهُم مِّن قَبْلُ وَإِيَّٰىَ ۖ أَتُهْلِكُنَا بِمَا فَعَلَ ٱلسُّفَهَآءُ مِنَّآ ۖ إِنْ هِىَ إِلَّا فِتْنَتُكَ تُضِلُّ بِهَا مَن تَشَآءُ وَتَهْدِى مَن تَشَآءُ ۖ أَنتَ وَلِيُّنَا فَٱغْفِرْ لَنَا وَٱرْحَمْنَا ۖ وَأَنتَ خَيْرُ ٱلْغَٰفِرِينَ (١٥٥) ۞ وَٱكْتُبْ لَنَا فِى هَٰذِهِ ٱلدُّنْيَا

حَسَنَةً وَفِى ٱلْءَاخِرَةِ إِنَّا هُدْنَآ إِلَيْكَ قَالَ عَذَابِى أُصِيبُ بِهِۦ مَنْ أَشَآءُ ۖ وَرَحْمَتِى وَسِعَتْ كُلَّ شَىْءٍ ۚ فَسَأَكْتُبُهَا لِلَّذِينَ يَتَّقُونَ وَيُؤْتُونَ ٱلزَّكَوٰةَ وَٱلَّذِينَ هُم بِـَٔايَٰتِنَا يُؤْمِنُونَ (١٥٦) ٱلَّذِينَ يَتَّبِعُونَ ٱلرَّسُولَ ٱلنَّبِىَّ ٱلْأُمِّىَّ ٱلَّذِى يَجِدُونَهُۥ مَكْتُوبًا عِندَهُمْ فِى ٱلتَّوْرَىٰةِ وَٱلْإِنجِيلِ يَأْمُرُهُم بِٱلْمَعْرُوفِ وَيَنْهَىٰهُمْ عَنِ ٱلْمُنكَرِ وَيُحِلُّ لَهُمُ ٱلطَّيِّبَٰتِ وَيُحَرِّمُ عَلَيْهِمُ ٱلْخَبَٰٓئِثَ وَيَضَعُ عَنْهُمْ إِصْرَهُمْ وَٱلْأَغْلَٰلَ ٱلَّتِى كَانَتْ عَلَيْهِمْ ۚ فَٱلَّذِينَ ءَامَنُوا۟ بِهِۦ وَعَزَّرُوهُ وَنَصَرُوهُ وَٱتَّبَعُوا۟ ٱلنُّورَ ٱلَّذِىٓ أُنزِلَ مَعَهُۥٓ ۙ أُو۟لَٰٓئِكَ هُمُ ٱلْمُفْلِحُونَ (١٥٧)

And Mûsa (Moses) chose out of his people seventy (of the best) men for Our appointed time and place of meeting, and when they were seized with a violent earthquake, he said: "O my Lord, if it had been Your Will, You could have destroyed them and me before; would You destroy us for the deeds of the foolish ones among us? It is only Your Trial by which You lead astray whom You will, and keep guided whom You will. You are our Walî (Protector), so forgive us and have Mercy on us, for You are the Best of those who forgive. (155) And ordain for us good in this world, and in the Hereafter. Certainly we have turned unto You." He said: (As to) My Punishment I afflict therewith whom I will and My Mercy embraces all things. That (Mercy) I shall ordain for those who are the Muttaqûn (pious -), and give Zakât; and those who believe in Our Ayât (proofs, evidences, verses, lessons, signs and revelations, etc.); (156) Those who *follow the Messenger, the Prophet who can neither read nor write (i.e. Muhammad) whom they find written with them in the Taurât (Torah) and the Injeel, - he commands them for Al-Ma'rûf (i.e. Islâmic Monotheism and all that Islâm has ordained); and forbids them from Al-Munkar (i.e. disbelief, polytheism of all kinds, and all that Islâm has forbidden); he allows them as lawful At-Tayyibât (i.e. all good and lawful as regards things, deeds, beliefs, persons, foods), and prohibits them as unlawful Al-Khabâ'ith (i.e. all evil and unlawful as regards things, deeds, beliefs, persons and foods), he releases them from their heavy burdens (of Allâh's Covenant with the children of Israel), and from the fetters (bindings) that were upon them. So those who believe in him (Muhammad), honour him, help him, and follow the light (the Qur'ân) which has been sent down with him, it is they who will be successful. (157)*

Quran 7:162-165

فَبَدَّلَ ٱلَّذِينَ ظَلَمُواْ مِنْهُمْ قَوْلاً غَيْرَ ٱلَّذِى قِيلَ لَهُمْ فَأَرْسَلْنَا عَلَيْهِمْ رِجْزًا مِّنَ ٱلسَّمَآءِ بِمَا كَانُواْ يَظْلِمُونَ (١٦٢) وَسْئَلْهُمْ عَنِ ٱلْقَرْيَةِ ٱلَّتِى كَانَتْ حَاضِرَةَ ٱلْبَحْرِ إِذْ يَعْدُونَ فِى ٱلسَّبْتِ إِذْ تَأْتِيهِمْ حِيتَانُهُمْ يَوْمَ سَبْتِهِمْ شُرَّعًا وَيَوْمَ لاَ يَسْبِتُونَ لاَ تَأْتِيهِمْ كَذَالِكَ نَبْلُوهُم بِمَا كَانُواْ يَفْسُقُونَ (١٦٣) وَإِذْ قَالَتْ أُمَّةٌ مِّنْهُمْ لِمَ تَعِظُونَ قَوْمًا ٱللَّهُ مُهْلِكُهُمْ أَوْ مُعَذِّبُهُمْ عَذَابًا شَدِيدًا قَالُواْ

مَعْذِرَةً إِلَىٰ رَبِّكُمْ وَلَعَلَّهُمْ يَتَّقُونَ (١٦٤) فَلَمَّا نَسُواْ مَا ذُكِّرُواْ بِهِۦ أَنجَيْنَا ٱلَّذِينَ يَنْهَوْنَ عَنِ ٱلسُّوٓءِ وَأَخَذْنَا ٱلَّذِينَ ظَلَمُواْ بِعَذَابٍۭ بَـِٔيسٍۭ بِمَا كَانُواْ يَفْسُقُونَ (١٦٥)

But those among them who did wrong changed the word that had been told to them. So We sent on them a torment from the heaven in return for their wrongdoings. (162) And ask them (O Muhammad) about the town that was by the sea; when they transgressed in the matter of the Sabbath (i.e. Saturday): when their fish came to them openly on the Sabbath day, and did not come to them on the day they had no Sabbath. Thus We made a trial of them, for they used to rebel against Allâh's Command (disobey Allâh). (163) And when a community among them said: "Why do you preach to a people whom Allâh is about to destroy or to punish with a severe torment?" (The preachers) said: "In order to be free from guilt before your Lord (Allâh), and perhaps they may fear Allâh." (164) So when they forgot the remindings that had been given to them, We rescued those who forbade evil, but We seized those who did wrong with a severe torment because they used to rebel against Allah's command (disobey Allâh). (165)

Quran 7:168-169

وَقَطَّعْنَٰهُمْ فِى ٱلْأَرْضِ أُمَمًا ۖ مِّنْهُمُ ٱلصَّٰلِحُونَ وَمِنْهُمْ دُونَ ذَٰلِكَ ۖ وَبَلَوْنَٰهُم بِٱلْحَسَنَٰتِ وَٱلسَّيِّـَٔاتِ لَعَلَّهُمْ يَرْجِعُونَ (١٦٨) فَخَلَفَ مِنۢ بَعْدِهِمْ خَلْفٌ وَرِثُوا۟ ٱلْكِتَٰبَ يَأْخُذُونَ عَرَضَ هَٰذَا ٱلْأَدْنَىٰ وَيَقُولُونَ سَيُغْفَرُ لَنَا وَإِن يَأْتِهِمْ عَرَضٌ مِّثْلُهُۥ يَأْخُذُوهُ ۚ أَلَمْ يُؤْخَذْ عَلَيْهِم مِّيثَٰقُ ٱلْكِتَٰبِ أَن لَّا يَقُولُوا۟ عَلَى ٱللَّهِ إِلَّا ٱلْحَقَّ وَدَرَسُوا۟ مَا فِيهِ ۗ وَٱلدَّارُ ٱلْءَاخِرَةُ خَيْرٌ لِّلَّذِينَ يَتَّقُونَ ۗ أَفَلَا تَعْقِلُونَ (١٦٩)

And We have broken them (i.e. the Jews) up into various separate groups on the earth, some of them are righteous and some are away from that. And We tried them with good (blessings) and evil (calamities) in order that they might turn (to Allâh's Obedience). (168) Then after them succeeded an (evil) generation, which inherited the Book, but they chose (for themselves) the goods of this low life (evil pleasures of this world) saying (as an excuse): "(Everything) will be forgiven to us." And if (again) the offer of the like (evil pleasures of this world) came their way, they would (again) seize them (would commit those sins). Was not the covenant of the Book taken from them that they would not say about Allâh anything but the truth? And they have studied what is in it (the Book). And the home of the Hereafter is better for those who are Al-Muttaqûn (the pious). Do not you then understand? (169)

Quran 7:175-178

وَٱتْلُ عَلَيْهِمْ نَبَأَ ٱلَّذِىٓ ءَاتَيْنَٰهُ ءَايَٰتِنَا فَٱنسَلَخَ مِنْهَا فَأَتْبَعَهُ ٱلشَّيْطَٰنُ فَكَانَ مِنَ ٱلْغَاوِينَ (١٧٥) وَلَوْ شِئْنَا لَرَفَعْنَٰهُ بِهَا وَلَٰكِنَّهُۥٓ أَخْلَدَ إِلَى ٱلْأَرْضِ وَٱتَّبَعَ هَوَىٰهُ ۚ فَمَثَلُهُۥ كَمَثَلِ ٱلْكَلْبِ إِن تَحْمِلْ عَلَيْهِ يَلْهَثْ أَوْ تَتْرُكْهُ يَلْهَث ۚ ذَّٰلِكَ مَثَلُ ٱلْقَوْمِ ٱلَّذِينَ كَذَّبُوا۟ بِـَٔايَٰتِنَا ۚ فَٱقْصُصِ ٱلْقَصَصَ لَعَلَّهُمْ يَتَفَكَّرُونَ (١٧٦) سَآءَ مَثَلًا ٱلْقَوْمُ ٱلَّذِينَ كَذَّبُوا۟ بِـَٔايَٰتِنَا وَأَنفُسَهُمْ كَانُوا۟ يَظْلِمُونَ (١٧٧) مَن يَهْدِ ٱللَّهُ فَهُوَ ٱلْمُهْتَدِى ۖ وَمَن يُضْلِلْ فَأُو۟لَٰٓئِكَ هُمُ ٱلْخَٰسِرُونَ (١٧٨)

And recite (O Muhammad) to them the story of him to whom We gave Our Ayât (proofs, evidences, verses, lessons, signs, revelations, etc.), but he threw them away, so Shaitân (Satan) followed him up, and he became of those who went astray. (175) And had We willed, We would surely have elevated him therewith but he clung to the earth and followed his own vain desire. So his parable is the parable of a dog: if you drive him away, he lolls his tongue out, or if you leave him alone, he (still) lolls his tongue out. Such is the parable of the people who reject Our Ayât (proofs, evidences, verses, lessons, signs, revelations, etc.). So relate the stories, perhaps they may reflect (176) Evil is the parable of the people who reject Our Ayât (proofs, evidences, verses and signs, etc.), and used to wrong their ownselves (177) Whomsoever Allâh guides, he is the guided one, and whomsoever He sends astray, then those! they are the losers (178)

Quran 7:181-186

وَمِمَّنْ خَلَقْنَآ أُمَّةٌ يَهْدُونَ بِٱلْحَقِّ وَبِهِۦ يَعْدِلُونَ (١٨١) وَٱلَّذِينَ كَذَّبُواْ بِـَٔايَٰتِنَا سَنَسْتَدْرِجُهُم مِّنْ حَيْثُ لَا يَعْلَمُونَ (١٨٢) وَأُمْلِى لَهُمْۚ إِنَّ كَيْدِى مَتِينٌ (١٨٣) أَوَلَمْ يَتَفَكَّرُواْۗ مَا بِصَاحِبِهِم مِّن جِنَّةٍۚ إِنْ هُوَ إِلَّا نَذِيرٌ مُّبِينٌ (١٨٤) أَوَلَمْ يَنظُرُواْ فِى مَلَكُوتِ ٱلسَّمَٰوَٰتِ وَٱلْأَرْضِ وَمَا خَلَقَ ٱللَّهُ مِن شَىْءٍ وَأَنْ عَسَىٰٓ أَن يَكُونَ قَدِ ٱقْتَرَبَ أَجَلُهُمْۖ فَبِأَىِّ حَدِيثٍۭ بَعْدَهُۥ يُؤْمِنُونَ (١٨٥) مَن يُضْلِلِ ٱللَّهُ فَلَا هَادِىَ لَهُۥۚ وَيَذَرُهُمْ فِى طُغْيَٰنِهِمْ يَعْمَهُونَ (١٨٦)

And of those whom We have created, there is a community who guides (others) with the truth, and establishes justice therewith. (181) Those who reject Our Ayât (proofs, evidences, verses, lessons, signs, revelations, etc.), We shall gradually seize them with punishment in ways they perceive not. (182) And I respite them; certainly My Plan is strong. (183) Do they not reflect? There is no madness in their companion (Muhammad). He is but a plain warner. (184) Do they not look in the dominion of the heavens and the earth and all things that Allâh has created, and that it may be that the end of their lives is near. In what message after this will they then believe? (185) Whomsoever Allâh sends astray, none can guide him; and He lets them wander blindly in their transgressions. (186)

Quran 7:198-202

وَإِن تَدْعُوهُمْ إِلَى ٱلْهُدَىٰ لَا يَسْمَعُوا۟ۖ وَتَرَىٰهُمْ يَنظُرُونَ إِلَيْكَ وَهُمْ لَا يُبْصِرُونَ (١٩٨) خُذِ ٱلْعَفْوَ وَأْمُرْ بِٱلْعُرْفِ وَأَعْرِضْ عَنِ ٱلْجَٰهِلِينَ (١٩٩) وَإِمَّا يَنزَغَنَّكَ مِنَ ٱلشَّيْطَٰنِ نَزْغٌ فَٱسْتَعِذْ بِٱللَّهِۚ إِنَّهُۥ سَمِيعٌ عَلِيمٌ (٢٠٠) إِنَّ ٱلَّذِينَ ٱتَّقَوْا۟ إِذَا مَسَّهُمْ طَٰٓئِفٌ مِّنَ ٱلشَّيْطَٰنِ تَذَكَّرُوا۟ فَإِذَا هُم مُّبْصِرُونَ (٢٠١) وَإِخْوَٰنُهُمْ يَمُدُّونَهُمْ فِى ٱلْغَىِّ ثُمَّ لَا يُقْصِرُونَ (٢٠٢)

And if you call them to guidance, they hear not and you will see them looking at you, yet they see not. (198) Show forgiveness, enjoin what is good, and turn away from the foolish (i.e. don't punish them). (199) And if an evil whisper comes to you from Shaitân (Satan) then seek refuge with Allâh. Verily, He is All-Hearer, All-Knower. (200) Verily, those who are Al-Muttaqûn (the pious), when an evil thought comes to them from Shaitân (Satan), they remember (Allâh), and (indeed) they then see (aright). (201) But (as for) their brothers (the devils) they (i.e. the devils) plunge them deeper into error, and they never stop short. (202)

Quran 8:13

ذَٰلِكَ بِأَنَّهُمْ شَآقُّوا۟ ٱللَّهَ وَرَسُولَهُۥۚ وَمَن يُشَاقِقِ ٱللَّهَ وَرَسُولَهُۥ فَإِنَّ ٱللَّهَ شَدِيدُ ٱلْعِقَابِ (١٣)

This is because they defied and disobeyed Allâh and His Messenger. And whoever defies and disobeys

Allâh and His Messenger, then verily, Allâh is Severe in punishment (13)

Quran 8:20-25

يَٰٓأَيُّهَا ٱلَّذِينَ ءَامَنُوٓاْ أَطِيعُواْ ٱللَّهَ وَرَسُولَهُۥ وَلَا تَوَلَّوْاْ عَنْهُ وَأَنتُمْ تَسْمَعُونَ (٢٠) وَلَا تَكُونُواْ كَٱلَّذِينَ قَالُواْ سَمِعْنَا وَهُمْ لَا يَسْمَعُونَ (٢١) ۞ إِنَّ شَرَّ ٱلدَّوَآبِّ عِندَ ٱللَّهِ ٱلصُّمُّ ٱلْبُكْمُ ٱلَّذِينَ لَا يَعْقِلُونَ (٢٢) وَلَوْ عَلِمَ ٱللَّهُ فِيهِمْ خَيْرًا لَّأَسْمَعَهُمْ وَلَوْ أَسْمَعَهُمْ لَتَوَلَّواْ وَّهُم مُّعْرِضُونَ (٢٣) يَٰٓأَيُّهَا ٱلَّذِينَ ءَامَنُواْ ٱسْتَجِيبُواْ لِلَّهِ وَلِلرَّسُولِ إِذَا دَعَاكُمْ لِمَا يُحْيِيكُمْ وَٱعْلَمُوٓاْ أَنَّ ٱللَّهَ يَحُولُ بَيْنَ ٱلْمَرْءِ وَقَلْبِهِۦ وَأَنَّهُۥٓ إِلَيْهِ تُحْشَرُونَ (٢٤) وَٱتَّقُواْ فِتْنَةً لَّا تُصِيبَنَّ ٱلَّذِينَ ظَلَمُواْ مِنكُمْ خَآصَّةً ۖ وَٱعْلَمُوٓاْ أَنَّ ٱللَّهَ شَدِيدُ ٱلْعِقَابِ (٢٥)

O you who believe! Obey Allâh and His Messenger, and turn not away from him (i.e. Messenger Muhammad) while you are hearing. (20) And be not like those who say: "We have heard," but they hear not. (21) Verily! The worst of (moving) living creatures with Allâh are the deaf and the dumb, who understand not (i.e. the disbelievers) (22) Had Allâh known of any good in them, He would indeed have made them listen; and even if He had made them listen, they would but have turned away with aversion (to the truth). (23) O you who believe! Answer Allâh (by obeying Him) and (His) Messenger when he calls you to that which will give you life, and know that Allâh comes in between a person and his heart (i.e. He prevents an evil person to decide anything). And verily to Him you shall (all) be gathered. (24) And fear the Fitnah (affliction and trial) which affects not in particular (only) those of you who do wrong (but it may afflict all the good and the bad people), and know that Allâh is Severe in punishment. (25)

Quran 8:27

يَـٰٓأَيُّهَا ٱلَّذِينَ ءَامَنُواْ لَا تَخُونُواْ ٱللَّهَ وَٱلرَّسُولَ وَتَخُونُوٓاْ أَمَـٰنَـٰتِكُمْ وَأَنتُمْ تَعْلَمُونَ (٢٧)

O you who believe! Betray not Allâh and His Messenger, nor betray knowingly your Amânât (things entrusted to you, and all the duties which Allâh has ordained for you). (27)

Quran 8:49-51

إِذْ يَقُولُ ٱلْمُنَـٰفِقُونَ وَٱلَّذِينَ فِى قُلُوبِهِم مَّرَضٌ غَرَّ هَـٰٓؤُلَاءِ دِينُهُمْ ۗ وَمَن يَتَوَكَّلْ عَلَى ٱللَّهِ فَإِنَّ ٱللَّهَ عَزِيزٌ حَكِيمٌ (٤٩) وَلَوْ تَرَىٰٓ إِذْ يَتَوَفَّى ٱلَّذِينَ كَفَرُواْ ٱلْمَلَـٰٓئِكَةُ يَضْرِبُونَ وُجُوهَهُمْ وَأَدْبَـٰرَهُمْ وَذُوقُواْ عَذَابَ ٱلْحَرِيقِ (٥٠) ذَٰلِكَ بِمَا قَدَّمَتْ أَيْدِيكُمْ وَأَنَّ ٱللَّهَ لَيْسَ بِظَلَّـٰمٍ لِّلْعَبِيدِ (٥١)

When the hypocrites and those in whose hearts was a disease (of disbelief) said: "These people (Muslims) are deceived by their religion." But whoever puts his trust in Allâh, then surely, Allâh is All-Mighty, All-

Wise (49) And if you could see when the angels take away the souls of those who disbelieve (at death), they smite their faces and their backs, (saying): "Taste the punishment of the blazing Fire." (50) "This is because of that which your hands had forwarded. And verily, Allâh is not unjust to His slaves." (51)

Quran 9:53-58

قُلْ أَنفِقُوا۟ طَوْعًا أَوْ كَرْهًا لَّن يُتَقَبَّلَ مِنكُمْ إِنَّكُمْ كُنتُمْ قَوْمًا فَـٰسِقِينَ (٥٣) وَمَا مَنَعَهُمْ أَن تُقْبَلَ مِنْهُمْ نَفَقَـٰتُهُمْ إِلَّآ أَنَّهُمْ كَفَرُوا۟ بِٱللَّهِ وَبِرَسُولِهِۦ وَلَا يَأْتُونَ ٱلصَّلَوٰةَ إِلَّا وَهُمْ كُسَالَىٰ وَلَا يُنفِقُونَ إِلَّا وَهُمْ كَـٰرِهُونَ (٥٤) فَلَا تُعْجِبْكَ أَمْوَٰلُهُمْ وَلَآ أَوْلَـٰدُهُمْ إِنَّمَا يُرِيدُ ٱللَّهُ لِيُعَذِّبَهُم بِهَا فِى ٱلْحَيَوٰةِ ٱلدُّنْيَا وَتَزْهَقَ أَنفُسُهُمْ وَهُمْ كَـٰفِرُونَ (٥٥) وَيَحْلِفُونَ بِٱللَّهِ إِنَّهُمْ لَمِنكُمْ وَمَا هُم مِّنكُمْ وَلَـٰكِنَّهُمْ قَوْمٌ يَفْرَقُونَ (٥٦) لَوْ يَجِدُونَ مَلْجَـًٔا أَوْ مَغَـٰرَٰتٍ أَوْ مُدَّخَلًا لَّوَلَّوْا۟ إِلَيْهِ وَهُمْ يَجْمَحُونَ (٥٧) وَمِنْهُم مَّن يَلْمِزُكَ فِى ٱلصَّدَقَـٰتِ فَإِنْ أُعْطُوا۟ مِنْهَا رَضُوا۟ وَإِن لَّمْ يُعْطَوْا۟ مِنْهَآ إِذَا هُمْ يَسْخَطُونَ (٥٨)

Say: "Spend (in Allâh's Cause) willingly or unwillingly, it will not be accepted from you. Verily, you are ever a people who are Fâsiqûn (rebellious, disobedient to Allâh)." (53) And nothing prevents their contributions from being accepted from them except that they disbelieved in Allâh and in His Messenger (Muhammad); and that they came not to As-Salât (the prayer) except in a lazy state; and that they offer not contributions but unwillingly. (54) So let not their wealth or their children amaze you (O Muhammad); in reality Allâh's Plan is to punish them with these things in the life of the this world, and that their souls shall depart (die) while they are disbelievers. (55) They swear by Allâh that they are truly of you while they are not of you, but they are a people (hypocrites) who are afraid (that you may kill them). (56) Should they find a refuge, or caves, or a place of concealment, they would turn straightway thereto with a swift rush. (57) And of them are some who accuse you (O Muhammad) in the matter of (the distribution of) the alms. If they are given part thereof, they are pleased, but if they are not given thereof, behold! They are enraged! (58)

Quran 9:61-69

وَمِنْهُمُ ٱلَّذِينَ يُؤْذُونَ ٱلنَّبِىَّ وَيَقُولُونَ هُوَ أُذُنٌ قُلْ أُذُنُ خَيْرٍ لَّكُمْ يُؤْمِنُ بِٱللَّهِ وَيُؤْمِنُ لِلْمُؤْمِنِينَ وَرَحْمَةٌ لِّلَّذِينَ ءَامَنُوا۟ مِنكُمْ وَٱلَّذِينَ يُؤْذُونَ رَسُولَ ٱللَّهِ لَهُمْ عَذَابٌ أَلِيمٌ (٦١) يَحْلِفُونَ بِٱللَّهِ لَكُمْ لِيُرْضُوكُمْ وَٱللَّهُ وَرَسُولُهُۥ أَحَقُّ أَن يُرْضُوهُ إِن كَانُوا۟ مُؤْمِنِينَ (٦٢) أَلَمْ يَعْلَمُوٓا۟ أَنَّهُۥ مَن يُحَادِدِ ٱللَّهَ وَرَسُولَهُۥ فَأَنَّ لَهُۥ نَارَ جَهَنَّمَ خَٰلِدًا فِيهَا ذَٰلِكَ ٱلْخِزْىُ ٱلْعَظِيمُ (٦٣) يَحْذَرُ ٱلْمُنَٰفِقُونَ أَن تُنَزَّلَ عَلَيْهِمْ سُورَةٌ تُنَبِّئُهُم بِمَا فِى قُلُوبِهِمْ قُلِ ٱسْتَهْزِءُوٓا۟ إِنَّ ٱللَّهَ مُخْرِجٌ مَّا تَحْذَرُونَ (٦٤) وَلَئِن سَأَلْتَهُمْ لَيَقُولُنَّ إِنَّمَا كُنَّا نَخُوضُ وَنَلْعَبُ قُلْ أَبِٱللَّهِ وَءَايَٰتِهِۦ وَرَسُولِهِۦ كُنتُمْ تَسْتَهْزِءُونَ (٦٥) لَا تَعْتَذِرُوا۟ قَدْ كَفَرْتُم بَعْدَ إِيمَٰنِكُمْ إِن نَّعْفُ عَن طَآئِفَةٍ مِّنكُمْ نُعَذِّبْ طَآئِفَةًۢ بِأَنَّهُمْ كَانُوا۟ مُجْرِمِينَ (٦٦) ٱلْمُنَٰفِقُونَ وَٱلْمُنَٰفِقَٰتُ بَعْضُهُم مِّنۢ

بَعْضٍۚ يَأْمُرُونَ بِٱلْمُنكَرِ وَيَنْهَوْنَ عَنِ ٱلْمَعْرُوفِ وَيَقْبِضُونَ أَيْدِيَهُمْۚ نَسُواْ ٱللَّهَ فَنَسِيَهُمْۗ إِنَّ ٱلْمُنَٰفِقِينَ هُمُ ٱلْفَٰسِقُونَ (٦٧) وَعَدَ ٱللَّهُ ٱلْمُنَٰفِقِينَ وَٱلْمُنَٰفِقَٰتِ وَٱلْكُفَّارَ نَارَ جَهَنَّمَ خَٰلِدِينَ فِيهَاۚ هِىَ حَسْبُهُمْۚ وَلَعَنَهُمُ ٱللَّهُۖ وَلَهُمْ عَذَابٌ مُّقِيمٌ (٦٨) كَٱلَّذِينَ مِن قَبْلِكُمْ كَانُوٓاْ أَشَدَّ مِنكُمْ قُوَّةً وَأَكْثَرَ أَمْوَٰلًا وَأَوْلَٰدًا فَٱسْتَمْتَعُواْ بِخَلَٰقِهِمْ فَٱسْتَمْتَعْتُم بِخَلَٰقِكُمْ كَمَا ٱسْتَمْتَعَ ٱلَّذِينَ مِن قَبْلِكُم بِخَلَٰقِهِمْ وَخُضْتُمْ كَٱلَّذِى خَاضُوٓاْۚ أُوْلَٰٓئِكَ حَبِطَتْ أَعْمَٰلُهُمْ فِى ٱلدُّنْيَا وَٱلْءَاخِرَةِۖ وَأُوْلَٰٓئِكَ هُمُ ٱلْخَٰسِرُونَ (٦٩)

And among them are men who annoy the Prophet (Muhammad) and say: "He is (lending his) ear (to every news)." Say: "He listens to what is best for you; he believes in Allâh; has faith in the believers; and is a mercy to those of you who believe." But those who hurt Allâh's Messenger (Muhammad) will have a painful torment. (61) They swear by Allâh to you (Muslims) in order to please you, but it is more fitting that they should please Allâh and His Messenger (Muhammad), if they are believers. (62) Know they not that whoever opposes and shows hostility to Allâh and His Messenger, certainly for him will be the Fire of Hell to abide therein. That is extreme disgrace. (63) The hypocrites fear lest a Sûrah (chapter of the Qur'ân) should be revealed about them, showing them what is in their hearts. Say: "(Go ahead and) mock! But certainly Allâh will bring to light all that you fear." (64) If you ask them (about this), they declare: "We were only talking idly and joking." Say: "Was it at Allâh, and His Ayât (proofs, evidences, verses, lessons, signs, revelations) and His Messenger that you were mocking?" (65) Make no excuse; you have disbelieved after you had believed. If We pardon some of you, We will punish others amongst you because they were Mujrimûn (disbelievers, polytheists, sinners, criminals). (66) The hypocrites, men and women, are one from another, they enjoin (on the people) Al-Munkar (i.e. disbelief and polytheism of all kinds and all that Islâm has forbidden), and forbid (people) from Al-Ma'rûf (i.e. Islâmic Monotheism and all that Islâm orders one to do), and they close their hands [from giving (spending in Allâh's Cause) alms]. They have forgotten Allâh, so He has forgotten them. Verily, the hypocrites are the Fâsiqûn (rebellious, disobedient to Allâh). (67) Allâh has promised the hypocrites — men and women — and the disbelievers, the Fire of Hell, therein shall they abide. It will suffice them. Allâh has cursed them and for them is the lasting torment. (68) Like those before you: they were mightier than you in power, and more abundant in wealth and children. They had enjoyed their portion (awhile), so enjoy your portion (awhile) as those before you enjoyed their portion (awhile); and you indulged in play and pastime (and in telling lies against Allâh and His Messenger Muhammad) as they indulged in play and pastime. Such are they whose deeds are in vain in this world and in the Hereafter. Such are they who are the losers. (69)

Quran 9:73-74

يَٰٓأَيُّهَا ٱلنَّبِىُّ جَٰهِدِ ٱلْكُفَّارَ وَٱلْمُنَٰفِقِينَ وَٱغْلُظْ عَلَيْهِمْ وَمَأْوَىٰهُمْ جَهَنَّمُ وَبِئْسَ ٱلْمَصِيرُ (٧٣) يَحْلِفُونَ بِٱللَّهِ مَا قَالُوا۟ وَلَقَدْ قَالُوا۟ كَلِمَةَ ٱلْكُفْرِ وَكَفَرُوا۟ بَعْدَ إِسْلَٰمِهِمْ وَهَمُّوا۟ بِمَا لَمْ يَنَالُوا۟ وَمَا نَقَمُوٓا۟ إِلَّآ أَنْ أَغْنَىٰهُمُ ٱللَّهُ وَرَسُولُهُۥ مِن فَضْلِهِۦ فَإِن يَتُوبُوا۟ يَكُ خَيْرًا لَّهُمْ وَإِن يَتَوَلَّوْا۟ يُعَذِّبْهُمُ ٱللَّهُ عَذَابًا أَلِيمًا فِى ٱلدُّنْيَا وَٱلْءَاخِرَةِ وَمَا لَهُمْ فِى ٱلْأَرْضِ مِن وَلِىٍّ وَلَا نَصِيرٍ (٧٤)

O Prophet (Muhammad)! Strive hard against the disbelievers and the hypocrites, and be harsh against them, their abode is Hell, - and worst indeed is that destination. (73) They swear by Allâh that they said nothing (bad), but really they said the word of disbelief, and they disbelieved after accepting Islâm, and they resolved that (plot to murder Prophet Muhammad) which they were unable to carry out, and they could not find any cause to do so except that Allâh and His Messenger had enriched them of His Bounty. If then they repent, it will be better for them, but if they turn away, Allâh will punish them with a painful torment in this worldly life and in the Hereafter. And there is none for them on earth as a Walî (supporter, protector) or a helper. (74)

Quran 9:96-97

يَحْلِفُونَ لَكُمْ لِتَرْضَوْا۟ عَنْهُمْ ۖ فَإِن تَرْضَوْا۟ عَنْهُمْ فَإِنَّ ٱللَّهَ لَا يَرْضَىٰ عَنِ ٱلْقَوْمِ ٱلْفَٰسِقِينَ (٩٦) ٱلْأَعْرَابُ أَشَدُّ كُفْرًا وَنِفَاقًا وَأَجْدَرُ أَلَّا يَعْلَمُوا۟ حُدُودَ مَآ أَنزَلَ ٱللَّهُ عَلَىٰ رَسُولِهِۦ ۗ وَٱللَّهُ عَلِيمٌ حَكِيمٌ (٩٧)

They (the hypocrites) swear to you (Muslims) that you may be pleased with them, but if you are pleased with them, certainly Allâh is not pleased with the people who are Al-Fâsiqûn (rebellious, disobedient to Allâh) (96) The bedouins are the worst in disbelief and hypocrisy, and more likely to be in ignorance of the limits (Allâh's Commandments and His Laws) which Allâh has revealed to His Messenger. And Allâh is All-Knower, All-Wise. (97)

Quran 9:107-110

وَٱلَّذِينَ ٱتَّخَذُوا۟ مَسْجِدًا ضِرَارًا وَكُفْرًا وَتَفْرِيقًۢا بَيْنَ ٱلْمُؤْمِنِينَ وَإِرْصَادًا لِّمَنْ حَارَبَ ٱللَّهَ وَرَسُولَهُۥ مِن قَبْلُ ۚ وَلَيَحْلِفُنَّ إِنْ أَرَدْنَآ إِلَّا ٱلْحُسْنَىٰ ۖ وَٱللَّهُ يَشْهَدُ إِنَّهُمْ لَكَٰذِبُونَ (١٠٧) لَا تَقُمْ فِيهِ أَبَدًا ۚ لَّمَسْجِدٌ أُسِّسَ عَلَى ٱلتَّقْوَىٰ مِنْ أَوَّلِ يَوْمٍ أَحَقُّ أَن تَقُومَ فِيهِ ۚ فِيهِ رِجَالٌ يُحِبُّونَ أَن يَتَطَهَّرُوا۟ ۚ وَٱللَّهُ يُحِبُّ ٱلْمُطَّهِّرِينَ (١٠٨) أَفَمَنْ أَسَّسَ بُنْيَٰنَهُۥ عَلَىٰ تَقْوَىٰ مِنَ ٱللَّهِ وَرِضْوَٰنٍ خَيْرٌ أَم مَّنْ أَسَّسَ بُنْيَٰنَهُۥ عَلَىٰ شَفَا جُرُفٍ هَارٍ فَٱنْهَارَ بِهِۦ فِى نَارِ جَهَنَّمَ

وَٱللَّهُ لَا يَهْدِى ٱلْقَوْمَ ٱلظَّٰلِمِينَ (١٠٩) لَا يَزَالُ بُنْيَٰنُهُمُ ٱلَّذِى بَنَوْا۟ رِيبَةً فِى قُلُوبِهِمْ إِلَّآ أَن تَقَطَّعَ قُلُوبُهُمْ ۗ وَٱللَّهُ عَلِيمٌ حَكِيمٌ (١١٠)

And as for those who put up a mosque by way of harm and disbelief, and to disunite the believers, and as an outpost for those who warred against Allâh and His Messenger (Muhammad) aforetime, they will indeed swear that their intention is nothing but good. Allâh bears witness that they are certainly liars. (107) Never stand you therein. Verily, the mosque whose foundation was laid from the first day on piety is more worthy that you stand therein (to pray). In it are men who love to clean and to purify themselves. And Allâh loves those who make themselves clean and pure. (108) Is it then he who laid the foundation of his building on piety to Allâh and His Good Pleasure better, or he who laid the foundation of his building on the brink of an undetermined precipice ready to crumble down, so that it crumbled to pieces with him into the Fire of Hell. And Allâh guides not the people who are the Zâlimûn (cruel, violent, proud, polytheist and wrong-doer). (109) The building which they built will never cease to be a cause of hypocrisy and doubt in their hearts, unless their hearts are cut to pieces. (i.e. till they die). And Allâh is All-Knowing, All-Wise. (110)

Quran 9:115

وَمَا كَانَ ٱللَّهُ لِيُضِلَّ قَوْمًۢا بَعْدَ إِذْ هَدَىٰهُمْ حَتَّىٰ يُبَيِّنَ لَهُم مَّا يَتَّقُونَ ۚ إِنَّ ٱللَّهَ بِكُلِّ شَىْءٍ عَلِيمٌ (١١٥)

And Allâh will never lead a people astray after He has guided them until He makes clear to them as to what they should avoid. Verily, Allâh is the All-Knower of everything.(115)

Quran 9:123-127

يَـٰٓأَيُّهَا ٱلَّذِينَ ءَامَنُوا۟ قَـٰتِلُوا۟ ٱلَّذِينَ يَلُونَكُم مِّنَ ٱلْكُفَّارِ وَلْيَجِدُوا۟ فِيكُمْ غِلْظَةً ۚ وَٱعْلَمُوٓا۟ أَنَّ ٱللَّهَ مَعَ ٱلْمُتَّقِينَ (١٢٣) وَإِذَا مَآ أُنزِلَتْ سُورَةٌ فَمِنْهُم مَّن يَقُولُ أَيُّكُمْ زَادَتْهُ هَـٰذِهِۦٓ إِيمَـٰنًا ۚ فَأَمَّا ٱلَّذِينَ ءَامَنُوا۟ فَزَادَتْهُمْ إِيمَـٰنًا وَهُمْ يَسْتَبْشِرُونَ (١٢٤) وَأَمَّا ٱلَّذِينَ فِى قُلُوبِهِم مَّرَضٌ فَزَادَتْهُمْ رِجْسًا إِلَىٰ رِجْسِهِمْ وَمَاتُوا۟ وَهُمْ كَـٰفِرُونَ (١٢٥) أَوَلَا يَرَوْنَ أَنَّهُمْ يُفْتَنُونَ فِى كُلِّ عَامٍ مَّرَّةً أَوْ مَرَّتَيْنِ ثُمَّ لَا يَتُوبُونَ وَلَا هُمْ يَذَّكَّرُونَ (١٢٦) وَإِذَا مَآ أُنزِلَتْ سُورَةٌ نَّظَرَ بَعْضُهُمْ إِلَىٰ بَعْضٍ هَلْ يَرَىٰكُم مِّنْ أَحَدٍ ثُمَّ ٱنصَرَفُوا۟ ۚ صَرَفَ ٱللَّهُ قُلُوبَهُم بِأَنَّهُمْ قَوْمٌ لَّا يَفْقَهُونَ (١٢٧)

O you who believe! Fight those of the disbelievers who are close to you, and let them find harshness in you, and know that Allâh is with those who are the Al-Muttaqûn (the pious). (123) And whenever there comes down a Sûrah (chapter from the Qur'ân), some of them (hypocrites) say: "Which of you has had his Faith increased by it?" As for those who believe, it has increased their Faith, and they rejoice. (124) But as for those in whose hearts is a disease (of doubt, disbelief and hypocrisy), it will add suspicion and doubt to their suspicion, disbelief and doubt, and they die while they are disbelievers. (125) See they not that they are put in trial once or twice every year (with different kinds of calamities, disease, famine)? Yet, they turn not in repentance, nor do they learn a lesson (from it). (126) And whenever there comes down a Sûrah (chapter from the Qur'ân), they look at one another (saying): "Does any one see you?" Then they turn away. Allâh has turned their hearts (from the light) because they are a people that understand not. (127)

Quran 10:15-19

وَإِذَا تُتْلَىٰ عَلَيْهِمْ ءَايَاتُنَا بَيِّنَاتٍ قَالَ ٱلَّذِينَ لَا يَرْجُونَ لِقَآءَنَا ٱئْتِ بِقُرْءَانٍ غَيْرِ هَٰذَآ أَوْ بَدِّلْهُ قُلْ مَا يَكُونُ لِىٓ أَنْ أُبَدِّلَهُۥ مِن تِلْقَآئِ نَفْسِىٓ إِنْ أَتَّبِعُ إِلَّا مَا يُوحَىٰٓ إِلَىَّ إِنِّىٓ أَخَافُ إِنْ عَصَيْتُ رَبِّى عَذَابَ يَوْمٍ عَظِيمٍ (١٥) قُل لَّوْ شَآءَ ٱللَّهُ مَا تَلَوْتُهُۥ عَلَيْكُمْ وَلَآ أَدْرَىٰكُم بِهِۦ فَقَدْ لَبِثْتُ فِيكُمْ عُمُرًا مِّن قَبْلِهِۦٓ أَفَلَا تَعْقِلُونَ (١٦) فَمَنْ أَظْلَمُ مِمَّنِ ٱفْتَرَىٰ عَلَى ٱللَّهِ كَذِبًا أَوْ كَذَّبَ بِـَٔايَـٰتِهِۦٓ إِنَّهُۥ لَا يُفْلِحُ ٱلْمُجْرِمُونَ (١٧) وَيَعْبُدُونَ مِن دُونِ ٱللَّهِ مَا لَا يَضُرُّهُمْ وَلَا يَنفَعُهُمْ وَيَقُولُونَ هَـٰٓؤُلَآءِ شُفَعَـٰٓؤُنَا عِندَ ٱللَّهِ قُلْ أَتُنَبِّـُٔونَ ٱللَّهَ بِمَا لَا يَعْلَمُ فِى ٱلسَّمَـٰوَاتِ وَلَا فِى ٱلْأَرْضِ سُبْحَـٰنَهُۥ وَتَعَـٰلَىٰ عَمَّا يُشْرِكُونَ (١٨) وَمَا كَانَ ٱلنَّاسُ إِلَّآ أُمَّةً وَاحِدَةً فَٱخْتَلَفُوا۟ وَلَوْلَا كَلِمَةٌ سَبَقَتْ مِن رَّبِّكَ لَقُضِىَ بَيْنَهُمْ فِيمَا فِيهِ يَخْتَلِفُونَ (١٩)

And when Our Clear Verses are recited unto them, those who hope not for their meeting with Us, say: Bring us a Qur'ân other than this, or change it." Say (O Muhammad): "It is not for me to change it on my own accord; I only follow that which is revealed unto me. Verily, I fear the torment of the Great Day (i.e. the Day of Resurrection). if I were to disobey my Lord." (15) Say (O Muhammad): "If Allâh had so willed, I should not have recited it to you nor would He have made it known to you. Verily, I have stayed amongst you a life time before this. Have you then no sense?" (16) So who does more wrong than he who forges a lie against Allâh or denies His Ayât (proofs, evidences, verses, lessons, signs, revelations, etc.)? Surely, the Mujrimûn (criminals, sinners, disbelievers and polytheists) will never be successful! (17) And they worship besides Allâh things that hurt them not, nor profit them, and they say: "These are our intercessors with Allâh." Say: "Do you inform Allâh of that which He knows not in the heavens and on the earth?" Glorified and Exalted is He above all that which they associate as partners (with Him)! (18) Mankind were but one community (i.e. on one religion - Islâmic Monotheism), then they differed (later), and had not it been for a Word that went forth before from your Lord, it would have been settled between them regarding what they differed (19)

Quran 10:36

وَمَا يَتَّبِعُ أَكْثَرُهُمْ إِلَّا ظَنًّا ۚ إِنَّ ٱلظَّنَّ لَا يُغْنِى مِنَ ٱلْحَقِّ شَيْئًا ۚ إِنَّ ٱللَّهَ عَلِيمٌ بِمَا يَفْعَلُونَ (٣٦)

And most of them follow nothing but conjecture. Certainly, conjecture can be of no avail against the truth. Surely, Allâh is All-Aware of what they do. (36)

Quran 11:113

وَلَا تَرْكَنُوٓاْ إِلَى ٱلَّذِينَ ظَلَمُواْ فَتَمَسَّكُمُ ٱلنَّارُ وَمَا لَكُم مِّن دُونِ ٱللَّهِ مِنْ أَوْلِيَآءَ ثُمَّ لَا تُنصَرُونَ (١١٣)

And incline not toward those who do wrong, lest the Fire should touch you, and you have no protectors other than Allâh, nor you would then be helped (113)

Quran 11:116-118

فَلَوْلَا كَانَ مِنَ ٱلْقُرُونِ مِن قَبْلِكُمْ أُوْلُواْ بَقِيَّةٍ يَنْهَوْنَ عَنِ ٱلْفَسَادِ فِى ٱلْأَرْضِ إِلَّا قَلِيلًا مِّمَّنْ أَنجَيْنَا مِنْهُمْ ۗ وَٱتَّبَعَ ٱلَّذِينَ ظَلَمُواْ مَآ أُتْرِفُواْ فِيهِ وَكَانُواْ مُجْرِمِينَ (١١٦) وَمَا كَانَ رَبُّكَ لِيُهْلِكَ ٱلْقُرَىٰ بِظُلْمٍ وَأَهْلُهَا مُصْلِحُونَ (١١٧) وَلَوْ شَآءَ رَبُّكَ لَجَعَلَ ٱلنَّاسَ أُمَّةً وَٰحِدَةً ۖ وَلَا يَزَالُونَ مُخْتَلِفِينَ (١١٨)

If only there had been among the generations before you, persons having wisdom, prohibiting (others) from Al-Fasâd (disbelief, polytheism, and all kinds of crimes and sins) in the earth, (but there were none) except a few of those whom We saved from among them. Those who did wrong pursued the enjoyment of good things of (this worldly) life, and were Mujrimûn (criminals, disbelievers in Allâh, polytheists, sinners). (116) And your Lord would never destroy the towns wrongfully, while their people were right-doers. (117) And if your Lord had so willed, He could surely have made mankind one Ummah [nation or community (following one religion only i.e. Islâm)], but they will not cease to disagree, – (118)

Quran 13:25

وَٱلَّذِينَ يَنقُضُونَ عَهْدَ ٱللَّهِ مِنۢ بَعْدِ مِيثَٰقِهِۦ وَيَقْطَعُونَ مَآ أَمَرَ ٱللَّهُ بِهِۦٓ أَن يُوصَلَ وَيُفْسِدُونَ فِى ٱلْأَرْضِ ۙ أُو۟لَٰٓئِكَ لَهُمُ ٱللَّعْنَةُ وَلَهُمْ سُوٓءُ ٱلدَّارِ (٢٥)

And those who break the Covenant of Allâh, after its ratification, and sever that which Allâh has commanded to be joined (i.e. they sever the bond of kinship and are not good to their relatives), and work mischief in the land, on them is the curse (i.e. they will be far away from Allâh's Mercy); and for them is the unhappy (evil) home (i.e. Hell) (25)

Quran 13:37

وَكَذَٰلِكَ أَنزَلْنَٰهُ حُكْمًا عَرَبِيًّا ۚ وَلَئِنِ ٱتَّبَعْتَ أَهْوَآءَهُم بَعْدَمَا جَآءَكَ مِنَ ٱلْعِلْمِ مَا لَكَ مِنَ ٱللَّهِ مِن وَلِىٍّ وَلَا وَاقٍ (٣٧)

And thus have We sent it (the Qur'ân) down to be a judgement of authority in Arabic. Were you (O Muhammad) to follow their (vain) desires after the knowledge which has come to you, then you will not have any Walî (protector) or Waq (defender) against Allâh. (37)

Quran 14:3

ٱلَّذِينَ يَسْتَحِبُّونَ ٱلْحَيَوٰةَ ٱلدُّنْيَا عَلَى ٱلْءَاخِرَةِ وَيَصُدُّونَ عَن سَبِيلِ ٱللَّهِ وَيَبْغُونَهَا عِوَجًا ۚ أُوْلَٰٓئِكَ فِى ضَلَٰلٍۭ بَعِيدٍ (٣)

Those who prefer the life of this world to of the Hereafter, and hinder (men) from the Path of Allâh (i.e.Islâm) and seek crookedness therein - they are far astray. (3)

Quran 14:21-22

وَبَرَزُواْ لِلَّهِ جَمِيعًا فَقَالَ ٱلضُّعَفَٰٓؤُاْ لِلَّذِينَ ٱسْتَكْبَرُوٓاْ إِنَّا كُنَّا لَكُمْ تَبَعًا فَهَلْ أَنتُم مُّغْنُونَ عَنَّا مِنْ عَذَابِ ٱللَّهِ مِن شَىْءٍ ۚ قَالُواْ لَوْ هَدَىٰنَا ٱللَّهُ لَهَدَيْنَٰكُمْ ۖ سَوَآءٌ عَلَيْنَآ أَجَزِعْنَآ أَمْ صَبَرْنَا مَا لَنَا مِن مَّحِيصٍ (٢١) وَقَالَ ٱلشَّيْطَٰنُ

لَمَّا قُضِىَ ٱلْأَمْرُ إِنَّ ٱللَّهَ وَعَدَكُمْ وَعْدَ ٱلْحَقِّ وَوَعَدتُّكُمْ فَأَخْلَفْتُكُمْ ۖ وَمَا كَانَ لِىَ عَلَيْكُم مِّن سُلْطَٰنٍ إِلَّآ أَن دَعَوْتُكُمْ فَٱسْتَجَبْتُمْ لِى ۖ فَلَا تَلُومُونِى وَلُومُوٓا۟ أَنفُسَكُم ۖ مَّآ أَنَا۠ بِمُصْرِخِكُمْ وَمَآ أَنتُم بِمُصْرِخِىَّ ۖ إِنِّى كَفَرْتُ بِمَآ أَشْرَكْتُمُونِ مِن قَبْلُ ۗ إِنَّ ٱلظَّٰلِمِينَ لَهُمْ عَذَابٌ أَلِيمٌ (٢٢)

And they all shall appear before Allâh (on the Day of Resurrection) then the weak will say to those who were arrogant (chiefs): "Verily, we were following you; can you avail us anything against Allâh's Torment?" They will say: "Had Allâh guided us, we would have guided you. It makes no difference to us (now) whether we rage, or bear (these torments) with patience, there is no place of refuge for us." (21) And Shaitân (Satan) will say when the matter has been decided: "Verily, Allâh promised you a promise of truth. And I too promised you, but I betrayed you. I had no authority over you except that I called you, so you responded to me. So blame me not, but blame yourselves. I cannot help you, nor can you help me. I deny your former act in associating me (Satan) as a partner with Allâh (by obeying me in the life of the world). Verily, there is a painful torment for the Zâlimûn (polytheists and wrong-doers)." (22)

Quran 14:24-28

أَلَمْ تَرَ كَيْفَ ضَرَبَ ٱللَّهُ مَثَلًا كَلِمَةً طَيِّبَةً كَشَجَرَةٍ طَيِّبَةٍ أَصْلُهَا ثَابِتٌ وَفَرْعُهَا فِى ٱلسَّمَآءِ (٢٤) تُؤْتِىٓ أُكُلَهَا كُلَّ حِينٍۭ بِإِذْنِ رَبِّهَا ۗ وَيَضْرِبُ ٱللَّهُ ٱلْأَمْثَالَ لِلنَّاسِ لَعَلَّهُمْ يَتَذَكَّرُونَ (٢٥) وَمَثَلُ كَلِمَةٍ خَبِيثَةٍ كَشَجَرَةٍ خَبِيثَةٍ ٱجْتُثَّتْ مِن فَوْقِ ٱلْأَرْضِ مَا لَهَا مِن قَرَارٍ (٢٦) يُثَبِّتُ ٱللَّهُ ٱلَّذِينَ ءَامَنُوا۟ بِٱلْقَوْلِ ٱلثَّابِتِ فِى ٱلْحَيَوٰةِ ٱلدُّنْيَا وَفِى ٱلْأَخِرَةِ ۖ وَيُضِلُّ ٱللَّهُ ٱلظَّالِمِينَ ۚ وَيَفْعَلُ ٱللَّهُ مَا يَشَآءُ (٢٧) ۞ أَلَمْ تَرَ إِلَى ٱلَّذِينَ بَدَّلُوا۟ نِعْمَتَ ٱللَّهِ كُفْرًا وَأَحَلُّوا۟ قَوْمَهُمْ دَارَ ٱلْبَوَارِ (٢٨)

See you not how Allâh sets forth a parable? - A goodly word as a goodly tree, whose root is firmly fixed, and its branches (reach) to the sky (i.e. very high). (24) Giving its fruit at all times, by the Leave of its Lord and Allâh sets forth parables for mankind in order that they may remember. (25) And the parable of an evil word is that of an evil tree uprooted from the surface of earth having no stability. (26) Allâh will keep firm those who believe, with the word that stands firm in this world (i.e. they will keep on worshipping Allâh Alone and none else), and in the Hereafter. And Allâh will cause to go astray those who are Zâlimûn (polytheists and wrong-doers, etc.), and Allâh does what He wills. (27) Have you not seen those who have changed the Blessings of Allâh into disbelief (by denying Prophet Muhammad and his Message of Islâm), and caused their people to dwell in the house of destruction? (28)

Quran 15:39-42

قَالَ رَبِّ بِمَآ أَغْوَيْتَنِى لَأُزَيِّنَنَّ لَهُمْ فِى ٱلْأَرْضِ وَلَأُغْوِيَنَّهُمْ أَجْمَعِينَ (٣٩) إِلَّا عِبَادَكَ مِنْهُمُ ٱلْمُخْلَصِينَ (٤٠) قَالَ هَٰذَا صِرَٰطٌ عَلَىَّ مُسْتَقِيمٌ (٤١) إِنَّ عِبَادِى لَيْسَ لَكَ عَلَيْهِمْ سُلْطَٰنٌ إِلَّا مَنِ ٱتَّبَعَكَ مِنَ ٱلْغَاوِينَ (٤٢)

[Iblîs (Satan)] said: "O my Lord! Because you misled me, I shall indeed adorn the path of error for them (mankind) on the earth, and I shall mislead them all. (39) "Except Your chosen, (guided) slaves among them." (40) (Allâh) said: "This is the Way which will lead straight to Me." (41) "Certainly, you shall have no authority over My slaves, except those who follow you of the Ghâwun (those who go astray, criminals, polytheists, and evil-doers) (42)

Quran 16:63-64

تَٱللَّهِ لَقَدْ أَرْسَلْنَآ إِلَىٰٓ أُمَمٍ مِّن قَبْلِكَ فَزَيَّنَ لَهُمُ ٱلشَّيْطَٰنُ أَعْمَٰلَهُمْ فَهُوَ وَلِيُّهُمُ ٱلْيَوْمَ وَلَهُمْ عَذَابٌ أَلِيمٌ (٦٣) وَمَآ أَنزَلْنَا عَلَيْكَ ٱلْكِتَٰبَ إِلَّا لِتُبَيِّنَ لَهُمُ ٱلَّذِى ٱخْتَلَفُوا۟ فِيهِ وَهُدًى وَرَحْمَةً لِّقَوْمٍ يُؤْمِنُونَ (٦٤)

By Allâh, We indeed sent (Messengers) to the nations before you (O Muhammad), but Shaitân (Satan) made their deeds fair-seeming to them. So he (Satan) is their Wali (helper) today (i.e. in this world), and theirs will be a painful torment. (63) And We have not sent down the Book (the Qur'an) to you (O

Muhammad), except that you may explain clearly unto them those things in which they differ, and (as) a guidance and a mercy for a folk who believe. (64)

Quran 16:91-100

وَأَوْفُواْ بِعَهْدِ ٱللَّهِ إِذَا عَـٰهَدتُّمْ وَلَا تَنقُضُواْ ٱلْأَيْمَـٰنَ بَعْدَ تَوْكِيدِهَا وَقَدْ جَعَلْتُمُ ٱللَّهَ عَلَيْكُمْ كَفِيلاً إِنَّ ٱللَّهَ يَعْلَمُ مَا تَفْعَلُونَ (٩١) وَلَا تَكُونُواْ كَٱلَّتِى نَقَضَتْ غَزْلَهَا مِنۢ بَعْدِ قُوَّةٍ أَنكَـٰثًا تَتَّخِذُونَ أَيْمَـٰنَكُمْ دَخَلاً بَيْنَكُمْ أَن تَكُونَ أُمَّةٌ هِىَ أَرْبَىٰ مِنْ أُمَّةٍ إِنَّمَا يَبْلُوكُمُ ٱللَّهُ بِهِۦ وَلَيُبَيِّنَنَّ لَكُمْ يَوْمَ ٱلْقِيَـٰمَةِ مَا كُنتُمْ فِيهِ تَخْتَلِفُونَ (٩٢) وَلَوْ شَآءَ ٱللَّهُ لَجَعَلَكُمْ أُمَّةً وَٰحِدَةً وَلَـٰكِن يُضِلُّ مَن يَشَآءُ وَيَهْدِى مَن يَشَآءُ وَلَتُسْـَٔلُنَّ عَمَّا كُنتُمْ تَعْمَلُونَ (٩٣) وَلَا تَتَّخِذُوٓاْ أَيْمَـٰنَكُمْ دَخَلاًۢ بَيْنَكُمْ فَتَزِلَّ قَدَمٌۢ بَعْدَ ثُبُوتِهَا وَتَذُوقُواْ ٱلسُّوٓءَ بِمَا صَدَدتُّمْ عَن سَبِيلِ ٱللَّهِ وَلَكُمْ عَذَابٌ عَظِيمٌ (٩٤) وَلَا تَشْتَرُواْ بِعَهْدِ ٱللَّهِ ثَمَنًا قَلِيلاً إِنَّمَا عِندَ ٱللَّهِ هُوَ خَيْرٌ لَّكُمْ إِن كُنتُمْ تَعْلَمُونَ (٩٥) مَا عِندَكُمْ يَنفَدُ وَمَا عِندَ ٱللَّهِ بَاقٍ وَلَنَجْزِيَنَّ ٱلَّذِينَ صَبَرُوٓاْ أَجْرَهُم بِأَحْسَنِ مَا كَانُواْ يَعْمَلُونَ (٩٦) مَنْ عَمِلَ صَـٰلِحًا مِّن ذَكَرٍ أَوْ أُنثَىٰ وَهُوَ مُؤْمِنٌ فَلَنُحْيِيَنَّهُۥ حَيَوٰةً طَيِّبَةً وَلَنَجْزِيَنَّهُمْ أَجْرَهُم بِأَحْسَنِ مَا كَانُواْ يَعْمَلُونَ (٩٧) فَإِذَا قَرَأْتَ ٱلْقُرْءَانَ فَٱسْتَعِذْ بِٱللَّهِ مِنَ ٱلشَّيْطَـٰنِ ٱلرَّجِيمِ (٩٨) إِنَّهُۥ لَيْسَ لَهُۥ سُلْطَـٰنٌ عَلَى ٱلَّذِينَ ءَامَنُواْ وَعَلَىٰ رَبِّهِمْ يَتَوَكَّلُونَ (٩٩) إِنَّمَا سُلْطَـٰنُهُۥ عَلَى ٱلَّذِينَ يَتَوَلَّوْنَهُۥ وَٱلَّذِينَ هُم بِهِۦ مُشْرِكُونَ (١٠٠)

And fulfill the Covenant of Allâh (Bai'a: pledge for Islâm) when you have covenanted, and break not the oaths after you have confirmed them, and indeed you have appointed Allâh your surety. Verily! Allâh knows what you do. (91) And be not like her who undoes the thread which she has spun after it has *become strong, by taking your oaths as a means of deception among yourselves, lest a nation should be more numerous than another nation. Allâh only tests you by this [i.e who obeys Allâh and fulfills Allâh's Covenant and who disobeys Allâh and breaks Allâh's Covenant]. And on the Day of Resurrection, He will certainly make clear to you that wherein you used to differ (92) And had Allâh willed, He could have made you (all) one nation, but He sends astray whom He wills and guides whom He wills. But you shall certainly be called to account for what you used to do. (93) And make not your oaths, a means of deception among yourselves, lest a foot should slip after being firmly planted, and you may have to taste the evil (punishment in this world) of having hindered (men) from the Path of Allâh (i.e. Belief in the Oneness of Allâh and His Messenger, Muhammad), and yours will be a great torment (i.e. the Fire of Hell in the Hereafter). (94) And purchase not a small gain at the cost of Allâh's Covenant. Verily! What is with Allâh is better for you if you did but know. (95) Whatever is with you, will be exhausted, and whatever is with Allâh will remain. And those who are patient, We will certainly pay them a reward in proportion to the best of what they used to do. (96) Whoever works* righteousness, whether male or female, while he (or she) is a true believer (of Islâmic Monotheism) verily, to him We will give a good life (in this world with respect, contentment and lawful provision), and We shall pay them certainly a reward in proportion to the best of what they used to do (i.e. Paradise in the Hereafter). (97) So when you want to recite the Qur'ân, seek refuge with Allâh from Shaitân (Satan), the outcast (the cursed one). (98) Verily! He has no power over those who believe and put their trust only in their Lord (Allâh). (99) His power is only over those who obey and follow him (Satan), and those who join partners with Him (Allâh) [those who are Mushrikûn - polytheists] (100)

Quran 16:105-109

إِنَّمَا يَفْتَرِى ٱلْكَذِبَ ٱلَّذِينَ لَا يُؤْمِنُونَ بِـَٔايَٰتِ ٱللَّهِ ۖ وَأُو۟لَٰٓئِكَ هُمُ ٱلْكَٰذِبُونَ (١٠٥) مَن كَفَرَ بِٱللَّهِ مِنۢ بَعْدِ إِيمَٰنِهِۦٓ إِلَّا مَنْ أُكْرِهَ وَقَلْبُهُۥ مُطْمَئِنٌّۢ بِٱلْإِيمَٰنِ وَلَٰكِن مَّن شَرَحَ بِٱلْكُفْرِ صَدْرًا فَعَلَيْهِمْ غَضَبٌ مِّنَ ٱللَّهِ وَلَهُمْ عَذَابٌ عَظِيمٌ (١٠٦) ذَٰلِكَ بِأَنَّهُمُ ٱسْتَحَبُّوا۟ ٱلْحَيَوٰةَ ٱلدُّنْيَا عَلَى ٱلْـَٔاخِرَةِ وَأَنَّ ٱللَّهَ لَا يَهْدِى ٱلْقَوْمَ ٱلْكَٰفِرِينَ (١٠٧) أُو۟لَٰٓئِكَ ٱلَّذِينَ طَبَعَ ٱللَّهُ عَلَىٰ قُلُوبِهِمْ وَسَمْعِهِمْ وَأَبْصَٰرِهِمْ ۖ وَأُو۟لَٰٓئِكَ هُمُ ٱلْغَٰفِلُونَ (١٠٨) لَا جَرَمَ أَنَّهُمْ فِى ٱلْـَٔاخِرَةِ هُمُ ٱلْخَٰسِرُونَ (١٠٩)

It is only those who believe not in the Ayât (proofs, evidences, verses, lessons, signs, revelations, etc.) of

Allâh, who fabricate falsehood, and it is they who are liars (105) Whoever disbelieved in Allâh after his belief, except him who is forced thereto and whose heart is at rest with Faith, but such as open their breasts to disbelief, on them is wrath from Allâh, and theirs will be a great torment. (106) That is because they loved and preferred the life of this world over that of the Hereafter. And Allâh guides not the people who disbelieve. (107) They are those upon whose hearts, hearing (ears) and sight (eyes) Allâh has set a seal. And they are the heedless! (108) No doubt, in the Hereafter, they will be the losers. (109)

Quran 16:116-117

وَلَا تَقُولُواْ لِمَا تَصِفُ أَلْسِنَتُكُمُ ٱلْكَذِبَ هَٰذَا حَلَٰلٌ وَهَٰذَا حَرَامٌ لِّتَفْتَرُواْ عَلَى ٱللَّهِ ٱلْكَذِبَ إِنَّ ٱلَّذِينَ يَفْتَرُونَ عَلَى ٱللَّهِ ٱلْكَذِبَ لَا يُفْلِحُونَ (١١٦) مَتَٰعٌ قَلِيلٌ وَلَهُمْ عَذَابٌ أَلِيمٌ (١١٧)

And say not concerning that which your tongues put forth falsely: "This is lawful and this is forbidden," so as to invent lies against Allâh. Verily, those who invent lies against Allâh will never prosper. (116) A passing brief enjoyment (will be theirs), but they will have a painful torment. (117)

Quran 17:53

وَقُل لِّعِبَادِى يَقُولُواْ ٱلَّتِى هِىَ أَحْسَنُ ۚ إِنَّ ٱلشَّيْطَٰنَ يَنزَغُ بَيْنَهُمْ ۚ إِنَّ ٱلشَّيْطَٰنَ كَانَ لِلْإِنسَٰنِ عَدُوًّا مُّبِينًا (٥٣)

And say to My slaves (i.e. the true believers of Islâmic Monotheism) that they should (only) say those words that are the best. (Because) Shaitân (Satan) verily, sows state of conflict and disagreements among them. Surely, Shaitân (Satan) is to man a plain enemy. (53)

Quran 17:62-64

قَالَ أَرَءَيْتَكَ هَٰذَا ٱلَّذِى كَرَّمْتَ عَلَىَّ لَئِنْ أَخَّرْتَنِ إِلَىٰ يَوْمِ ٱلْقِيَٰمَةِ لَأَحْتَنِكَنَّ ذُرِّيَّتَهُۥٓ إِلَّا قَلِيلًا (٦٢) قَالَ ٱذْهَبْ فَمَن تَبِعَكَ مِنْهُمْ فَإِنَّ جَهَنَّمَ جَزَآؤُكُمْ جَزَآءً مَّوْفُورًا (٦٣) وَٱسْتَفْزِزْ مَنِ ٱسْتَطَعْتَ مِنْهُم بِصَوْتِكَ وَأَجْلِبْ عَلَيْهِم بِخَيْلِكَ وَرَجِلِكَ وَشَارِكْهُمْ فِى ٱلْأَمْوَٰلِ وَٱلْأَوْلَٰدِ وَعِدْهُمْ ۚ وَمَا يَعِدُهُمُ ٱلشَّيْطَٰنُ إِلَّا غُرُورًا (٦٤)

[Iblîs (Satan)] said: "See this one whom You have honoured above me, if You give me respite (keep me alive) to the Day of Resurrection, I will surely seize and mislead his offspring (by sending them astray) all but a few!" (62) (Allâh) said: "Go, and whosoever of them follows you, surely! Hell will be the recompense of you (all) - an ample recompense. (63) "And befool them gradually those whom you can among them with your voice (i.e. songs, music, and any other call for Allâh's disobedience), make assaults on them with your cavalry and your infantry, share with them wealth and children (by tempting them to earn money by illegal ways - usury or by committing illegal sexual intercourse), and make promises to them." But Satan promises them nothing but deceit (64)

Quran 17:73-75

وَإِن كَادُوا۟ لَيَفْتِنُونَكَ عَنِ ٱلَّذِىٓ أَوْحَيْنَآ إِلَيْكَ لِتَفْتَرِىَ عَلَيْنَا غَيْرَهُۥ ۖ وَإِذًا لَّٱتَّخَذُوكَ خَلِيلًا (٧٣) وَلَوْلَآ أَن ثَبَّتْنَٰكَ لَقَدْ كِدتَّ تَرْكَنُ إِلَيْهِمْ شَيْـًٔا قَلِيلًا (٧٤) إِذًا لَّأَذَقْنَٰكَ ضِعْفَ ٱلْحَيَوٰةِ وَضِعْفَ ٱلْمَمَاتِ ثُمَّ لَا تَجِدُ لَكَ عَلَيْنَا نَصِيرًا (٧٥)

Verily, they were about to tempt you away from that which We have revealed (the Qur'ân) unto you (O Muhammad), to fabricate something other than it against Us, and then they would certainly have taken you a Khalil (an intimate friend)! (73) And had We not made you stand firm, you would nearly have inclined to them a little. (74) In that case, We would have made you taste a double portion (of punishment) in this life and a double portion (of punishment) after death. And then you would have found none to help you against Us. (75)

Quran 18:54-57

وَلَقَدْ صَرَّفْنَا فِى هَٰذَا ٱلْقُرْءَانِ لِلنَّاسِ مِن كُلِّ مَثَلٍ وَكَانَ ٱلْإِنسَٰنُ أَكْثَرَ شَىْءٍ جَدَلًا (٥٤) وَمَا مَنَعَ ٱلنَّاسَ أَن يُؤْمِنُوٓا۟ إِذْ جَآءَهُمُ ٱلْهُدَىٰ وَيَسْتَغْفِرُوا۟ رَبَّهُمْ إِلَّآ أَن تَأْتِيَهُمْ سُنَّةُ ٱلْأَوَّلِينَ أَوْ يَأْتِيَهُمُ ٱلْعَذَابُ قُبُلًا (٥٥) وَمَا نُرْسِلُ ٱلْمُرْسَلِينَ إِلَّا مُبَشِّرِينَ وَمُنذِرِينَ وَيُجَٰدِلُ ٱلَّذِينَ كَفَرُوا۟ بِٱلْبَٰطِلِ لِيُدْحِضُوا۟ بِهِ ٱلْحَقَّ وَٱتَّخَذُوٓا۟ ءَايَٰتِى وَمَآ أُنذِرُوا۟ هُزُوًا (٥٦) وَمَنْ أَظْلَمُ مِمَّن ذُكِّرَ بِـَٔايَٰتِ رَبِّهِ فَأَعْرَضَ عَنْهَا وَنَسِىَ مَا قَدَّمَتْ يَدَاهُ إِنَّا جَعَلْنَا عَلَىٰ قُلُوبِهِمْ أَكِنَّةً أَن يَفْقَهُوهُ وَفِىٓ ءَاذَانِهِمْ وَقْرًا وَإِن تَدْعُهُمْ إِلَى ٱلْهُدَىٰ فَلَن يَهْتَدُوٓا۟ إِذًا أَبَدًا (٥٧)

And indeed We have put forth every kind of example in this Qur'ân, for mankind. But, man is ever more quarrelsome than anything. (54) And nothing prevents men from believing, (now) when the guidance (the Qur'ân) has come to them, and from asking Forgiveness of their Lord, except that the ways of the ancients be repeated with them (i.e. their destruction decreed by Allâh), or the torment be brought to them face to face? (55) And We send not the Messengers except as givers of glad tidings and warners. But those who disbelieve, dispute with false argument, in order to refute the truth thereby. And they treat My Ayât (proofs, evidences, verses, lessons, signs, revelations, etc.), and that with which they are warned, as jest and mockery! (56) And who does more wrong than he who is reminded of the Ayât (proofs, evidences, verses, lessons, signs, revelations, etc.) of his Lord, but turns away from them forgetting what (deeds) his hands have sent forth. Truly, We have set veils over their hearts lest they should understand this (the Qur'ân), and in their ears, deafness. And if you (O Muhammad) call them to guidance, even then they will never be guided. (57)

Quran 18:103-106

قُلْ هَلْ نُنَبِّئُكُم بِٱلْأَخْسَرِينَ أَعْمَـٰلًا (١٠٣) ٱلَّذِينَ ضَلَّ سَعْيُهُمْ فِى ٱلْحَيَوٰةِ ٱلدُّنْيَا وَهُمْ يَحْسَبُونَ أَنَّهُمْ يُحْسِنُونَ صُنْعًا (١٠٤) أُوْلَـٰٓئِكَ ٱلَّذِينَ كَفَرُواْ بِـَٔايَـٰتِ رَبِّهِمْ وَلِقَآئِهِۦ فَحَبِطَتْ أَعْمَـٰلُهُمْ فَلَا نُقِيمُ لَهُمْ يَوْمَ ٱلْقِيَـٰمَةِ وَزْنًا (١٠٥) ذَٰلِكَ جَزَآؤُهُمْ جَهَنَّمُ بِمَا كَفَرُواْ وَٱتَّخَذُوٓاْ ءَايَـٰتِى وَرُسُلِى هُزُوًا (١٠٦)

Say (O Muhammad): "Shall We tell you the greatest losers in respect of (their) deeds? (103) "Those whose efforts have been wasted in this life while they thought that they were acquiring good by their deeds! (104) "They are those who deny the Ayât (proofs, evidences, verses, lessons, signs, revelations, etc.) of their Lord and the Meeting with Him (in the Hereafter). So their works are in vain, and on the Day of Resurrection, We shall assign not weight for them. (105) "That shall be their recompense, Hell; because they disbelieved and took My Ayât (proofs, evidences, verses, lessons, signs, revelations, etc.) and My Messengers by way of jest and mockery. (106)

Quran 19:68-70

فَوَرَبِّكَ لَنَحْشُرَنَّهُمْ وَٱلشَّيَٰطِينَ ثُمَّ لَنُحْضِرَنَّهُمْ حَوْلَ جَهَنَّمَ جِثِيًّا (٦٨) ثُمَّ لَنَنزِعَنَّ مِن كُلِّ شِيعَةٍ أَيُّهُمْ أَشَدُّ عَلَى ٱلرَّحْمَٰنِ عِتِيًّا (٦٩) ثُمَّ لَنَحْنُ أَعْلَمُ بِٱلَّذِينَ هُمْ أَوْلَىٰ بِهَا صِلِيًّا (٧٠)

So by your Lord, surely, We shall gather them together, and (also) the Shayâtin (devils) (with them), then We shall bring them round Hell on their knees. (68) Then indeed We shall drag out from every sect all those who were worst in obstinate rebellion against the Most Gracious (Allâh). (69) Then, verily, We know best those who are most worthy of being burnt therein. (70)

Quran 19:75

قُلْ مَن كَانَ فِى ٱلضَّلَٰلَةِ فَلْيَمْدُدْ لَهُ ٱلرَّحْمَٰنُ مَدًّا حَتَّىٰٓ إِذَا رَأَوْاْ مَا يُوعَدُونَ إِمَّا ٱلْعَذَابَ وَإِمَّا ٱلسَّاعَةَ فَسَيَعْلَمُونَ مَنْ هُوَ شَرٌّ مَّكَانًا وَأَضْعَفُ جُندًا (٧٥)

Say (O Muhammad) whoever is in error, the Most Gracious (Allâh) will extend (the rope) to him, until, when they see that which they were promised, either the torment or the Hour, they will come to know who is worst in position, and who is weaker in forces. (75)

Quran 19:83-84

أَلَمْ تَرَ أَنَّا أَرْسَلْنَا ٱلشَّيَٰطِينَ عَلَى ٱلْكَٰفِرِينَ تَؤُزُّهُمْ أَزًّا (٨٣) فَلَا تَعْجَلْ عَلَيْهِمْ ۖ إِنَّمَا نَعُدُّ لَهُمْ عَدًّا (٨٤)

See you not that We have sent the Shayâtin (devils) against the disbelievers to push them to do evil. (83) So make no haste against them; We only count out to them a (limited) number (of the days of the life of this world and delay their term so that they may increase in evil and sins). (84)

Quran 20:61

قَالَ لَهُم مُّوسَىٰ وَيْلَكُمْ لَا تَفْتَرُوا۟ عَلَى ٱللَّهِ كَذِبًا فَيُسْحِتَكُم بِعَذَابٍ ۖ وَقَدْ خَابَ مَنِ ٱفْتَرَىٰ (٦١)

Mûsa (Moses) said to them: "Woe unto you! Invent not a lie against Allâh, lest He should destroy you completely by a torment. And surely, he who invents a lie (against Allâh) will fail miserably." (61)

Quran 20:85-97

قَالَ فَإِنَّا قَدْ فَتَنَّا قَوْمَكَ مِنۢ بَعْدِكَ وَأَضَلَّهُمُ ٱلسَّامِرِيُّ (٨٥) فَرَجَعَ مُوسَىٰٓ إِلَىٰ قَوْمِهِۦ غَضْبَٰنَ أَسِفًا ۚ قَالَ يَٰقَوْمِ أَلَمْ يَعِدْكُمْ رَبُّكُمْ وَعْدًا حَسَنًا ۚ أَفَطَالَ عَلَيْكُمُ ٱلْعَهْدُ أَمْ أَرَدتُّمْ أَن يَحِلَّ عَلَيْكُمْ غَضَبٌ مِّن رَّبِّكُمْ فَأَخْلَفْتُم مَّوْعِدِى (٨٦) قَالُوا۟ مَآ أَخْلَفْنَا مَوْعِدَكَ بِمَلْكِنَا وَلَٰكِنَّا حُمِّلْنَآ أَوْزَارًا مِّن زِينَةِ ٱلْقَوْمِ فَقَذَفْنَٰهَا فَكَذَٰلِكَ أَلْقَى ٱلسَّامِرِيُّ (٨٧) فَأَخْرَجَ لَهُمْ عِجْلًا جَسَدًا لَّهُۥ خُوَارٌ فَقَالُوا۟ هَٰذَآ إِلَٰهُكُمْ وَإِلَٰهُ مُوسَىٰ فَنَسِىَ (٨٨) أَفَلَا يَرَوْنَ أَلَّا

يَرْجِعُ إِلَيْهِمْ قَوْلاً وَلاَ يَمْلِكُ لَهُمْ ضَرًّا وَلاَ نَفْعًا (٨٩) وَلَقَدْ قَالَ لَهُمْ هَارُونُ مِن قَبْلُ يَاقَوْمِ إِنَّمَا فُتِنتُم بِهِ ۖ وَإِنَّ رَبَّكُمُ ٱلرَّحْمَـٰنُ فَٱتَّبِعُونِى وَأَطِيعُوٓاْ أَمْرِى (٩٠) قَالُواْ لَن نَّبْرَحَ عَلَيْهِ عَـٰكِفِينَ حَتَّىٰ يَرْجِعَ إِلَيْنَا مُوسَىٰ (٩١) قَالَ يَـٰهَـٰرُونُ مَا مَنَعَكَ إِذْ رَأَيْتَهُمْ ضَلُّوٓاْ (٩٢) أَلاَّ تَتَّبِعَنِ ۖ أَفَعَصَيْتَ أَمْرِى (٩٣) قَالَ يَبْنَؤُمَّ لاَ تَأْخُذْ بِلِحْيَتِى وَلاَ بِرَأْسِىٓ ۖ إِنِّى خَشِيتُ أَن تَقُولَ فَرَّقْتَ بَيْنَ بَنِىٓ إِسْرَٰءِيلَ وَلَمْ تَرْقُبْ قَوْلِى (٩٤) قَالَ فَمَا خَطْبُكَ يَـٰسَـٰمِرِىُّ (٩٥) قَالَ بَصُرْتُ بِمَا لَمْ يَبْصُرُواْ بِهِۦ فَقَبَضْتُ قَبْضَةً مِّنْ أَثَرِ ٱلرَّسُولِ فَنَبَذْتُهَا وَكَذَٰلِكَ سَوَّلَتْ لِى نَفْسِى (٩٦) قَالَ فَٱذْهَبْ فَإِنَّ لَكَ فِى ٱلْحَيَوٰةِ أَن تَقُولَ لاَ مِسَاسَ ۖ وَإِنَّ لَكَ مَوْعِدًا لَّن تُخْلَفَهُ ۖ وَٱنظُرْ إِلَىٰٓ إِلَـٰهِكَ ٱلَّذِى ظَلْتَ عَلَيْهِ عَاكِفًا ۖ لَّنُحَرِّقَنَّهُۥ ثُمَّ لَنَنسِفَنَّهُۥ فِى ٱلْيَمِّ نَسْفًا (٩٧)

(Allâh) said: "Verily! we have tried your people in your absence, and As-Samiri has led them astray." (85) Then Mûsa (Moses) returned to his people in a state of anger and sorrow. He said: "O my people! Did not your Lord promise you a fair promise? Did then the promise seem to you long in coming? Or did you desire that wrath should descend from your Lord on you, that you broke your promise to me (i.e disbelieving in Allâh and worshipping the calf)?" (86) They said: "We broke not the promise to you, of our own will, but we were made to carry the weight of the ornaments of the [Fir'aun's (Pharaoh)] people, then we cast them (into the fire), and that was what As-Samiri suggested." (87) Then he took out (of the

fire) for them (a statue of) a calf which seemed to low. They said: "This is your ilâh (god), and the ilâh (god) of Mûsa (Moses), but [Mûsa (Moses)] has forgotten (his god).'" (88) Did they not see that it could not return them a word (for answer), and that it had no power either to harm them or to do them good?
(89) And Hârûn (Aaron) indeed had said to them beforehand: "O my people! You are being tried in this, and verily, your Lord is (Allâh) the Most Gracious, so follow me and obey my order."
(90) They said: "We will not stop worshipping it (i.e. the calf), until Mûsa (Moses) returns to us."
(91) [Mûsa (Moses)] said: "O Hârûn (Aaron)! What prevented you when you saw them going astray;
(92) "That you followed me not (according to my advice to you)? Have you then disobeyed my order?"
(93) He [Hârûn (Aaron)] said: "O son of my mother! Seize (me) not by my beard, nor by my head! Verily, I feared lest you should say: 'You have caused a division among the Children of Israel, and you have not respected my word!' " (94) [Mûsa (Moses)] said: "And what is the matter with you. O Samiri? (i.e. why did you do so?)" (95) (Samiri) said: "I saw what they saw not, so I took a handful (of dust) from the (hoof) print of the messenger [Jibril's (Gabriel) horse]

and threw it [into the fire in which were put the ornaments of the Fir'aun's (Pharaoh) people, or into the calf]. Thus my inner-self suggested to me." (96) Mûsa (Moses) said: "Then go away! And verily, your (punishment) in this life will be that you will say: "Touch me not (i.e. you will live alone exiled away from mankind); and verily (for a future torment), you have a promise that will not fail. And look at your ilâh (god), to which you have been devoted. We will certainly burn it, and scatter its particles in the sea." (97)

Quran 22:3-4

وَمِنَ ٱلنَّاسِ مَن يُجَٰدِلُ فِى ٱللَّهِ بِغَيْرِ عِلْمٍ وَيَتَّبِعُ كُلَّ شَيْطَٰنٍ مَّرِيدٍ (٣) كُتِبَ عَلَيْهِ أَنَّهُ ۥ مَن تَوَلَّاهُ فَأَنَّهُ ۥ يُضِلُّهُ ۥ وَيَهْدِيهِ إِلَىٰ عَذَابِ ٱلسَّعِيرِ (٤)

And among mankind is he who disputes concerning Allâh, without knowledge, and follows every rebellious (disobedient to Allâh) Shaitân (devil) (devoid of every kind of good). (3) For him (the devil) it is decreed that whosoever follows him, he will mislead him, and will drive him to the torment of the Fire. (4)

Quran 22:8-11

وَمِنَ ٱلنَّاسِ مَن يُجَٰدِلُ فِى ٱللَّهِ بِغَيْرِ عِلْمٍ وَلَا هُدًى وَلَا كِتَٰبٍ مُّنِيرٍ (٨) ثَانِىَ عِطْفِهِۦ لِيُضِلَّ عَن سَبِيلِ ٱللَّهِ ۖ لَهُۥ فِى ٱلدُّنْيَا خِزْىٌ ۖ وَنُذِيقُهُۥ يَوْمَ ٱلْقِيَٰمَةِ عَذَابَ ٱلْحَرِيقِ (٩) ذَٰلِكَ بِمَا قَدَّمَتْ يَدَاكَ وَأَنَّ ٱللَّهَ لَيْسَ بِظَلَّٰمٍ لِّلْعَبِيدِ (١٠) وَمِنَ ٱلنَّاسِ مَن يَعْبُدُ ٱللَّهَ عَلَىٰ حَرْفٍ ۖ فَإِنْ أَصَابَهُۥ خَيْرٌ ٱطْمَأَنَّ بِهِۦ ۖ وَإِنْ أَصَابَتْهُ فِتْنَةٌ ٱنقَلَبَ عَلَىٰ وَجْهِهِۦ خَسِرَ ٱلدُّنْيَا وَٱلْءَاخِرَةَ ۚ ذَٰلِكَ هُوَ ٱلْخُسْرَانُ ٱلْمُبِينُ (١١)

And among men is he who disputes about Allâh, without knowledge or guidance, or a Book giving light (from Allâh), (8) Bending his neck in pride (far astray from the Path of Allâh), and leading (others) too (far) astray from the Path of Allâh. For him there is disgrace in this worldly life, and on the Day of Resurrection We shall make him taste the torment of burning (Fire). (9) That is because of what your hands have sent forth, and verily, Allâh is not unjust to (His) slaves. (10) And among mankind is he who worships Allâh as it were, upon the edge (i.e. in doubt); if good befalls him, he is content therewith; but if a trial befalls him, he turns back on his face (i.e. reverts back to disbelief after embracing Islâm). He loses both this world and the Hereafter. That is the evident loss. (11)

Quran 22:51-55

وَٱلَّذِينَ سَعَوْاْ فِىٓ ءَايَٰتِنَا مُعَٰجِزِينَ أُوْلَٰٓئِكَ أَصْحَٰبُ ٱلْجَحِيمِ (٥١) وَمَآ أَرْسَلْنَا مِن قَبْلِكَ مِن رَّسُولٍ وَلَا نَبِىٍّ إِلَّآ إِذَا تَمَنَّىٰٓ أَلْقَى ٱلشَّيْطَٰنُ فِىٓ

أُمْنِيَّتِهِۦ فَيَنسَخُ ٱللَّهُ مَا يُلْقِى ٱلشَّيْطَٰنُ ثُمَّ يُحْكِمُ ٱللَّهُ ءَايَٰتِهِۦ ۗ وَٱللَّهُ عَلِيمٌ حَكِيمٌ (٥٢) لِّيَجْعَلَ مَا يُلْقِى ٱلشَّيْطَٰنُ فِتْنَةً لِّلَّذِينَ فِى قُلُوبِهِم مَّرَضٌ وَٱلْقَاسِيَةِ قُلُوبُهُمْ ۗ وَإِنَّ ٱلظَّٰلِمِينَ لَفِى شِقَاقٍۭ بَعِيدٍ (٥٣) وَلِيَعْلَمَ ٱلَّذِينَ أُوتُوا۟ ٱلْعِلْمَ أَنَّهُ ٱلْحَقُّ مِن رَّبِّكَ فَيُؤْمِنُوا۟ بِهِۦ فَتُخْبِتَ لَهُۥ قُلُوبُهُمْ ۗ وَإِنَّ ٱللَّهَ لَهَادِ ٱلَّذِينَ ءَامَنُوٓا۟ إِلَىٰ صِرَٰطٍ مُّسْتَقِيمٍ (٥٤) وَلَا يَزَالُ ٱلَّذِينَ كَفَرُوا۟ فِى مِرْيَةٍ مِّنْهُ حَتَّىٰ تَأْتِيَهُمُ ٱلسَّاعَةُ بَغْتَةً أَوْ يَأْتِيَهُمْ عَذَابُ يَوْمٍ عَقِيمٍ (٥٥)

But those who strive against Our Ayât (proofs, evidences, verses, lessons, signs, revelations, etc.), to frustrate them, they will be dwellers of the Hell-fire. (51) Never did We send a Messenger or a Prophet before you, but; when he did recite the revelation or narrated or spoke, Shaitân (Satan) threw (some falsehood) in it. But Allâh abolishes that which Shaitân (Satan) throws in. Then Allâh establishes His Revelations. And Allâh is All-Knower, All-Wise: (52) That He (Allâh) may make what is thrown in by Shaitân (Satan) a trial for those in whose hearts is a disease (of hypocrisy and disbelief) and whose hearts are hardened. And certainly, the Zalimûn (polytheists and wrong-doers) are in an opposition far-off (from the truth against Allâh's Messenger and the believers). (53) And that those who have been given knowledge may know that it (this Qur'ân) is the truth from your Lord, so that they may believe therein, and their hearts may submit to it with humility. And verily, Allâh is the Guide of those who believe, to the Straight Path. (54) And those who disbelieved will not cease to be in doubt about it (this Qur'ân) until the Hour comes suddenly upon them, or there comes to them the torment of the Day after which there will be no night (i.e. the Day of Resurrection). (55)

Quran 23:53-56

فَتَقَطَّعُوٓا۟ أَمْرَهُم بَيْنَهُمْ زُبُرًا ۖ كُلُّ حِزْبٍۭ بِمَا لَدَيْهِمْ فَرِحُونَ (٥٣) فَذَرْهُمْ فِى غَمْرَتِهِمْ حَتَّىٰ حِينٍ (٥٤) أَيَحْسَبُونَ أَنَّمَا نُمِدُّهُم بِهِۦ مِن مَّالٍ وَبَنِينَ (٥٥) نُسَارِعُ لَهُمْ فِى ٱلْخَيْرَٰتِ ۚ بَل لَّا يَشْعُرُونَ (٥٦)

But they (men) have broken their religion among them into sects, each group rejoicing in what is with it (as its belief). (53) So leave them in their error for a time. (54) Do they think that in wealth and children with which We enlarge them (55) We hasten unto them with good things (Nay it is Fitnah (trail) in this worldly life so that they will have no share of good things in the Hereafter)? but they perceive not. (56)

Quran 23:71

وَلَوِ ٱتَّبَعَ ٱلْحَقُّ أَهْوَآءَهُمْ لَفَسَدَتِ ٱلسَّمَٰوَٰتُ وَٱلْأَرْضُ وَمَن فِيهِنَّ ۚ بَلْ أَتَيْنَٰهُم بِذِكْرِهِمْ فَهُمْ عَن ذِكْرِهِم مُّعْرِضُونَ (٧١)

And if the truth had been in accordance with their desires, verily, the heavens and the earth, and whosoever is therein would have been corrupted! Nay, We have brought them their reminder, but they turn away from their reminder. (71)

Quran 23:96-98

ٱدْفَعْ بِٱلَّتِى هِىَ أَحْسَنُ ٱلسَّيِّئَةَ نَحْنُ أَعْلَمُ بِمَا يَصِفُونَ (٩٦) وَقُل رَّبِّ أَعُوذُ بِكَ مِنْ هَمَزَٰتِ ٱلشَّيَٰطِينِ (٩٧) وَأَعُوذُ بِكَ رَبِّ أَن يَحْضُرُونِ (٩٨)

Repel evil with that which is better. We are Best-Acquainted with the things they utter. (96) And say: "My Lord! I seek refuge with You from the whisperings (suggestions) of the Shayâtin (devils). (97) "And I seek refuge with You, My Lord! lest they (should come near) me." (98)

Quran 24:11-18

إِنَّ ٱلَّذِينَ جَآءُو بِٱلْإِفْكِ عُصْبَةٌ مِّنكُمْ ۚ لَا تَحْسَبُوهُ شَرًّا لَّكُم ۖ بَلْ هُوَ خَيْرٌ لَّكُمْ ۚ لِكُلِّ ٱمْرِئٍ مِّنْهُم مَّا ٱكْتَسَبَ مِنَ ٱلْإِثْمِ ۚ وَٱلَّذِى تَوَلَّىٰ كِبْرَهُۥ مِنْهُمْ لَهُۥ عَذَابٌ عَظِيمٌ (١١) لَّوْلَآ إِذْ سَمِعْتُمُوهُ ظَنَّ ٱلْمُؤْمِنُونَ وَٱلْمُؤْمِنَٰتُ بِأَنفُسِهِمْ خَيْرًا وَقَالُوا۟ هَٰذَآ إِفْكٌ مُّبِينٌ (١٢) لَّوْلَا جَآءُو عَلَيْهِ بِأَرْبَعَةِ شُهَدَآءَ ۚ فَإِذْ لَمْ يَأْتُوا۟ بِٱلشُّهَدَآءِ فَأُو۟لَٰٓئِكَ عِندَ ٱللَّهِ هُمُ ٱلْكَٰذِبُونَ (١٣) وَلَوْلَا فَضْلُ ٱللَّهِ عَلَيْكُمْ وَرَحْمَتُهُۥ فِى ٱلدُّنْيَا وَٱلْءَاخِرَةِ لَمَسَّكُمْ فِى مَآ أَفَضْتُمْ فِيهِ عَذَابٌ عَظِيمٌ (١٤) إِذْ تَلَقَّوْنَهُۥ بِأَلْسِنَتِكُمْ وَتَقُولُونَ بِأَفْوَاهِكُم مَّا لَيْسَ لَكُم بِهِۦ عِلْمٌ وَتَحْسَبُونَهُۥ هَيِّنًا وَهُوَ عِندَ ٱللَّهِ عَظِيمٌ (١٥) وَلَوْلَآ إِذْ سَمِعْتُمُوهُ قُلْتُم

مَّا يَكُونُ لَنَآ أَن نَّتَكَلَّمَ بِهَٰذَا سُبْحَٰنَكَ هَٰذَا بُهْتَٰنٌ عَظِيمٌ (١٦) يَعِظُكُمُ ٱللَّهُ أَن تَعُودُوا۟ لِمِثْلِهِۦٓ أَبَدًا إِن كُنتُم مُّؤْمِنِينَ (١٧) وَيُبَيِّنُ ٱللَّهُ لَكُمُ ٱلْءَايَٰتِ ۚ وَٱللَّهُ عَلِيمٌ حَكِيمٌ (١٨)

Verily! those who brought forth the slander (against 'Aishah the wife of the Prophet) are a group among you. Consider it not a bad thing for you. Nay, it is good for you. Unto every man among them will be paid that which he had earned of the sin, and as for him among them who had the greater share therein, his will be a great torment. (11) Why then, did not the believers, men and women, when you heard it (the slander) think good of their own people and say: "This (charge) is an obvious lie?" (12) Why did they not produce four witnesses? Since they (the slanderers) have not produced witnesses! Then with Allâh they are the liars. (13) Had it not been for the Grace of Allâh and His Mercy unto you in this world and in the Hereafter, a great torment would have touched you for that whereof you had spoken. (14) When you were propagating it with your tongues, and uttering with your mouths that whereof you had no knowledge, you counted it a little thing, while with Allâh it was very great. (15) And why did you not, when you heard it, say "It is not right for us to speak of this. Glory is to You (O Allâh) this is a great lie." (16) Allâh forbids you from it and warns you not to repeat the like of it forever, if you are believers. (17) And Allâh makes the Ayât (proofs, evidences, verses, lessons, signs, revelations.) plain to you, and Allâh is All-Knowing, All-Wise. (18)

Quran 24:21

يَٰٓأَيُّهَا ٱلَّذِينَ ءَامَنُوا۟ لَا تَتَّبِعُوا۟ خُطُوَٰتِ ٱلشَّيْطَٰنِ وَمَن يَتَّبِعْ خُطُوَٰتِ ٱلشَّيْطَٰنِ فَإِنَّهُۥ يَأْمُرُ بِٱلْفَحْشَآءِ وَٱلْمُنكَرِ وَلَوْلَا فَضْلُ ٱللَّهِ عَلَيْكُمْ وَرَحْمَتُهُۥ مَا زَكَىٰ مِنكُم مِّنْ أَحَدٍ أَبَدًا وَلَٰكِنَّ ٱللَّهَ يُزَكِّى مَن يَشَآءُ وَٱللَّهُ سَمِيعٌ عَلِيمٌ (٢١)

O you who believe! Follow not the footsteps of Shaitân (Satan). And whosoever follows the footsteps of Shaitân (Satan), then, verily he commands Al-Fahshâ' [i.e. to commit indecency (illegal sexual intercourse)], and Al-Munkar [disbelief and polytheism (i.e. to do evil and wicked deeds; and to speak or to do what is forbidden in Islâm)]. And had it not been for the Grace of Allâh and His Mercy on you, not one of you would ever have been pure from sins. But Allâh purifies (guides to Islâm) whom He wills, and Allâh is All-Hearer, All-Knower. (21)

Quran 24:47-54

وَيَقُولُونَ ءَامَنَّا بِٱللَّهِ وَبِٱلرَّسُولِ وَأَطَعْنَا ثُمَّ يَتَوَلَّىٰ فَرِيقٌ مِّنْهُم مِّنۢ بَعْدِ ذَٰلِكَ وَمَآ أُو۟لَٰٓئِكَ بِٱلْمُؤْمِنِينَ (٤٧) وَإِذَا دُعُوٓا۟ إِلَى ٱللَّهِ وَرَسُولِهِۦ لِيَحْكُمَ

بَيْنَهُمْ إِذَا فَرِيقٌ مِّنْهُم مُّعْرِضُونَ ﴿٤٨﴾ وَإِن يَكُن لَّهُمُ ٱلْحَقُّ يَأْتُوٓا۟ إِلَيْهِ مُذْعِنِينَ ﴿٤٩﴾ أَفِى قُلُوبِهِم مَّرَضٌ أَمِ ٱرْتَابُوٓا۟ أَمْ يَخَافُونَ أَن يَحِيفَ ٱللَّهُ عَلَيْهِمْ وَرَسُولُهُۥ ۚ بَلْ أُو۟لَٰٓئِكَ هُمُ ٱلظَّٰلِمُونَ ﴿٥٠﴾ إِنَّمَا كَانَ قَوْلَ ٱلْمُؤْمِنِينَ إِذَا دُعُوٓا۟ إِلَى ٱللَّهِ وَرَسُولِهِۦ لِيَحْكُمَ بَيْنَهُمْ أَن يَقُولُوا۟ سَمِعْنَا وَأَطَعْنَا ۚ وَأُو۟لَٰٓئِكَ هُمُ ٱلْمُفْلِحُونَ ﴿٥١﴾ وَمَن يُطِعِ ٱللَّهَ وَرَسُولَهُۥ وَيَخْشَ ٱللَّهَ وَيَتَّقْهِ فَأُو۟لَٰٓئِكَ هُمُ ٱلْفَآئِزُونَ ﴿٥٢﴾ ۞ وَأَقْسَمُوا۟ بِٱللَّهِ جَهْدَ أَيْمَٰنِهِمْ لَئِنْ أَمَرْتَهُمْ لَيَخْرُجُنَّ ۖ قُل لَّا تُقْسِمُوا۟ ۖ طَاعَةٌ مَّعْرُوفَةٌ ۚ إِنَّ ٱللَّهَ خَبِيرٌۢ بِمَا تَعْمَلُونَ ﴿٥٣﴾ قُلْ أَطِيعُوا۟ ٱللَّهَ وَأَطِيعُوا۟ ٱلرَّسُولَ ۖ فَإِن تَوَلَّوْا۟ فَإِنَّمَا عَلَيْهِ مَا حُمِّلَ وَعَلَيْكُم مَّا حُمِّلْتُمْ ۖ وَإِن تُطِيعُوهُ تَهْتَدُوا۟ ۚ وَمَا عَلَى ٱلرَّسُولِ إِلَّا ٱلْبَلَٰغُ ٱلْمُبِينُ ﴿٥٤﴾

They (hypocrites) say: "We have believed in Allâh and in the Messenger (Muhammad), and we obey," then a party of them turn away thereafter, such are not believers. (47) And when they are called to Allâh (i.e. His Words, the Qur'ân) and His Messenger, to judge between them, lo! a party of them refuse (to come) and turn away. (48) But if the truth is on their sides, they come to him willingly with submission. (49) Is there a disease in their hearts? Or do they doubt or fear lest Allâh and His Messenger should wrong them in judgement. Nay, it is they themselves who are the Zâlimûn (polytheists, hypocrites and wrong-doers). (50) The only saying of the faithful believers, when they are called to Allâh (His Words, the Qur'ân) and His Messenger, to judge between them, is that they say: "We hear and we obey." And such are the successful (who will live forever in Paradise). (51) And whosoever obeys Allâh and His Messenger, fears Allâh, and keeps his duty (to Him), such are the successful. (52) They swear by Allâh their strongest oaths, that if only you would order them, they would leave (their homes for fighting in Allâh's Cause). Say: "Swear you not; (this) obedience (of yours) is known (to be false). Verily, Allâh knows well what you do." (53) Say: "Obey Allâh and obey the Messenger, but if you turn away, he (Messenger Muhammad) is only responsible for the duty placed on him (i.e. to convey Allâh's Message) and you for that placed on you. If you obey him, you shall be on the right guidance. The Messenger's duty is only to convey (the message) in a clear way (i.e. to preach in a plain way)." (54)

Quran 24:63

لَا تَجْعَلُوا۟ دُعَآءَ ٱلرَّسُولِ بَيْنَكُمْ كَدُعَآءِ بَعْضِكُم بَعْضًا ۚ قَدْ يَعْلَمُ ٱللَّهُ ٱلَّذِينَ يَتَسَلَّلُونَ مِنكُمْ لِوَاذًا ۚ فَلْيَحْذَرِ ٱلَّذِينَ يُخَالِفُونَ عَنْ أَمْرِهِۦٓ أَن تُصِيبَهُمْ فِتْنَةٌ أَوْ يُصِيبَهُمْ عَذَابٌ أَلِيمٌ (٦٣)

Make not the calling of the Messenger (Muhammad) among you as your calling one of another. Allâh knows those of you who slip away under shelter (of some excuse without taking the permission to leave, from the Messenger). And let those who oppose the Messenger's (Muhammad) commandment (i.e. his Sunnah — legal ways, orders, acts of worship, statements) (among the sects) beware, lest some Fitnah (disbelief, trials, afflictions, earthquakes, killing, overpowered by a tyrant) should befall them or a painful torment be inflicted on them. (63)

Quran 25:27-31

وَيَوْمَ يَعَضُّ ٱلظَّالِمُ عَلَىٰ يَدَيْهِ يَقُولُ يَٰلَيْتَنِى ٱتَّخَذْتُ مَعَ ٱلرَّسُولِ سَبِيلاً (٢٧) يَٰوَيْلَتَىٰ لَيْتَنِى لَمْ أَتَّخِذْ فُلَانًا خَلِيلاً (٢٨) لَقَدْ أَضَلَّنِى عَنِ ٱلذِّكْرِ بَعْدَ إِذْ جَآءَنِى ۗ وَكَانَ ٱلشَّيْطَٰنُ لِلْإِنسَٰنِ خَذُولاً (٢٩) وَقَالَ ٱلرَّسُولُ يَٰرَبِّ إِنَّ قَوْمِى ٱتَّخَذُوا۟ هَٰذَا ٱلْقُرْءَانَ مَهْجُورًا (٣٠) وَكَذَٰلِكَ جَعَلْنَا لِكُلِّ نَبِىٍّ عَدُوًّا مِّنَ ٱلْمُجْرِمِينَ ۗ وَكَفَىٰ بِرَبِّكَ هَادِيًا وَنَصِيرًا (٣١)

And (remember) the Day when the Zâlim (wrong-doer, oppressor, polytheist) will bite at his hands, he will say: "Oh! Would that I had taken a path with the Messenger (Muhammad). (27) "Ah! Woe to me! Would that I had never taken so-and-so as a Khalil (an intimate friend)! (28) "He indeed led me astray from the Reminder (this Qur'ân) after it had come to me. And Shaitân (Satan) is to man ever a deserter in the hour of need." (29) And the Messenger (Muhammad) will say: "O my Lord! Verily, my people deserted this Qur'ân (neither listened to it, nor acted on its laws and teachings). (30) Thus have We made for every Prophet an enemy among the Mujrimûn (disbelievers, polytheists, criminals). But Sufficient is your Lord as a Guide and Helper. (31)

Quran 25:43

أَرَءَيْتَ مَنِ ٱتَّخَذَ إِلَٰهَهُۥ هَوَىٰهُ أَفَأَنتَ تَكُونُ عَلَيْهِ وَكِيلًا (٤٣)

Have you (O Muhammad) seen him who has taken as his ilâh (god) his own vain desire? Would you then be a Wakîl (a disposer of his affairs or a watcher) over him? (43)

Quran 26:221-223

هَلْ أُنَبِّئُكُمْ عَلَىٰ مَن تَنَزَّلُ ٱلشَّيَٰطِينُ (٢٢١) تَنَزَّلُ عَلَىٰ كُلِّ أَفَّاكٍ أَثِيمٍ (٢٢٢) يُلْقُونَ ٱلسَّمْعَ وَأَكْثَرُهُمْ كَٰذِبُونَ (٢٢٣)

Shall I inform you (O people!) upon whom the Shayâtin (devils) descend? (221) They descend on every lying, sinful person. (222) Who gives ear, and most of them are liars. (223)

Quran 27:76-85

إِنَّ هَٰذَا ٱلْقُرْءَانَ يَقُصُّ عَلَىٰ بَنِىٓ إِسْرَٰٓءِيلَ أَكْثَرَ ٱلَّذِى هُمْ فِيهِ يَخْتَلِفُونَ (٧٦) وَإِنَّهُۥ لَهُدًى وَرَحْمَةٌ لِّلْمُؤْمِنِينَ (٧٧) إِنَّ رَبَّكَ يَقْضِى بَيْنَهُم بِحُكْمِهِۦ وَهُوَ ٱلْعَزِيزُ ٱلْعَلِيمُ (٧٨) فَتَوَكَّلْ عَلَى ٱللَّهِ إِنَّكَ عَلَى ٱلْحَقِّ

ٱلْمُبِينِ (٧٩) إِنَّكَ لَا تُسْمِعُ ٱلْمَوْتَىٰ وَلَا تُسْمِعُ ٱلصُّمَّ ٱلدُّعَآءَ إِذَا وَلَّوْاْ مُدْبِرِينَ (٨٠) وَمَآ أَنتَ بِهَـٰدِى ٱلْعُمْىِ عَن ضَلَـٰلَتِهِمْ إِن تُسْمِعُ إِلَّا مَن يُؤْمِنُ بِـَٔايَـٰتِنَا فَهُم مُّسْلِمُونَ (٨١) ۞ وَإِذَا وَقَعَ ٱلْقَوْلُ عَلَيْهِمْ أَخْرَجْنَا لَهُمْ دَآبَّةً مِّنَ ٱلْأَرْضِ تُكَلِّمُهُمْ أَنَّ ٱلنَّاسَ كَانُواْ بِـَٔايَـٰتِنَا لَا يُوقِنُونَ (٨٢) وَيَوْمَ نَحْشُرُ مِن كُلِّ أُمَّةٍ فَوْجًا مِّمَّن يُكَذِّبُ بِـَٔايَـٰتِنَا فَهُمْ يُوزَعُونَ (٨٣) حَتَّىٰٓ إِذَا جَآءُو قَالَ أَكَذَّبْتُم بِـَٔايَـٰتِى وَلَمْ تُحِيطُواْ بِهَا عِلْمًا أَمَّاذَا كُنتُمْ تَعْمَلُونَ (٨٤) وَوَقَعَ ٱلْقَوْلُ عَلَيْهِم بِمَا ظَلَمُواْ فَهُمْ لَا يَنطِقُونَ (٨٥)

Verily, this Qur'ân narrates to the Children of Israel most of that in which they differ. (76) And truly, it (this Qur'ân) is a guide and a mercy for the believers. (77) Verily, your Lord will decide between them (various sects) by His Judgement. And He is the All-Mighty, the All-Knowing. (78) So put your trust in Allâh; surely, you (O Muhammad) are on manifest truth. (79) Verily, you cannot make the dead to hear nor can you make the deaf to hear the call (i.e. benefit them and similarly the disbelievers). when they flee, turning their backs. (80) Nor can you lead the blind out of their error, you can only make to hear those who believe in Our Ayât (proofs, evidences, verses, lessons, signs, revelations, etc.), and who have submitted (themselves to Allâh in Islâm as Muslims) (81) And when the Word (of torment) is fulfilled against them, We shall bring out from the earth a beast for them, to speak to them because mankind believed not with certainty in Our Ayât (Verses of the Qur'ân and Prophet Muhammad) (82) And (remember) the Day when We shall gather out of every nation a troop of those who denied Our Ayât (proofs, evidences, verses, lessons, signs, revelations, etc.), and (then) they (all) shall be set in array (gathered and driven to the place of reckoning), (83) Till, when they come (before their Lord at the place of reckoning), He will say: "Did you deny My Ayât (proofs, evidences, verses, lessons, signs, revelations, etc.) where as you comprehended them not by knowledge (of their truth or falsehood), or what (else) was it that you used to do?" (84) And the Word (of torment) will be fulfilled against them, because they have done wrong, and they will be unable to speak (in order to defend themselves). (85)

Quran 28:15-18

وَدَخَلَ ٱلْمَدِينَةَ عَلَىٰ حِينِ غَفْلَةٍ مِّنْ أَهْلِهَا فَوَجَدَ فِيهَا رَجُلَيْنِ يَقْتَتِلَانِ هَٰذَا مِن شِيعَتِهِۦ وَهَٰذَا مِنْ عَدُوِّهِۦ ۖ فَٱسْتَغَٰثَهُ ٱلَّذِى مِن شِيعَتِهِۦ عَلَى ٱلَّذِى مِنْ عَدُوِّهِۦ فَوَكَزَهُۥ مُوسَىٰ فَقَضَىٰ عَلَيْهِ ۖ قَالَ هَٰذَا مِنْ عَمَلِ ٱلشَّيْطَٰنِ ۖ إِنَّهُۥ عَدُوٌّ مُّضِلٌّ مُّبِينٌ (١٥) قَالَ رَبِّ إِنِّى ظَلَمْتُ نَفْسِى فَٱغْفِرْ لِى فَغَفَرَ لَهُۥٓ ۚ إِنَّهُۥ هُوَ ٱلْغَفُورُ ٱلرَّحِيمُ (١٦) قَالَ رَبِّ بِمَآ أَنْعَمْتَ عَلَىَّ فَلَنْ أَكُونَ ظَهِيرًا لِّلْمُجْرِمِينَ (١٧) فَأَصْبَحَ فِى ٱلْمَدِينَةِ خَآئِفًا يَتَرَقَّبُ فَإِذَا ٱلَّذِى ٱسْتَنصَرَهُۥ بِٱلْأَمْسِ يَسْتَصْرِخُهُۥ ۚ قَالَ لَهُۥ مُوسَىٰٓ إِنَّكَ لَغَوِىٌّ مُّبِينٌ (١٨)

And he entered the city at a time of unawareness of its people, and he found there two men fighting, - one of his party (his religion - from the Children of Israel), and the other of his foes. The man of his (own) party asked him for help against his foe, so Mûsa (Moses) struck him with his fist and killed him. He said: "This is of Shaitân's (Satan) doing, verily, he is a plain misleading enemy." (15) He said: "My Lord! Verily, I have wronged myself, so forgive me." Then He forgave him. Verily, He is the Oft-Forgiving, the Most Merciful. (16) He said: "My Lord! For that with which You have favored me, I will never more be a helper of the Mujrimûn (criminals, disbelievers polytheists, sinners)!" (17) So he became afraid, looking about in the city (waiting as to what will be the result of his crime of killing), when behold, the man who had sought his help the day before, called for his help (again). Mûsa (Moses) said to him: "Verily, you are a plain misleader!" (18)

Quran 29:2-4

أَحَسِبَ ٱلنَّاسُ أَن يُتْرَكُوٓا۟ أَن يَقُولُوٓا۟ ءَامَنَّا وَهُمْ لَا يُفْتَنُونَ (٢) وَلَقَدْ فَتَنَّا ٱلَّذِينَ مِن قَبْلِهِمْ فَلَيَعْلَمَنَّ ٱللَّهُ ٱلَّذِينَ صَدَقُوا۟ وَلَيَعْلَمَنَّ ٱلْكَٰذِبِينَ (٣) أَمْ حَسِبَ ٱلَّذِينَ يَعْمَلُونَ ٱلسَّيِّـَٔاتِ أَن يَسْبِقُونَاۚ سَآءَ مَا يَحْكُمُونَ (٤)

Do people think that they will be left alone because they say: "We believe," and will not be tested (2) And We indeed tested those who were before them. And Allâh will certainly make (it) known (the truth of) those who are true, and will certainly make (it) known (the falsehood of) those who are liars, (although Allâh knows all that before putting them to test). (3) Or think those who do evil deeds that they can outstrip Us (i.e. escape Our Punishment)? Evil is that which they judge! (4)

Quran 29:10-13

وَمِنَ ٱلنَّاسِ مَن يَقُولُ ءَامَنَّا بِٱللَّهِ فَإِذَآ أُوذِىَ فِى ٱللَّهِ جَعَلَ فِتْنَةَ ٱلنَّاسِ كَعَذَابِ ٱللَّهِ وَلَئِن جَآءَ نَصْرٌ مِّن رَّبِّكَ لَيَقُولُنَّ إِنَّا كُنَّا مَعَكُمْ أَوَلَيْسَ ٱللَّهُ بِأَعْلَمَ بِمَا فِى صُدُورِ ٱلْعَٰلَمِينَ (١٠) وَلَيَعْلَمَنَّ ٱللَّهُ ٱلَّذِينَ ءَامَنُواْ وَلَيَعْلَمَنَّ ٱلْمُنَٰفِقِينَ (١١) وَقَالَ ٱلَّذِينَ كَفَرُواْ لِلَّذِينَ ءَامَنُواْ ٱتَّبِعُواْ سَبِيلَنَا وَلْنَحْمِلْ خَطَٰيَٰكُمْ وَمَا هُم بِحَٰمِلِينَ مِنْ خَطَٰيَٰهُم مِّن شَىْءٍ إِنَّهُمْ لَكَٰذِبُونَ (١٢) وَلَيَحْمِلُنَّ أَثْقَالَهُمْ وَأَثْقَالًا مَّعَ أَثْقَالِهِمْ وَلَيُسْـَٔلُنَّ يَوْمَ ٱلْقِيَٰمَةِ عَمَّا كَانُواْ يَفْتَرُونَ (١٣)

Of mankind are some who say: "We believe in Allâh," but if they are made to suffer for the sake of Allâh, they consider the trial of mankind as Allâh's punishment, and if victory comes from your Lord, (the hypocrites) will say: "Verily! We were with you (helping you)." Is not Allâh Best Aware of what is in the breast of the 'Alamîn (mankind and jinn). (10) Verily, Allâh knows those who believe, and verily, He knows the hypocrites [Allâh will test the people with good and hard days to discriminate the good from the wicked although Allâh knows all that before putting them to test)]. (11) And those who disbelieve say to those who believe: "Follow our way and we will verily bear your sins," never will they bear anything of their sins. Surely, they are liars. (12) And verily, they shall bear their own loads, and other loads besides their own, and verily, they shall be questioned on the Day of Resurrection about that which they used to fabricate. (13)

Quran 31:21

وَإِذَا قِيلَ لَهُمُ ٱتَّبِعُواْ مَآ أَنزَلَ ٱللَّهُ قَالُواْ بَلْ نَتَّبِعُ مَا وَجَدْنَا عَلَيْهِ ءَابَآءَنَآ أَوَلَوْ كَانَ ٱلشَّيْطَٰنُ يَدْعُوهُمْ إِلَىٰ عَذَابِ ٱلسَّعِيرِ (٢١)

And when it is said to them: "Follow that which Allâh has sent down", they say: "Nay, we shall follow that which we found our fathers (following)." (Would they do so) even if Shaitân (Satan) invites them to the torment of the Fire? (21)

Quran 33:14

وَلَوْ دُخِلَتْ عَلَيْهِم مِّنْ أَقْطَارِهَا ثُمَّ سُئِلُوا۟ ٱلْفِتْنَةَ لَأَتَوْهَا وَمَا تَلَبَّثُوا۟ بِهَآ إِلَّا يَسِيرًا (١٤)

And if the enemy had entered from all sides (of the city), and they had been exhorted to Al¬Fitnah (i.e. to renegade from Islâm to polytheism) they would surely have committed it and would have hesitated thereupon but little. (14)

Quran 33:36

وَمَا كَانَ لِمُؤْمِنٍ وَلَا مُؤْمِنَةٍ إِذَا قَضَى ٱللَّهُ وَرَسُولُهُۥٓ أَمْرًا أَن يَكُونَ لَهُمُ ٱلْخِيَرَةُ مِنْ أَمْرِهِمْ ۗ وَمَن يَعْصِ ٱللَّهَ وَرَسُولَهُۥ فَقَدْ ضَلَّ ضَلَٰلًا مُّبِينًا (٣٦)

It is not for a believer, man or woman, when Allâh and His Messenger have decreed a matter that they should have any option in their decision. And whoever disobeys Allâh and His Messenger, he has indeed strayed in to a plain error. (36)

Quran 33:48

وَلَا تُطِعِ ٱلْكَٰفِرِينَ وَٱلْمُنَٰفِقِينَ وَدَعْ أَذَىٰهُمْ وَتَوَكَّلْ عَلَى ٱللَّهِ وَكَفَىٰ بِٱللَّهِ وَكِيلًا (٤٨)

And obey not the disbelievers and the hypocrites, and harm them not (in revenge for their harming you till you are ordered). And put your trust in Allâh, and

Sufficient is Allâh as a Wakîl (Trustee, or Disposer of affairs). (48)

Quran 33:60-62

﴿ لَّئِن لَّمْ يَنتَهِ ٱلْمُنَٰفِقُونَ وَٱلَّذِينَ فِى قُلُوبِهِم مَّرَضٌ وَٱلْمُرْجِفُونَ فِى ٱلْمَدِينَةِ لَنُغْرِيَنَّكَ بِهِمْ ثُمَّ لَا يُجَاوِرُونَكَ فِيهَآ إِلَّا قَلِيلًا (٦٠) مَّلْعُونِينَ ۖ أَيْنَمَا ثُقِفُوٓا۟ أُخِذُوا۟ وَقُتِّلُوا۟ تَقْتِيلًا (٦١) سُنَّةَ ٱللَّهِ فِى ٱلَّذِينَ خَلَوْا۟ مِن قَبْلُ ۖ وَلَن تَجِدَ لِسُنَّةِ ٱللَّهِ تَبْدِيلًا (٦٢)

If the hypocrites, and those in whose hearts is a disease (evil desire for adultery), and those who spread false news among the people in Al¬Madinah, stop not, We shall certainly let you overpower them; then they will not be able to stay in it as your neighbours but a little while. (60) Accursed, they shall be seized wherever found and killed with a (terrible) slaughter. (61) That was the Way of Allâh in the case of those who passed away of old, and you will not find any change in the Way of Allâh. (62)

Quran 33:66-69

يَوْمَ تُقَلَّبُ وُجُوهُهُمْ فِى ٱلنَّارِ يَقُولُونَ يَٰلَيْتَنَآ أَطَعْنَا ٱللَّهَ وَأَطَعْنَا ٱلرَّسُولَا۠ (٦٦) وَقَالُوا۟ رَبَّنَآ إِنَّآ أَطَعْنَا سَادَتَنَا وَكُبَرَآءَنَا فَأَضَلُّونَا ٱلسَّبِيلَا۠ (٦٧) رَبَّنَآ ءَاتِهِمْ ضِعْفَيْنِ مِنَ ٱلْعَذَابِ وَٱلْعَنْهُمْ لَعْنًا كَبِيرًا (٦٨) يَٰٓأَيُّهَا ٱلَّذِينَ ءَامَنُوا۟ لَا تَكُونُوا۟ كَٱلَّذِينَ ءَاذَوْا۟ مُوسَىٰ فَبَرَّأَهُ ٱللَّهُ مِمَّا قَالُوا۟ ۚ وَكَانَ عِندَ ٱللَّهِ وَجِيهًا (٦٩)

On the Day when their faces will be turned over in the Fire, they will say: "Oh, would that we had obeyed Allâh and obeyed the Messenger (Muhammad)." (66) And they will say: "Our Lord! Verily, we obeyed our chiefs and our great ones, and they misled us from the (Right) Way. (67) Our Lord! Give them double torment and curse them with a mighty curse!" (68) O you who believe! Be not like those who annoyed Mûsa (Moses), but Allâh cleared him of that which they alleged, and he was honourable before Allâh (69)

Quran 35:4-8

وَإِن يُكَذِّبُوكَ فَقَدْ كُذِّبَتْ رُسُلٌ مِّن قَبْلِكَ وَإِلَى ٱللَّهِ تُرْجَعُ ٱلْأُمُورُ (٤) يَٰٓأَيُّهَا ٱلنَّاسُ إِنَّ وَعْدَ ٱللَّهِ حَقٌّ ۖ فَلَا تَغُرَّنَّكُمُ ٱلْحَيَوٰةُ ٱلدُّنْيَا وَلَا يَغُرَّنَّكُم بِٱللَّهِ ٱلْغَرُورُ (٥) إِنَّ ٱلشَّيْطَٰنَ لَكُمْ عَدُوٌّ فَٱتَّخِذُوهُ عَدُوًّا ۚ إِنَّمَا يَدْعُواْ حِزْبَهُۥ لِيَكُونُواْ مِنْ أَصْحَٰبِ ٱلسَّعِيرِ (٦) ٱلَّذِينَ كَفَرُواْ لَهُمْ عَذَابٌ شَدِيدٌ ۖ وَٱلَّذِينَ ءَامَنُواْ وَعَمِلُواْ ٱلصَّٰلِحَٰتِ لَهُم مَّغْفِرَةٌ وَأَجْرٌ كَبِيرٌ (٧) أَفَمَن زُيِّنَ لَهُۥ سُوٓءُ عَمَلِهِۦ فَرَءَاهُ حَسَنًا ۖ فَإِنَّ ٱللَّهَ يُضِلُّ مَن يَشَآءُ وَيَهْدِى مَن يَشَآءُ ۖ فَلَا تَذْهَبْ نَفْسُكَ عَلَيْهِمْ حَسَرَٰتٍ ۚ إِنَّ ٱللَّهَ عَلِيمٌۢ بِمَا يَصْنَعُونَ (٨)

And if they belie you (O Muhammad), so were Messengers belied before you. And to Allâh return all matters (for decision). (4) O mankind! Verily, the Promise of Allâh is true. So let not this present life deceive you, and let not the chief deceiver (Satan) deceive you about Allâh. (5) Surely, Shaitân (Satan) is an enemy to you, so take (treat) him as an enemy. He only invites his Hizb (followers) that they may become the dwellers of the blazing Fire. (6) Those who disbelieve, theirs will be a severe torment; and those who believe (in the Oneness of Allâh Islâmic Monotheism) and do righteous good deeds, theirs will be forgiveness and a great reward (i.e. Paradise). (7) Is he, then, to whom the evil of his deeds made fair¬seeming, so that he considers it as good (equal to one who is rightly guided)? Verily, Allâh sends astray whom He wills, and guides whom He wills. So destroy not yourself (O Muhammad) in sorrow for them. Truly, Allâh is the All¬Knower of what they do! (8)

Quran 41:36

وَإِمَّا يَنزَغَنَّكَ مِنَ ٱلشَّيْطَٰنِ نَزْغٌ فَٱسْتَعِذْ بِٱللَّهِ ۚ إِنَّهُ هُوَ ٱلسَّمِيعُ ٱلْعَلِيمُ (٣٦)

And if an evil whisper from Shaitân (Satan) tries to turn you away (O Muhammad) (from doing good), then seek refuge in Allâh. Verily, He is the All-Hearer, the All-Knower. (36)

Quran 41:45

وَلَقَدْ ءَاتَيْنَا مُوسَى ٱلْكِتَٰبَ فَٱخْتُلِفَ فِيهِ ۚ وَلَوْلَا كَلِمَةٌ سَبَقَتْ مِن رَّبِّكَ لَقُضِىَ بَيْنَهُمْ ۚ وَإِنَّهُمْ لَفِى شَكٍّ مِّنْهُ مُرِيبٍ (٤٥)

And indeed We gave Mûsa (Moses) the Scripture, but dispute arose therein. And had it not been for a Word that went forth before from your Lord, (the torment would have overtaken them) and the matter would have been settled between them. But truly, they are in grave doubt thereto (i.e. about the Qur'ân). (45)

Quran 42:13-16

۞ شَرَعَ لَكُم مِّنَ ٱلدِّينِ مَا وَصَّىٰ بِهِۦ نُوحًا وَٱلَّذِىٓ أَوْحَيْنَآ إِلَيْكَ وَمَا وَصَّيْنَا بِهِۦٓ إِبْرَٰهِيمَ وَمُوسَىٰ وَعِيسَىٰٓ ۖ أَنْ أَقِيمُوا۟ ٱلدِّينَ وَلَا تَتَفَرَّقُوا۟ فِيهِ ۚ كَبُرَ عَلَى ٱلْمُشْرِكِينَ مَا تَدْعُوهُمْ إِلَيْهِ ۚ ٱللَّهُ يَجْتَبِىٓ إِلَيْهِ مَن يَشَآءُ وَيَهْدِىٓ إِلَيْهِ مَن يُنِيبُ (١٣) وَمَا تَفَرَّقُوٓا۟ إِلَّا مِنۢ بَعْدِ مَا جَآءَهُمُ ٱلْعِلْمُ بَغْيًۢا بَيْنَهُمْ ۚ وَلَوْلَا كَلِمَةٌ سَبَقَتْ مِن رَّبِّكَ إِلَىٰٓ أَجَلٍ مُّسَمًّى لَّقُضِىَ بَيْنَهُمْ ۚ وَإِنَّ ٱلَّذِينَ أُورِثُوا۟ ٱلْكِتَٰبَ مِنۢ بَعْدِهِمْ لَفِى شَكٍّ مِّنْهُ مُرِيبٍ (١٤) فَلِذَٰلِكَ فَٱدْعُ ۖ وَٱسْتَقِمْ كَمَآ أُمِرْتَ ۖ وَلَا تَتَّبِعْ أَهْوَآءَهُمْ ۖ وَقُلْ ءَامَنتُ بِمَآ أَنزَلَ ٱللَّهُ مِن كِتَٰبٍ ۖ وَأُمِرْتُ لِأَعْدِلَ بَيْنَكُمُ ۖ ٱللَّهُ رَبُّنَا وَرَبُّكُمْ ۖ لَنَآ أَعْمَٰلُنَا وَلَكُمْ أَعْمَٰلُكُمْ ۖ لَا حُجَّةَ بَيْنَنَا وَبَيْنَكُمُ ۖ ٱللَّهُ يَجْمَعُ بَيْنَنَا ۖ وَإِلَيْهِ ٱلْمَصِيرُ (١٥) وَٱلَّذِينَ يُحَآجُّونَ فِى ٱللَّهِ مِنۢ بَعْدِ مَا ٱسْتُجِيبَ لَهُۥ حُجَّتُهُمْ دَاحِضَةٌ عِندَ رَبِّهِمْ وَعَلَيْهِمْ غَضَبٌ وَلَهُمْ عَذَابٌ شَدِيدٌ (١٦)

He (Allâh) has ordained for you the same religion (Islâmic Monothesim) which He ordained for Nûh (Noah), and that which We have revealed to you (O

Muhammad), and that which We ordained for Ibrahîm (Abraham), Mûsa (Moses) and 'Īsā (Jesus) saying you should establish religion (i.e. to do what it orders you to do practically), and make no divisions in it (religion) (i.e. various sects in religion). Intolerable for the Mushrikûn , is that (Islâmic Monothesim) to which you (O Muhammad) call them. Allâh chooses for Himself whom He wills, and guides unto Himself who turns to Him in repentance and in obedience. (13) And they divided not till after knowledge had come to them, through (selfish) transgression between themselves. And had it not been for a Word that went forth before from your Lord for an appointed term, the matter would have been settled between them. And verily, those who were made to inherit the Scripture [i.e. the Taurâh (Torah) and the Injeel] after them (i.e. Jews and Christians) are in grave doubt concerning it (i.e. Allâh's true religion — Islâm or the Qur'ân). (14) So unto this (religion of Islâm alone and this Qur'ân) then invite (people) (O Muhammad), and stand firm [on Islâmic Monotheism by performing all that is ordained by Allâh (good deeds), and by abstaining from all that is forbidden by Allâh (sins and evil deeds)], as you are commanded, and follow not their desires but say: "I believe in whatsoever Allâh has sent down of the Book [all the holy Books, - this Qur'ân and the Books of the old from the Taurât (Torah), or the Injeel or the Pages of Ibrâhîm (Abraham)] and I am commanded to do justice among you. Allâh is our Lord and your Lord. For us our deeds and for you your deeds. There is no dispute between us and you. Allâh will assemble us (all), and to Him is the final return." (15) And those who dispute concerning Allâh (His religion of Islâmic Monotheism, with which Muhammad has been sent), after it has been accepted (by the people), of no use is their dispute before their Lord, and on them is wrath, and for them will be a severe torment. (16)

Quran 43:36-39

وَمَن يَعْشُ عَن ذِكْرِ ٱلرَّحْمَٰنِ نُقَيِّضْ لَهُۥ شَيْطَٰنًا فَهُوَ لَهُۥ قَرِينٌ (٣٦) وَإِنَّهُمْ لَيَصُدُّونَهُمْ عَنِ ٱلسَّبِيلِ وَيَحْسَبُونَ أَنَّهُم مُّهْتَدُونَ (٣٧) حَتَّىٰٓ إِذَا جَآءَنَا قَالَ يَٰلَيْتَ بَيْنِى وَبَيْنَكَ بُعْدَ ٱلْمَشْرِقَيْنِ فَبِئْسَ ٱلْقَرِينُ (٣٨) وَلَن يَنفَعَكُمُ ٱلْيَوْمَ إِذ ظَّلَمْتُمْ أَنَّكُمْ فِى ٱلْعَذَابِ مُشْتَرِكُونَ (٣٩)

And whosoever turns away blindly from the remembrance of the Most Gracious (Allâh) (i.e. this Qur'ân and worship of Allâh), We appoint for him Shaitân (Satan devil) to be a Qarîn (a intimate companion) to him. (36) And verily, they (Satans /

devils) hinder them from the Path (of Allâh), but they think that they are guided aright! (37) Till, when (such a one) comes to Us, he says [to his Qarîn (Satan / devil companion)] "Would that between me and you were the distance of the two easts (or the east and west)" a worst (type of) companion (indeed)! (38) It will profit you not this Day (O you who turn away from Allâh's remembrance and His worship) as you did wrong, (and) that you will be sharers (you and your Qarîn) in the punishment. (39)

Quran 43:62-65

وَلَا يَصُدَّنَّكُمُ ٱلشَّيْطَٰنُ إِنَّهُۥ لَكُمْ عَدُوٌّ مُّبِينٌ (٦٢) وَلَمَّا جَآءَ عِيسَىٰ بِٱلْبَيِّنَٰتِ قَالَ قَدْ جِئْتُكُم بِٱلْحِكْمَةِ وَلِأُبَيِّنَ لَكُم بَعْضَ ٱلَّذِى تَخْتَلِفُونَ فِيهِ ۖ فَٱتَّقُوا۟ ٱللَّهَ وَأَطِيعُونِ (٦٣) إِنَّ ٱللَّهَ هُوَ رَبِّى وَرَبُّكُمْ فَٱعْبُدُوهُ ۚ هَٰذَا صِرَٰطٌ مُّسْتَقِيمٌ (٦٤) فَٱخْتَلَفَ ٱلْأَحْزَابُ مِنۢ بَيْنِهِمْ ۖ فَوَيْلٌ لِّلَّذِينَ ظَلَمُوا۟ مِنْ عَذَابِ يَوْمٍ أَلِيمٍ (٦٥)

And let not Shaitân (Satan) hinder you (from the right religion, i.e. Islâmic Monotheism), Verily, he (Satan) to you is a plain enemy. (62) And when 'Īsā (Jesus) came with (Our) clear Proofs, he said: "I have come to you with Al-Hikmah (Prophethood), and in order to make clear to you some of the (points) in which you differ, Therefore fear Allâh and obey me, (63) "Verily, Allâh! He is my Lord (God) and your

Lord (God). So worship Him (Alone). This is the (only) Straight Path (i.e. Allâh's religion of true Islâmic Monotheism)." (64) But the sects from among themselves differed. So woe to those who do wrong (by ascribing things to 'Īsā (Jesus) that are not true) from the torment of a painful Day (i.e. the Day of Resurrection)! (65)

Quran 45:16-23

وَلَقَدْ ءَاتَيْنَا بَنِىٓ إِسْرَٰٓءِيلَ ٱلْكِتَٰبَ وَٱلْحُكْمَ وَٱلنُّبُوَّةَ وَرَزَقْنَٰهُم مِّنَ ٱلطَّيِّبَٰتِ وَفَضَّلْنَٰهُمْ عَلَى ٱلْعَٰلَمِينَ (١٦) وَءَاتَيْنَٰهُم بَيِّنَٰتٍ مِّنَ ٱلْأَمْرِ ۖ فَمَا ٱخْتَلَفُوٓاْ إِلَّا مِنۢ بَعْدِ مَا جَآءَهُمُ ٱلْعِلْمُ بَغْيًۢا بَيْنَهُمْ ۚ إِنَّ رَبَّكَ يَقْضِى بَيْنَهُمْ يَوْمَ ٱلْقِيَٰمَةِ فِيمَا كَانُواْ فِيهِ يَخْتَلِفُونَ (١٧) ثُمَّ جَعَلْنَٰكَ عَلَىٰ شَرِيعَةٍ مِّنَ ٱلْأَمْرِ فَٱتَّبِعْهَا وَلَا تَتَّبِعْ أَهْوَآءَ ٱلَّذِينَ لَا يَعْلَمُونَ (١٨) إِنَّهُمْ لَن يُغْنُواْ عَنكَ مِنَ ٱللَّهِ شَيْـًٔا ۚ وَإِنَّ ٱلظَّٰلِمِينَ بَعْضُهُمْ أَوْلِيَآءُ بَعْضٍ ۖ وَٱللَّهُ وَلِىُّ ٱلْمُتَّقِينَ (١٩) هَٰذَا بَصَٰٓئِرُ لِلنَّاسِ وَهُدًى وَرَحْمَةٌ لِّقَوْمٍ يُوقِنُونَ (٢٠) أَمْ حَسِبَ ٱلَّذِينَ ٱجْتَرَحُواْ ٱلسَّيِّـَٔاتِ أَن نَّجْعَلَهُمْ كَٱلَّذِينَ ءَامَنُواْ وَعَمِلُواْ ٱلصَّٰلِحَٰتِ سَوَآءً مَّحْيَاهُمْ وَمَمَاتُهُمْ ۚ سَآءَ مَا يَحْكُمُونَ (٢١) وَخَلَقَ ٱللَّهُ ٱلسَّمَٰوَٰتِ وَٱلْأَرْضَ بِٱلْحَقِّ وَلِتُجْزَىٰ كُلُّ نَفْسٍۭ بِمَا كَسَبَتْ وَهُمْ لَا يُظْلَمُونَ (٢٢) أَفَرَءَيْتَ مَنِ ٱتَّخَذَ إِلَٰهَهُۥ هَوَىٰهُ وَأَضَلَّهُ ٱللَّهُ عَلَىٰ عِلْمٍ وَخَتَمَ عَلَىٰ سَمْعِهِۦ وَقَلْبِهِۦ وَجَعَلَ عَلَىٰ بَصَرِهِۦ غِشَٰوَةً فَمَن يَهْدِيهِ مِنۢ بَعْدِ ٱللَّهِ ۚ أَفَلَا تَذَكَّرُونَ (٢٣)

And indeed We gave the Children of Israel the Scripture, and the understanding of the Scripture and its laws, and the Prophethood; and provided them with good things, and preferred them above the 'Alamîn (mankind and jinn of their time, during that period), (16) And gave them clear proofs in matters [by revealing to them the Taurât (Torah)]. And they differed not until after the knowledge came to them, through envy among themselves. Verily, Your Lord will judge between them on the Day of Resurrection about that wherein they used to differ. (17) Then We have put you (O Muhammad) on a (plain) way of (Our) commandment [like the one which We commanded Our Messengers before you (i.e. legal ways and laws of the Islâmic Monotheism)]. So follow you that (Islâmic Monotheism and its laws), and follow not the desires of those who know not. (18) Verily, they can avail you nothing against Allâh (if He wants to punish you). Verily, the Zâlimûn (polytheists, wrong-doers) are Auliyâ' (protectors, helpers) of one another, but Allâh is the Walî (Helper, Protector) of the Muttaqûn (pious). (19) This (Qur'ân) is a clear insight and evidence for mankind, and a guidance and a mercy for people who have Faith with certainty. (20) Or do those who earn evil deeds think that We shall hold them equal with those who believe (in the Oneness of Allâh — Islâmic Monotheism) and do righteous good deeds, in their present life and after their death? Worst is the judgement that they make. (21) And Allâh has created the heavens and the earth with truth, in order that each person may be recompensed what he has earned, and they will not be wronged. (22) Have you seen him who takes his own lust (vain desires) as his ilâh (god)? and Allâh knowing (him as such), left him astray, and sealed his hearing and his heart, and put a cover on his sight. Who then will guide him after Allâh? Will you not then remember? (23)

Quran 47:21-34

طَاعَةٌ وَقَوْلٌ مَّعْرُوفٌ فَإِذَا عَزَمَ ٱلْأَمْرُ فَلَوْ صَدَقُوا۟ ٱللَّهَ لَكَانَ خَيْرًا لَّهُمْ (٢١) فَهَلْ عَسَيْتُمْ إِن تَوَلَّيْتُمْ أَن تُفْسِدُوا۟ فِى ٱلْأَرْضِ وَتُقَطِّعُوٓا۟ أَرْحَامَكُمْ (٢٢) أُو۟لَـٰٓئِكَ ٱلَّذِينَ لَعَنَهُمُ ٱللَّهُ فَأَصَمَّهُمْ وَأَعْمَىٰٓ أَبْصَـٰرَهُمْ (٢٣) أَفَلَا يَتَدَبَّرُونَ ٱلْقُرْءَانَ أَمْ عَلَىٰ قُلُوبٍ أَقْفَالُهَآ (٢٤) إِنَّ ٱلَّذِينَ ٱرْتَدُّوا۟ عَلَىٰٓ أَدْبَـٰرِهِم مِّنۢ بَعْدِ مَا تَبَيَّنَ لَهُمُ ٱلْهُدَى ٱلشَّيْطَـٰنُ سَوَّلَ لَهُمْ وَأَمْلَىٰ لَهُمْ (٢٥) ذَٰلِكَ بِأَنَّهُمْ قَالُوا۟ لِلَّذِينَ كَرِهُوا۟ مَا نَزَّلَ ٱللَّهُ سَنُطِيعُكُمْ فِى بَعْضِ ٱلْأَمْرِ ۖ وَٱللَّهُ يَعْلَمُ إِسْرَارَهُمْ (٢٦) فَكَيْفَ إِذَا تَوَفَّتْهُمُ ٱلْمَلَـٰٓئِكَةُ يَضْرِبُونَ وُجُوهَهُمْ وَأَدْبَـٰرَهُمْ (٢٧) ذَٰلِكَ بِأَنَّهُمُ ٱتَّبَعُوا۟ مَآ أَسْخَطَ ٱللَّهَ وَكَرِهُوا۟ رِضْوَٰنَهُۥ فَأَحْبَطَ أَعْمَـٰلَهُمْ (٢٨) أَمْ حَسِبَ ٱلَّذِينَ فِى قُلُوبِهِم مَّرَضٌ أَن لَّن يُخْرِجَ ٱللَّهُ أَضْغَـٰنَهُمْ (٢٩) وَلَوْ نَشَآءُ لَأَرَيْنَـٰكَهُمْ فَلَعَرَفْتَهُم بِسِيمَـٰهُمْ ۚ وَلَتَعْرِفَنَّهُمْ فِى لَحْنِ ٱلْقَوْلِ ۚ وَٱللَّهُ يَعْلَمُ أَعْمَـٰلَكُمْ (٣٠) وَلَنَبْلُوَنَّكُمْ حَتَّىٰ نَعْلَمَ ٱلْمُجَـٰهِدِينَ مِنكُمْ وَٱلصَّـٰبِرِينَ وَنَبْلُوَا۟ أَخْبَارَكُمْ (٣١) إِنَّ ٱلَّذِينَ كَفَرُوا۟ وَصَدُّوا۟ عَن سَبِيلِ ٱللَّهِ وَشَآقُّوا۟ ٱلرَّسُولَ مِنۢ بَعْدِ مَا تَبَيَّنَ لَهُمُ ٱلْهُدَىٰ لَن يَضُرُّوا۟ ٱللَّهَ شَيْـًٔا وَسَيُحْبِطُ أَعْمَـٰلَهُمْ (٣٢) ۞ يَـٰٓأَيُّهَا ٱلَّذِينَ ءَامَنُوٓا۟ أَطِيعُوا۟ ٱللَّهَ وَأَطِيعُوا۟ ٱلرَّسُولَ وَلَا تُبْطِلُوٓا۟ أَعْمَـٰلَكُمْ (٣٣) إِنَّ ٱلَّذِينَ كَفَرُوا۟ وَصَدُّوا۟ عَن سَبِيلِ ٱللَّهِ ثُمَّ مَاتُوا۟ وَهُمْ كُفَّارٌ فَلَن يَغْفِرَ ٱللَّهُ لَهُمْ (٣٤)

Obedience and good words (were better for them). And when the matter (preparation for Jihâd) is resolved on, then if they had been true to Allâh, it would have been better for them. (21) Would you then, if you were given the authority, do mischief in the land, and sever your ties of kinship? (22) Such are they whom Allâh has cursed, so that He has made them deaf and blinded their sight. (23) Do they not then think deeply in the Qur'ân, or are their hearts locked up (from understanding it)? (24) Verily, those who have turned back (have apostatize) as disbelievers after the guidance has been manifested to them — Shaitân (Satan) has beautified for them (their false hopes), and (Allâh) prolonged their term (age). (25) This is because they said to those who hate what Allâh has sent down: "We will obey you in part of the matter," but Allâh knows their secrets. (26) Then how (will it be) when the angels will take their souls at death, smiting their faces and their backs? (27) That is because they followed that which angered Allâh, and hated that which pleased Him. So He made their deeds fruitless. (28) Or do those in whose hearts is a disease (of hypocrisy), think that Allâh will not bring to light all their hidden ill-wills? (29) Had We willed, We could have shown them to you, and you should have known them by their marks; but surely, you will know them by the tone of their speech! And Allâh knows (all) your deeds. (30) And surely, We shall try you till We test those who strive hard (for the Cause of Allâh) and As-Sabirun (the patient ones), and We shall test your facts (i.e. the one who is a liar, and the one who is truthful). (31) Verily, those who disbelieve, and hinder (men) from the Path of Allâh (i.e. Islâm), and oppose the Messenger after the guidance has been clearly shown to them, they will not hurt Allâh in the least, but He will make their deeds fruitless, (32) O you who believe! Obey Allâh, and obey the Messenger (Muhammad) and render not vain your deeds. (33) Verily, those who disbelieve, and hinder (men) from the Path of Allâh (i.e. Islâm); then die while they are disbelievers, - Allâh will not forgive them. (34)

Quran 47:38

هَـٰٓأَنتُمْ هَـٰٓؤُلَآءِ تُدْعَوْنَ لِتُنفِقُواْ فِى سَبِيلِ ٱللَّهِ فَمِنكُم مَّن يَبْخَلُۖ وَمَن يَبْخَلْ فَإِنَّمَا يَبْخَلُ عَن نَّفْسِهِۦۚ وَٱللَّهُ ٱلْغَنِىُّ وَأَنتُمُ ٱلْفُقَرَآءُۚ وَإِن تَتَوَلَّوْاْ يَسْتَبْدِلْ قَوْمًا غَيْرَكُمْ ثُمَّ لَا يَكُونُوٓاْ أَمْثَـٰلَكُم (٣٨)

Behold! You are those who are called to spend in the Cause of Allâh, yet among you are some who are niggardly. And whoever is niggardly, it is only at the expense of his ownself. But Allâh is Rich (Free of all needs), and you (mankind) are poor. And if you turn away (from Islâm and the obedience to Allâh), He will exchange you for some other people, and they will not be your likes. (38)

Quran 47:13

وَمَن لَّمْ يُؤْمِنۢ بِٱللَّهِ وَرَسُولِهِۦ فَإِنَّآ أَعْتَدْنَا لِلْكَٰفِرِينَ سَعِيرًا (١٣)

And whosoever does not believe in Allâh and His Messenger (Muhammad), then verily, We have prepared for the disbelievers a blazing Fire. (13)

Quran 48:28-29

هُوَ ٱلَّذِىٓ أَرْسَلَ رَسُولَهُۥ بِٱلْهُدَىٰ وَدِينِ ٱلْحَقِّ لِيُظْهِرَهُۥ عَلَى ٱلدِّينِ كُلِّهِۦ وَكَفَىٰ بِٱللَّهِ شَهِيدًا (٢٨) مُّحَمَّدٌ رَّسُولُ ٱللَّهِ وَٱلَّذِينَ مَعَهُۥٓ أَشِدَّآءُ عَلَى ٱلْكُفَّارِ رُحَمَآءُ بَيْنَهُمْ تَرَىٰهُمْ رُكَّعًا سُجَّدًا يَبْتَغُونَ فَضْلًا مِّنَ ٱللَّهِ وَرِضْوَٰنًا سِيمَاهُمْ فِى وُجُوهِهِم مِّنْ أَثَرِ ٱلسُّجُودِ ذَٰلِكَ مَثَلُهُمْ فِى ٱلتَّوْرَىٰةِ وَمَثَلُهُمْ فِى ٱلْإِنجِيلِ كَزَرْعٍ أَخْرَجَ شَطْـَٔهُۥ فَـَٔازَرَهُۥ فَٱسْتَغْلَظَ فَٱسْتَوَىٰ عَلَىٰ سُوقِهِۦ يُعْجِبُ ٱلزُّرَّاعَ لِيَغِيظَ بِهِمُ ٱلْكُفَّارَ وَعَدَ ٱللَّهُ ٱلَّذِينَ ءَامَنُوا۟ وَعَمِلُوا۟ ٱلصَّٰلِحَٰتِ مِنْهُم مَّغْفِرَةً وَأَجْرًا عَظِيمًۢا (٢٩)

He it is Who has sent His Messenger (Muhammad) with guidance and the religion of truth (Islâm), that He may make it (Islâm) superior over all religions. And All-Sufficient is Allâh as a Witness.

(28) Muhammad is the Messenger of Allâh, And those who are with him are severe against disbelievers, and merciful among themselves. You see them bowing and falling down prostrate (in prayer), seeking Bounty from Allâh and (His) Good Pleasure. The mark of them (i.e. of their Faith) is on their faces (foreheads) from the traces of prostration (during prayers). This is their description in the Taurât (Torah). But their description in the Injeel is like a (sown) seed which sends forth its shoot, then makes it strong, and becomes thick, and it stands straight on its stem, delighting the sowers that He may enrage the disbelievers with them. Allâh has promised those among them who believe (i.e. all those who follow Islâmic Monotheism, the religion of Prophet Muhammad till the Day of Resurrection) and do righteous good deeds, forgiveness and a mighty reward (i.e. Paradise). (29)

Quran 49:1-3

يَٰٓأَيُّهَا ٱلَّذِينَ ءَامَنُواْ لَا تُقَدِّمُواْ بَيْنَ يَدَيِ ٱللَّهِ وَرَسُولِهِۦ ۖ وَٱتَّقُواْ ٱللَّهَ ۚ إِنَّ ٱللَّهَ سَمِيعٌ عَلِيمٌ (١) يَٰٓأَيُّهَا ٱلَّذِينَ ءَامَنُواْ لَا تَرْفَعُوٓاْ أَصْوَٰتَكُمْ فَوْقَ صَوْتِ ٱلنَّبِيِّ وَلَا تَجْهَرُواْ لَهُۥ بِٱلْقَوْلِ كَجَهْرِ بَعْضِكُمْ لِبَعْضٍ أَن تَحْبَطَ أَعْمَٰلُكُمْ وَأَنتُمْ لَا تَشْعُرُونَ (٢) إِنَّ ٱلَّذِينَ يَغُضُّونَ أَصْوَٰتَهُمْ عِندَ رَسُولِ ٱللَّهِ أُوْلَٰٓئِكَ ٱلَّذِينَ ٱمْتَحَنَ ٱللَّهُ قُلُوبَهُمْ لِلتَّقْوَىٰ ۚ لَهُم مَّغْفِرَةٌ وَأَجْرٌ عَظِيمٌ (٣)

O you who believe! Make not (a decision) in advance before Allâh and His Messenger, and fear Allâh. Verily! Allâh is All-Hearing, All-Knowing. (1) O you who believe! Raise not your voices above the voice of the Prophet, nor speak aloud to him in talk as you speak aloud to one another, lest your deeds may be rendered fruitless while you perceive not. (2) Verily, those who lower their voices in the presence of Allâh's Messenger, they are the ones whose hearts Allâh has tested for piety. For them is forgiveness and a great reward. (3)

Quran 49:6-9

يَـٰٓأَيُّهَا ٱلَّذِينَ ءَامَنُوٓاْ إِن جَآءَكُمْ فَاسِقٌۢ بِنَبَإٍ فَتَبَيَّنُوٓاْ أَن تُصِيبُواْ قَوْمًۢا بِجَهَـٰلَةٍ فَتُصْبِحُواْ عَلَىٰ مَا فَعَلْتُمْ نَـٰدِمِينَ (٦) وَٱعْلَمُوٓاْ أَنَّ فِيكُمْ رَسُولَ ٱللَّهِ ۚ لَوْ يُطِيعُكُمْ فِى كَثِيرٍ مِّنَ ٱلْأَمْرِ لَعَنِتُّمْ وَلَـٰكِنَّ ٱللَّهَ حَبَّبَ إِلَيْكُمُ ٱلْإِيمَـٰنَ وَزَيَّنَهُۥ فِى قُلُوبِكُمْ وَكَرَّهَ إِلَيْكُمُ ٱلْكُفْرَ وَٱلْفُسُوقَ وَٱلْعِصْيَانَ ۚ أُوْلَـٰٓئِكَ هُمُ ٱلرَّٰشِدُونَ (٧) فَضْلًا مِّنَ ٱللَّهِ وَنِعْمَةً ۚ وَٱللَّهُ عَلِيمٌ حَكِيمٌ (٨) وَإِن طَآئِفَتَانِ مِنَ ٱلْمُؤْمِنِينَ ٱقْتَتَلُواْ فَأَصْلِحُواْ بَيْنَهُمَا ۖ فَإِنۢ بَغَتْ إِحْدَىٰهُمَا عَلَى ٱلْأُخْرَىٰ فَقَـٰتِلُواْ ٱلَّتِى تَبْغِى حَتَّىٰ تَفِىٓءَ إِلَىٰٓ أَمْرِ ٱللَّهِ ۚ فَإِن فَآءَتْ فَأَصْلِحُواْ بَيْنَهُمَا بِٱلْعَدْلِ وَأَقْسِطُوٓاْ ۖ إِنَّ ٱللَّهَ يُحِبُّ ٱلْمُقْسِطِينَ (٩)

O you who believe! If a Fasiq (liar — evil person) comes to you with any news, verify it, lest you should harm people in ignorance, and afterwards you become regretful for what you have done. (6) And know that, among you there is the Messenger of Allâh. If he were to obey you (i.e. follow your opinions and desires) in much of the matter, you would surely be in trouble, But Allâh has endeared the Faith to you and has beautified it in your hearts, and has made disbelief, wickedness and disobedience (to Allâh and His Messenger) hateful to you. Such are they who are the rightly guided, (7) (This is) a Grace from Allâh and His Favour. And Allâh is All-Knowing, All-Wise. (8) And if two parties or groups among the believers fall to fighting, then make peace between them both, But if one of them outrages against the other, then fight you (all) against the one that which outrages till it complies with the Command of Allâh; then if it complies, then make reconciliation between them justly, and be equitable. Verily! Allâh loves those who are equitable. (9)

Quran 49:14-16

۞ قَالَتِ ٱلۡأَعۡرَابُ ءَامَنَّاۖ قُل لَّمۡ تُؤۡمِنُواْ وَلَٰكِن قُولُوٓاْ أَسۡلَمۡنَا وَلَمَّا يَدۡخُلِ ٱلۡإِيمَٰنُ فِى قُلُوبِكُمۡۖ وَإِن تُطِيعُواْ ٱللَّهَ وَرَسُولَهُۥ لَا يَلِتۡكُم مِّنۡ أَعۡمَٰلِكُمۡ شَيۡـًٔاۚ إِنَّ ٱللَّهَ غَفُورٞ رَّحِيمٌ (١٤) إِنَّمَا ٱلۡمُؤۡمِنُونَ ٱلَّذِينَ ءَامَنُواْ بِٱللَّهِ وَرَسُولِهِۦ ثُمَّ لَمۡ يَرۡتَابُواْ وَجَٰهَدُواْ بِأَمۡوَٰلِهِمۡ وَأَنفُسِهِمۡ فِى سَبِيلِ ٱللَّهِۚ أُوْلَٰٓئِكَ هُمُ ٱلصَّٰدِقُونَ (١٥) قُلۡ أَتُعَلِّمُونَ ٱللَّهَ بِدِينِكُمۡ وَٱللَّهُ يَعۡلَمُ مَا فِى ٱلسَّمَٰوَٰتِ وَمَا فِى ٱلۡأَرۡضِۚ وَٱللَّهُ بِكُلِّ شَىۡءٍ عَلِيمٌ (١٦)

The bedouins say: "We believe." Say: "You believe not but you only say, 'We have surrendered (in Islâm),' for Faith has not yet entered your hearts. But if you obey Allâh and His Messenger, He will not decrease anything in reward for your deeds. Verily, Allâh is Oft-Forgiving, Most Merciful." (14) Only those are the believers who have believed in Allâh and His Messenger, and afterward doubt not but strive with their wealth and their lives for the Cause of Allâh. Those! They are the truthful. (15) Say: "Will you inform Allâh of your religion While Allâh knows all that is in the heavens and all that is in the earth, and Allâh is All-Aware of everything. (16)

Quran 53:19-24

أَفَرَءَيْتُمُ ٱللَّـٰتَ وَٱلْعُزَّىٰ (١٩) وَمَنَوٰةَ ٱلثَّالِثَةَ ٱلْأُخْرَىٰٓ (٢٠) أَلَكُمُ ٱلذَّكَرُ وَلَهُ ٱلْأُنثَىٰ (٢١) تِلْكَ إِذًا قِسْمَةٌ ضِيزَىٰٓ (٢٢) إِنْ هِىَ إِلَّآ أَسْمَآءٌ سَمَّيْتُمُوهَآ أَنتُمْ وَءَابَآؤُكُم مَّآ أَنزَلَ ٱللَّهُ بِهَا مِن سُلْطَـٰنٍ إِن يَتَّبِعُونَ إِلَّا ٱلظَّنَّ وَمَا تَهْوَى ٱلْأَنفُسُ وَلَقَدْ جَآءَهُم مِّن رَّبِّهِمُ ٱلْهُدَىٰٓ (٢٣) أَمْ لِلْإِنسَـٰنِ مَا تَمَنَّىٰ (٢٤)

Have you then considered Al-Lât, and Al-'Uzza (two idols of the pagan Arabs) (19) And Manât (another idol of the pagan Arabs), the other third? (20) Is it for you the males and for Him the females? (21) That indeed is a division most unfair! (22) They are but names which you have named — you and your fathers — for which Allâh has sent down no authority. They follow but a guess and that which they themselves desire, whereas there has surely come to them the Guidance from their Lord! (23) Or shall man have what he wishes? (24)

Quran 53:28-30

وَمَا لَهُم بِهِۦ مِنْ عِلْمٍ ۖ إِن يَتَّبِعُونَ إِلَّا ٱلظَّنَّ ۖ وَإِنَّ ٱلظَّنَّ لَا يُغْنِى مِنَ ٱلْحَقِّ شَيْـًٔا (٢٨) فَأَعْرِضْ عَن مَّن تَوَلَّىٰ عَن ذِكْرِنَا وَلَمْ يُرِدْ إِلَّا ٱلْحَيَوٰةَ ٱلدُّنْيَا (٢٩) ذَٰلِكَ مَبْلَغُهُم مِّنَ ٱلْعِلْمِ ۚ إِنَّ رَبَّكَ هُوَ أَعْلَمُ بِمَن ضَلَّ عَن سَبِيلِهِۦ وَهُوَ أَعْلَمُ بِمَنِ ٱهْتَدَىٰ (٣٠)

But they have no knowledge thereof. They follow but a guess, and verily, guess is no substitute for the truth. (28) Therefore withdraw (O Muhammad) from him who turns away from Our Reminder (this Qur'ân) and desires nothing but the life of this world. (29) That is what they could reach of knowledge. Verily, your Lord it is He Who knows best him who goes astray from His Path, and He knows best him who receives guidance. (30)

Quran 57:13-16

يَوْمَ يَقُولُ ٱلْمُنَٰفِقُونَ وَٱلْمُنَٰفِقَٰتُ لِلَّذِينَ ءَامَنُوا۟ ٱنظُرُونَا نَقْتَبِسْ مِن نُّورِكُمْ قِيلَ ٱرْجِعُوا۟ وَرَآءَكُمْ فَٱلْتَمِسُوا۟ نُورًا فَضُرِبَ بَيْنَهُم بِسُورٍ لَّهُۥ بَابٌ بَاطِنُهُۥ فِيهِ ٱلرَّحْمَةُ وَظَٰهِرُهُۥ مِن قِبَلِهِ ٱلْعَذَابُ (١٣) يُنَادُونَهُمْ أَلَمْ نَكُن

مَّعَكُمْ قَالُوا بَلَىٰ وَلَٰكِنَّكُمْ فَتَنتُمْ أَنفُسَكُمْ وَتَرَبَّصْتُمْ وَٱرْتَبْتُمْ وَغَرَّتْكُمُ ٱلْأَمَانِيُّ حَتَّىٰ جَآءَ أَمْرُ ٱللَّهِ وَغَرَّكُم بِٱللَّهِ ٱلْغَرُورُ ﴿١٤﴾ فَٱلْيَوْمَ لَا يُؤْخَذُ مِنكُمْ فِدْيَةٌ وَلَا مِنَ ٱلَّذِينَ كَفَرُوا ۚ مَأْوَىٰكُمُ ٱلنَّارُ ۖ هِىَ مَوْلَىٰكُمْ ۖ وَبِئْسَ ٱلْمَصِيرُ ﴿١٥﴾ ۞ أَلَمْ يَأْنِ لِلَّذِينَ ءَامَنُوٓا أَن تَخْشَعَ قُلُوبُهُمْ لِذِكْرِ ٱللَّهِ وَمَا نَزَلَ مِنَ ٱلْحَقِّ وَلَا يَكُونُوا كَٱلَّذِينَ أُوتُوا ٱلْكِتَٰبَ مِن قَبْلُ فَطَالَ عَلَيْهِمُ ٱلْأَمَدُ فَقَسَتْ قُلُوبُهُمْ ۖ وَكَثِيرٌ مِّنْهُمْ فَٰسِقُونَ ﴿١٦﴾

On the Day when the hypocrites men and women will say to the believers: "Wait for us! Let us get something from your light!" It will be said: "Go back to your rear! Then seek a light!" So a wall will be put up between them, with a gate therein. Inside it will be mercy, and outside it will be torment." (13) (The hypocrites) will call the believers: "Were we not with you?" The believers will reply: "Yes! But you led yourselves into temptations, you looked forward for our destruction; you doubted (in Faith); and you were deceived by false desires, till the Command of Allâh came to pass. And the chief deceiver (Satan) deceived you in respect of Allâh." (14) So this Day no ransom shall be taken from you (hypocrites), nor of those who disbelieved, (in the Oneness of Allâh Islâmic Monotheism). Your abode is the Fire, That is your maula (friend — proper place), and worst indeed is that destination. (15) Has not the time come for the hearts of those who believe (in the Oneness of

Allâh - Islâmic Monotheism) to be affected by Allâh's Reminder (this Qur'ân), and that which has been revealed of the truth, lest they become as those who received the Scripture [the Taurât (Torah) and the Injeel] before (i.e. Jews and Christians), and the term was prolonged for them and so their hearts were hardened? And many of them were Fâsiqûn (the rebellious, the disobedient to Allâh). (16)

Quran 57:25-27

لَقَدْ أَرْسَلْنَا رُسُلَنَا بِٱلْبَيِّنَٰتِ وَأَنزَلْنَا مَعَهُمُ ٱلْكِتَٰبَ وَٱلْمِيزَانَ لِيَقُومَ ٱلنَّاسُ بِٱلْقِسْطِ ۖ وَأَنزَلْنَا ٱلْحَدِيدَ فِيهِ بَأْسٌ شَدِيدٌ وَمَنَٰفِعُ لِلنَّاسِ وَلِيَعْلَمَ ٱللَّهُ مَن يَنصُرُهُۥ وَرُسُلَهُۥ بِٱلْغَيْبِ ۚ إِنَّ ٱللَّهَ قَوِيٌّ عَزِيزٌ (٢٥) وَلَقَدْ أَرْسَلْنَا نُوحًا وَإِبْرَٰهِيمَ وَجَعَلْنَا فِى ذُرِّيَّتِهِمَا ٱلنُّبُوَّةَ وَٱلْكِتَٰبَ ۖ فَمِنْهُم مُّهْتَدٍ ۖ وَكَثِيرٌ مِّنْهُمْ فَٰسِقُونَ (٢٦) ثُمَّ قَفَّيْنَا عَلَىٰٓ ءَاثَٰرِهِم بِرُسُلِنَا وَقَفَّيْنَا بِعِيسَى ٱبْنِ مَرْيَمَ وَءَاتَيْنَٰهُ ٱلْإِنجِيلَ وَجَعَلْنَا فِى قُلُوبِ ٱلَّذِينَ ٱتَّبَعُوهُ رَأْفَةً وَرَحْمَةً وَرَهْبَانِيَّةً ٱبْتَدَعُوهَا مَا كَتَبْنَٰهَا عَلَيْهِمْ إِلَّا ٱبْتِغَآءَ رِضْوَٰنِ ٱللَّهِ فَمَا رَعَوْهَا حَقَّ رِعَايَتِهَا ۖ فَـَٔاتَيْنَا ٱلَّذِينَ ءَامَنُوا۟ مِنْهُمْ أَجْرَهُمْ ۖ وَكَثِيرٌ مِّنْهُمْ فَٰسِقُونَ (٢٧)

Indeed We have sent Our Messengers with clear proofs, and revealed with them the Scripture and the Balance (justice) that mankind may keep up justice. And We brought forth iron wherein is mighty power (in matters of war), as well as many benefits for mankind, that Allâh may test who it is that will help Him (His religion), and His Messengers in the unseen. Verily, Allâh is All-Strong, All-Mighty.

(25) And indeed, We sent Nûh (Noah) and Ibrahîm (Abraham), and placed in their offspring Prophethood and Scripture, And among them there are some who are guided, but many of them are Fâsiqûn (rebellious, disobedient to Allâh). (26) Then, We sent after them, Our Messengers, and We sent 'Īsā (Jesus) son of Maryam (Mary), and gave him the Injeel. And We ordained in the hearts of those who followed him, compassion and mercy. But the monasticism which they invented for themselves, We did not prescribe for them, but (they sought it) only to please Allâh therewith, but they did not observe it with the right observance. So We gave those among them who believed, their (due) reward, but many of them are Fâsiqûn (rebellious, disobedient to Allâh). (27)

Quran 58:5-10

إِنَّ ٱلَّذِينَ يُحَآدُّونَ ٱللَّهَ وَرَسُولَهُۥ كُبِتُوا۟ كَمَا كُبِتَ ٱلَّذِينَ مِن قَبْلِهِمْ ۚ وَقَدْ أَنزَلْنَآ ءَايَٰتٍۭ بَيِّنَٰتٍ ۚ وَلِلْكَٰفِرِينَ عَذَابٌ مُّهِينٌ (٥) يَوْمَ يَبْعَثُهُمُ ٱللَّهُ جَمِيعًا فَيُنَبِّئُهُم بِمَا عَمِلُوٓا۟ ۚ أَحْصَىٰهُ ٱللَّهُ وَنَسُوهُ ۚ وَٱللَّهُ عَلَىٰ كُلِّ شَىْءٍ شَهِيدٌ (٦) أَلَمْ تَرَ أَنَّ ٱللَّهَ يَعْلَمُ مَا فِى ٱلسَّمَٰوَٰتِ وَمَا فِى ٱلْأَرْضِ ۖ مَا يَكُونُ مِن نَّجْوَىٰ ثَلَٰثَةٍ إِلَّا هُوَ رَابِعُهُمْ وَلَا خَمْسَةٍ إِلَّا هُوَ سَادِسُهُمْ وَلَآ أَدْنَىٰ مِن ذَٰلِكَ وَلَآ أَكْثَرَ إِلَّا هُوَ مَعَهُمْ أَيْنَ مَا كَانُوا۟ ۖ ثُمَّ يُنَبِّئُهُم بِمَا عَمِلُوا۟ يَوْمَ ٱلْقِيَٰمَةِ ۚ إِنَّ ٱللَّهَ بِكُلِّ شَىْءٍ عَلِيمٌ (٧) أَلَمْ تَرَ إِلَى ٱلَّذِينَ نُهُوا۟ عَنِ ٱلنَّجْوَىٰ ثُمَّ يَعُودُونَ لِمَا نُهُوا۟ عَنْهُ وَيَتَنَٰجَوْنَ بِٱلْإِثْمِ وَٱلْعُدْوَٰنِ وَمَعْصِيَتِ ٱلرَّسُولِ وَإِذَا جَآءُوكَ حَيَّوْكَ بِمَا لَمْ يُحَيِّكَ بِهِ ٱللَّهُ وَيَقُولُونَ فِىٓ أَنفُسِهِمْ لَوْلَا يُعَذِّبُنَا ٱللَّهُ بِمَا نَقُولُ

حَسْبُهُمْ جَهَنَّمُ يَصْلَوْنَهَا فَبِئْسَ ٱلْمَصِيرُ (٨) يَـٰٓأَيُّهَا ٱلَّذِينَ ءَامَنُوٓا۟ إِذَا تَنَـٰجَيْتُمْ فَلَا تَتَنَـٰجَوْا۟ بِٱلْإِثْمِ وَٱلْعُدْوَٰنِ وَمَعْصِيَتِ ٱلرَّسُولِ وَتَنَـٰجَوْا۟ بِٱلْبِرِّ وَٱلتَّقْوَىٰ وَٱتَّقُوا۟ ٱللَّهَ ٱلَّذِىٓ إِلَيْهِ تُحْشَرُونَ (٩) إِنَّمَا ٱلنَّجْوَىٰ مِنَ ٱلشَّيْطَـٰنِ لِيَحْزُنَ ٱلَّذِينَ ءَامَنُوا۟ وَلَيْسَ بِضَآرِّهِمْ شَيْـًٔا إِلَّا بِإِذْنِ ٱللَّهِ وَعَلَى ٱللَّهِ فَلْيَتَوَكَّلِ ٱلْمُؤْمِنُونَ (١٠)

Verily, those who oppose Allâh and His Messenger (Muhammad) will be disgraced, as those before them (among the past nation), were disgraced. And We have sent down clear Ayât (proofs, evidences, verses, lessons, signs, revelations, etc.). And for the disbelievers is a disgracing torment. (5) On the Day when Allâh will resurrect them all together (i.e. on the Day of Resurrection) and inform them of what they did. Allâh has kept account of it, while they have forgotten it. And Allâh is Witness over all things. (6) Have you not seen that Allâh knows whatsoever is in the heavens and whatsoever is on the earth? There is no Najwa (secret counsel) of three, but He is their fourth (with His Knowledge, while He Himself is over the Throne, over the seventh heaven), nor of five but He is their sixth (with His Knowledge), not of less than that or more, but He is with them (with His Knowledge) wheresoever they may be; And afterwards on the Day of Resurrection, He will inform them of what they did. Verily, Allâh is the

All-Knower of everything. (7) Have you not seen those who were forbidden to hold secret counsels, and afterwards returned to that which they had been forbidden, and conspired together for sin and wrong doing and disobedience to the Messenger (Muhammad). And when they come to you, they greet you with a greeting wherewith Allâh greets you not, and say within themselves: "Why should Allâh punish us not for what we say?" Hell will be sufficient for them, they will burn therein, and worst indeed is that destination! (8) O you who believe! When you hold secret counsel, do it not for sin and wrong-doing, and disobedience towards the Messenger (Muhammad) but do it for Al-Birr (righteousness) and Taqwa (virtues and piety); and fear Allâh unto Whom you shall be gathered.
(9) Secret counsels (conspiracies) are only from Shaitân (Satan), in order that he may cause grief to the believers. But he cannot harm them in the least, except as Allâh permits, and in Allâh let the believers put their trust (10)

Quran 58:14-20

۞ أَلَمْ تَرَ إِلَى ٱلَّذِينَ تَوَلَّوْا۟ قَوْمًا غَضِبَ ٱللَّهُ عَلَيْهِم مَّا هُم مِّنكُمْ وَلَا مِنْهُمْ وَيَحْلِفُونَ عَلَى ٱلْكَذِبِ وَهُمْ يَعْلَمُونَ (١٤) أَعَدَّ ٱللَّهُ لَهُمْ عَذَابًا شَدِيدًا إِنَّهُمْ سَآءَ مَا كَانُوا۟ يَعْمَلُونَ (١٥) ٱتَّخَذُوٓا۟ أَيْمَـٰنَهُمْ جُنَّةً فَصَدُّوا۟ عَن سَبِيلِ ٱللَّهِ

فَلَهُمْ عَذَابٌ مُّهِينٌ ﴿١٦﴾ لَّن تُغْنِىَ عَنْهُمْ أَمْوَٰلُهُمْ وَلَآ أَوْلَٰدُهُم مِّنَ ٱللَّهِ شَيْـًٔا ۚ أُو۟لَٰٓئِكَ أَصْحَٰبُ ٱلنَّارِ ۖ هُمْ فِيهَا خَٰلِدُونَ ﴿١٧﴾ يَوْمَ يَبْعَثُهُمُ ٱللَّهُ جَمِيعًا فَيَحْلِفُونَ لَهُۥ كَمَا يَحْلِفُونَ لَكُمْ ۖ وَيَحْسَبُونَ أَنَّهُمْ عَلَىٰ شَىْءٍ ۚ أَلَآ إِنَّهُمْ هُمُ ٱلْكَٰذِبُونَ ﴿١٨﴾ ٱسْتَحْوَذَ عَلَيْهِمُ ٱلشَّيْطَٰنُ فَأَنسَىٰهُمْ ذِكْرَ ٱللَّهِ ۚ أُو۟لَٰٓئِكَ حِزْبُ ٱلشَّيْطَٰنِ ۚ أَلَآ إِنَّ حِزْبَ ٱلشَّيْطَٰنِ هُمُ ٱلْخَٰسِرُونَ ﴿١٩﴾ إِنَّ ٱلَّذِينَ يُحَآدُّونَ ٱللَّهَ وَرَسُولَهُۥٓ أُو۟لَٰٓئِكَ فِى ٱلْأَذَلِّينَ ﴿٢٠﴾

Have you (O Muhammad) not seen those (hypocrites) who take as friends a people upon whom is the Wrath of Allâh (i.e. Jews)? They are neither of you (Muslims) nor of them (Jews), and they swear to a lie while they know. (14) Allâh has prepared for them a severe torment. Evil indeed is that which they used to do. (15) They have made their oaths a screen (for their evil actions). Thus they hinder (men) from the Path of Allâh, so they shall have a humiliating torment. (16) Their children and their wealth will avail them nothing against Allâh. They will be the dwellers of the Fire, to dwell therein forever. (17) On the Day when Allâh will resurrect them all together (for their account), then they will swear to Him as they swear to you (O Muslims). And they think that they have something (to stand upon). Verily, they are liars! (18) Shaitân (Satan) has overpowered them. So he has made them forget the remembrance of Allâh. They are the party of Shaitân (Satan). Verily, it is the party of Shaitân (Satan) that will be the losers! (19) Those who oppose Allâh and His Messenger (Muhammad), they will be among the lowest (most humiliated). (20)

Quran 60:1

يَٰٓأَيُّهَا ٱلَّذِينَ ءَامَنُوا۟ لَا تَتَّخِذُوا۟ عَدُوِّى وَعَدُوَّكُمْ أَوْلِيَآءَ تُلْقُونَ إِلَيْهِم بِٱلْمَوَدَّةِ وَقَدْ كَفَرُوا۟ بِمَا جَآءَكُم مِّنَ ٱلْحَقِّ يُخْرِجُونَ ٱلرَّسُولَ وَإِيَّاكُمْ أَن تُؤْمِنُوا۟ بِٱللَّهِ رَبِّكُمْ إِن كُنتُمْ خَرَجْتُمْ جِهَٰدًا فِى سَبِيلِى وَٱبْتِغَآءَ مَرْضَاتِى تُسِرُّونَ إِلَيْهِم بِٱلْمَوَدَّةِ وَأَنَا۠ أَعْلَمُ بِمَآ أَخْفَيْتُمْ وَمَآ أَعْلَنتُمْ وَمَن يَفْعَلْهُ مِنكُمْ فَقَدْ ضَلَّ سَوَآءَ ٱلسَّبِيلِ (١)

O you who believe! Take not My enemies and your enemies as friends, showing affection towards them, while they have disbelieved in what has come to you of the truth (i.e. Islâmic Monotheism, this Qur'ân, and Muhammad), and have driven out the Messenger and yourselves because you believe in Allâh your Lord! If you have come forth to strive in My Cause and to seek My Good Pleasure, (then take not these disbelievers and polytheists, as your friends). You show friendship to them in secret, while I am All-Aware of what you conceal and what you reveal. And whosoever of you (Muslims) does that, then indeed he has gone (far) astray, from the Straight Path. (1)

Quran 61:5-9

وَإِذْ قَالَ مُوسَىٰ لِقَوْمِهِ يَٰقَوْمِ لِمَ تُؤْذُونَنِى وَقَد تَّعْلَمُونَ أَنِّى رَسُولُ ٱللَّهِ إِلَيْكُمْ فَلَمَّا زَاغُوٓا۟ أَزَاغَ ٱللَّهُ قُلُوبَهُمْ وَٱللَّهُ لَا يَهْدِى ٱلْقَوْمَ ٱلْفَٰسِقِينَ (٥) وَإِذْ قَالَ عِيسَى ٱبْنُ مَرْيَمَ يَٰبَنِىٓ إِسْرَٰٓءِيلَ إِنِّى رَسُولُ ٱللَّهِ إِلَيْكُم مُّصَدِّقًا لِّمَا بَيْنَ يَدَىَّ مِنَ ٱلتَّوْرَىٰةِ وَمُبَشِّرًۢا بِرَسُولٍ يَأْتِى مِنۢ بَعْدِى ٱسْمُهُۥٓ أَحْمَدُ فَلَمَّا جَآءَهُم بِٱلْبَيِّنَٰتِ قَالُوا۟ هَٰذَا سِحْرٌ مُّبِينٌ (٦) وَمَنْ أَظْلَمُ مِمَّنِ ٱفْتَرَىٰ عَلَى ٱللَّهِ ٱلْكَذِبَ وَهُوَ يُدْعَىٰٓ إِلَى ٱلْإِسْلَٰمِ وَٱللَّهُ لَا يَهْدِى ٱلْقَوْمَ ٱلظَّٰلِمِينَ (٧) يُرِيدُونَ لِيُطْفِـُٔوا۟ نُورَ ٱللَّهِ بِأَفْوَٰهِهِمْ وَٱللَّهُ مُتِمُّ نُورِهِۦ وَلَوْ كَرِهَ ٱلْكَٰفِرُونَ (٨) هُوَ ٱلَّذِىٓ أَرْسَلَ رَسُولَهُۥ بِٱلْهُدَىٰ وَدِينِ ٱلْحَقِّ لِيُظْهِرَهُۥ عَلَى ٱلدِّينِ كُلِّهِۦ وَلَوْ كَرِهَ ٱلْمُشْرِكُونَ (٩)

And (remember) when Mûsa (Moses) said to his people: "O my people! Why do you annoy me while you know certainly that I am the Messenger of Allâh to you? So when they turned away (from the Path of Allâh), Allâh turned their hearts away (from the Right Path). And Allâh guides not the people who are Fâsiqûn (the rebellious, the disobedient to Allâh). (5) And (remember) when 'Īsā (Jesus), son of Maryam (Mary), said: "O Children of Israel! I am the Messenger of Allâh unto you confirming the Taurât [(Torah) which came] before me, and giving glad tidings of a Messenger to come after me, whose name shall be Ahmed . But when he (Ahmed i.e. Muhammad) came to them with clear proofs, they said: "This is plain magic." (6) And who does more wrong than the one who invents a lie against Allâh, while he is being invited to Islâm? And Allâh guides not the people who are Zâlimûn (polytheists, wrong-doers and disbelievers) folk. (7) They intend to put out the Light of Allâh (i.e. the Religion of Islâm, this Qur'ân, and the Prophet Muhammad) with their mouths. But Allâh will bring His Light to perfection even though the disbelievers hate (it). (8) He it is Who has sent His Messenger (Muhammad) with guidance and the religion of truth (Islâmic Monotheism) to make it victorious over all (other) religions even though the Mushrikûn (polytheists, pagans, idolaters, and disbelievers in the Oneness of Allâh and in His Messenger Muhammed) hate (it). (9)

Quran 61:14

يَٰٓأَيُّهَا ٱلَّذِينَ ءَامَنُوا۟ كُونُوٓا۟ أَنصَارَ ٱللَّهِ كَمَا قَالَ عِيسَى ٱبْنُ مَرْيَمَ لِلْحَوَارِيِّۦنَ مَنْ أَنصَارِىٓ إِلَى ٱللَّهِۖ قَالَ ٱلْحَوَارِيُّونَ نَحْنُ أَنصَارُ ٱللَّهِۖ فَـَٔامَنَت طَّآئِفَةٌ مِّنۢ بَنِىٓ إِسْرَٰٓءِيلَ وَكَفَرَت طَّآئِفَةٌۖ فَأَيَّدْنَا ٱلَّذِينَ ءَامَنُوا۟ عَلَىٰ عَدُوِّهِمْ فَأَصْبَحُوا۟ ظَٰهِرِينَ (١٤)

O you who believe! Be you helpers (in the Cause) of Allâh as said 'Īsā (Jesus), son of Maryam (Mary), to the Hawârîyyun (the disciples) : "Who are my helpers (in the Cause) of Allâh?" The Hawârîyyun (the disciples) said: "We are Allâh's helpers" (i.e. we will strive in His Cause!). Then a group of the Children of Israel believed and a group disbelieved. So We gave power to those who believed against their enemies, and they became the victorious (uppermost). (14)

Quran 62:5

مَثَلُ ٱلَّذِينَ حُمِّلُواْ ٱلتَّوْرَىٰةَ ثُمَّ لَمْ يَحْمِلُوهَا كَمَثَلِ ٱلْحِمَارِ يَحْمِلُ أَسْفَارًا ۢ بِئْسَ مَثَلُ ٱلْقَوْمِ ٱلَّذِينَ كَذَّبُواْ بِـَٔايَـٰتِ ٱللَّهِ ۚ وَٱللَّهُ لَا يَهْدِى ٱلْقَوْمَ ٱلظَّـٰلِمِينَ (٥)

The likeness of those who were entrusted with the (obligation of the) Taurât (Torah) (i.e. to obey its commandments and to practise its laws), but who subsequently failed in those (obligations), is as the likeness of a donkey which carries huge burdens of books (but understands nothing from them). How bad is the example of people who deny the Ayât (proofs, evidences, verses, signs, revelations) of Allâh. And Allâh guides not the people who are Zâlimûn (polytheists, wrong-doers, disbelievers). (5)

Quran 63:1-7

إِذَا جَآءَكَ ٱلْمُنَـٰفِقُونَ قَالُواْ نَشْهَدُ إِنَّكَ لَرَسُولُ ٱللَّهِ ۗ وَٱللَّهُ يَعْلَمُ إِنَّكَ لَرَسُولُهُۥ وَٱللَّهُ يَشْهَدُ إِنَّ ٱلْمُنَـٰفِقِينَ لَكَـٰذِبُونَ (١) ٱتَّخَذُوٓاْ أَيْمَـٰنَهُمْ جُنَّةً فَصَدُّواْ عَن سَبِيلِ ٱللَّهِ ۚ إِنَّهُمْ سَآءَ مَا كَانُواْ يَعْمَلُونَ (٢) ذَٰلِكَ بِأَنَّهُمْ ءَامَنُواْ ثُمَّ كَفَرُواْ فَطُبِعَ عَلَىٰ قُلُوبِهِمْ فَهُمْ لَا يَفْقَهُونَ (٣) ۞ وَإِذَا رَأَيْتَهُمْ تُعْجِبُكَ أَجْسَامُهُمْ ۖ

وَإِن يَقُولُوا۟ تَسْمَعْ لِقَوْلِهِمْ ۖ كَأَنَّهُمْ خُشُبٌ مُّسَنَّدَةٌ ۖ يَحْسَبُونَ كُلَّ صَيْحَةٍ عَلَيْهِمْ ۚ هُمُ ٱلْعَدُوُّ فَٱحْذَرْهُمْ ۚ قَـٰتَلَهُمُ ٱللَّهُ ۖ أَنَّىٰ يُؤْفَكُونَ (٤) وَإِذَا قِيلَ لَهُمْ تَعَالَوْا۟ يَسْتَغْفِرْ لَكُمْ رَسُولُ ٱللَّهِ لَوَّوْا۟ رُءُوسَهُمْ وَرَأَيْتَهُمْ يَصُدُّونَ وَهُم مُّسْتَكْبِرُونَ (٥) سَوَآءٌ عَلَيْهِمْ أَسْتَغْفَرْتَ لَهُمْ أَمْ لَمْ تَسْتَغْفِرْ لَهُمْ لَن يَغْفِرَ ٱللَّهُ لَهُمْ ۚ إِنَّ ٱللَّهَ لَا يَهْدِى ٱلْقَوْمَ ٱلْفَـٰسِقِينَ (٦) هُمُ ٱلَّذِينَ يَقُولُونَ لَا تُنفِقُوا۟ عَلَىٰ مَنْ عِندَ رَسُولِ ٱللَّهِ حَتَّىٰ يَنفَضُّوا۟ ۗ وَلِلَّهِ خَزَآئِنُ ٱلسَّمَـٰوَٰتِ وَٱلْأَرْضِ وَلَـٰكِنَّ ٱلْمُنَـٰفِقِينَ لَا يَفْقَهُونَ (٧)

When the hypocrites come to you (O Muhammad), they say: "We bear witness that you are indeed the Messenger of Allâh." Allâh knows that you are indeed His Messenger and Allâh bears witness that the hypocrites are liars indeed. (1) They have made their oaths a screen (for their hypocrisy). Thus they hinder (men) from the Path of Allâh. Verily, evil is what they used to do. (2) That is because they believed, then disbelieved, therefore their hearts are sealed, so they understand not. (3) And when you look at them, their bodies please you; and when they speak, you listen to their words. They are as blocks of wood propped up. They think that every cry is against them. They are the enemies, so beware of them. May Allâh curse them! How are they denying (or deviating from) the Right Path? (4) And when it is said to them: "Come, so that the Messenger of Allâh may ask forgiveness from Allâh for you", they twist their heads, and you would see them turning away their faces in pride. (5) It is equal to them whether you (Muhammad) ask forgiveness or ask not forgiveness for them. Verily, Allâh guides not the people who are the Fâsiqîn (the rebellious, the disobedient to Allâh)(6) They are the ones who say: "Spend not on those who are with Allâh's Messenger, until they desert him." And to Allâh belong the treasures of the heavens and the earth, but the hypocrites comprehend not. (7)

Quran 72:4-5

وَأَنَّهُ كَانَ يَقُولُ سَفِيهُنَا عَلَى ٱللَّهِ شَطَطًا (٤) وَأَنَّا ظَنَنَّا أَن لَّن تَقُولَ ٱلْإِنسُ وَٱلْجِنُّ عَلَى ٱللَّهِ كَذِبًا (٥) وَأَنَّهُ كَانَ رِجَالٌ مِّنَ ٱلْإِنسِ يَعُوذُونَ بِرِجَالٍ مِّنَ ٱلْجِنِّ فَزَادُوهُمْ رَهَقًا (٦)

'And that the foolish among us used to utter against Allâh that which was an enormity in falsehood. (4) 'And verily, we thought that men and jinn would not utter a lie against Allâh. (5)

Quran 72:11

وَأَنَّا مِنَّا ٱلصَّٰلِحُونَ وَمِنَّا دُونَ ذَٰلِكَ كُنَّا طَرَآئِقَ قِدَدًا (١١)

'There are among us some that are righteous, and some the contrary; we are groups each having a different ways (religious sects). (11)

Quran 74:31

وَمَا جَعَلْنَا أَصْحَٰبَ ٱلنَّارِ إِلَّا مَلَٰٓئِكَةً ۙ وَمَا جَعَلْنَا عِدَّتَهُمْ إِلَّا فِتْنَةً لِّلَّذِينَ كَفَرُواْ لِيَسْتَيْقِنَ ٱلَّذِينَ أُوتُواْ ٱلْكِتَٰبَ وَيَزْدَادَ ٱلَّذِينَ ءَامَنُوٓاْ إِيمَٰنًا ۙ وَلَا يَرْتَابَ ٱلَّذِينَ أُوتُواْ ٱلْكِتَٰبَ وَٱلْمُؤْمِنُونَ ۙ وَلِيَقُولَ ٱلَّذِينَ فِى قُلُوبِهِم مَّرَضٌ وَٱلْكَٰفِرُونَ مَاذَآ أَرَادَ ٱللَّهُ بِهَٰذَا مَثَلًا ۚ كَذَٰلِكَ يُضِلُّ ٱللَّهُ مَن يَشَآءُ وَيَهْدِى مَن يَشَآءُ ۚ وَمَا يَعْلَمُ جُنُودَ رَبِّكَ إِلَّا هُوَ ۚ وَمَا هِىَ إِلَّا ذِكْرَىٰ لِلْبَشَرِ (٣١)

And We have set none but angels as guardians of the Fire, and We have fixed number (19) only as a trial for the disbelievers, in order that the people of the Scripture (Jews and Christians) may arrive at a certainty [that this Qur'ân is the truth as it agrees with their Books regarding their number (19) which is written in the Taurât (Torah) and the Injeel] and that the believers may increase in Faith (as this Qur'ân is the truth) and that no doubt may be left for the people of the Scripture and the believers, and that those in whose hearts is a disease (of hypocrisy) and the disbelievers may say: "What Allâh intends by this (curious) example?" Thus Allâh leads astray whom He wills and guides whom He wills. And none can know the hosts of your Lord but He. And this (Hell) is nothing else than a (warning) reminder to mankind. (31)

Quran 98:1-6

لَمْ يَكُنِ ٱلَّذِينَ كَفَرُوا۟ مِنْ أَهْلِ ٱلْكِتَٰبِ وَٱلْمُشْرِكِينَ مُنفَكِّينَ حَتَّىٰ تَأْتِيَهُمُ ٱلْبَيِّنَةُ (١) رَسُولٌ مِّنَ ٱللَّهِ يَتْلُوا۟ صُحُفًا مُّطَهَّرَةً (٢) فِيهَا كُتُبٌ قَيِّمَةٌ (٣) وَمَا تَفَرَّقَ ٱلَّذِينَ أُوتُوا۟ ٱلْكِتَٰبَ إِلَّا مِنۢ بَعْدِ مَا جَآءَتْهُمُ ٱلْبَيِّنَةُ (٤) وَمَآ أُمِرُوٓا۟ إِلَّا لِيَعْبُدُوا۟ ٱللَّهَ مُخْلِصِينَ لَهُ ٱلدِّينَ حُنَفَآءَ وَيُقِيمُوا۟ ٱلصَّلَوٰةَ وَيُؤْتُوا۟ ٱلزَّكَوٰةَ ۚ وَذَٰلِكَ دِينُ ٱلْقَيِّمَةِ (٥) إِنَّ ٱلَّذِينَ كَفَرُوا۟ مِنْ أَهْلِ ٱلْكِتَٰبِ وَٱلْمُشْرِكِينَ فِى نَارِ جَهَنَّمَ خَٰلِدِينَ فِيهَآ ۚ أُو۟لَٰٓئِكَ هُمْ شَرُّ ٱلْبَرِيَّةِ (٦)

Those who disbelieve from among the people of the Scripture (Jews and Christians) and Al-Mushrikûn, were not going to leave (their disbelief) until there came to them clear evidence (1) A Messenger (Muhammad) from Allâh, reciting (the Qur'ân) purified pages [purified from Al-Bâtil (falsehood)] (2) Wherein are correct and straight laws from Allâh. (3) And the people of the Scripture (Jews and Christians) differed not until after there came to them clear evidence. (i.e. Prophet Muhammad and whatever was revealed to him). (4) And they were commanded not, but that they should worship Allâh, and worship none but Him Alone (abstaining from ascribing partners to Him), and perform As-Salât (Iqâmat-as-Salât) and give Zakât: and that is the right religion. (5) Verily, those who disbelieve (in the religion of Islâm, the Qur'ân and Prophet Muhammad) from among the people of the Scripture

(Jews and Christians) and Al-Mushrikûn will abide in the Fire of Hell. They are the worst of creatures.(6)

Quran 104:1

وَيْلٌ لِّكُلِّ هُمَزَةٍ لُّمَزَةٍ (١)

Woe to every slanderer and backbiter. (1)

Quran 107:4-7

فَوَيْلٌ لِّلْمُصَلِّينَ (٤) ٱلَّذِينَ هُمْ عَن صَلَاتِهِمْ سَاهُونَ (٥) ٱلَّذِينَ هُمْ يُرَآءُونَ (٦) وَيَمْنَعُونَ ٱلْمَاعُونَ (٧)

So woe unto those performers of Salât (prayers) (hypocrites), (4) Those who delay their Salât (prayer from their stated fixed times), (5) Those who do good deeds only to be seen (of men), (6) And prevent Al-Mâ'ûn. (7)

Quran 108

إِنَّآ أَعْطَيْنَاكَ ٱلْكَوْثَرَ (١) فَصَلِّ لِرَبِّكَ وَٱنْحَرْ (٢) إِنَّ شَانِئَكَ هُوَ ٱلْأَبْتَرُ (٣)

Verily, We have granted you (O Muhammad) Al-Kauthar (1) Therefore turn in prayer to your Lord and sacrifice (to Him only) (2) For he who hates you (O Muhammad), he will be cut off from every posterity (good thing in this world and in the Hereafter). (3)

Quran 114:1-6

قُلْ أَعُوذُ بِرَبِّ ٱلنَّاسِ (١) مَلِكِ ٱلنَّاسِ (٢) إِلَـٰهِ ٱلنَّاسِ (٣) مِن شَرِّ ٱلْوَسْوَاسِ ٱلْخَنَّاسِ (٤) ٱلَّذِى يُوَسْوِسُ فِى صُدُورِ ٱلنَّاسِ (٥) مِنَ ٱلْجِنَّةِ وَٱلنَّاسِ (٦)

Say: "I seek refuge with (Allâh) the Lord of mankind, (1) "The King of mankind (2) "The Ilâh (God) of mankind, (3) "From the evil of the whisperer (devil who whispers evil in the hearts of men) who withdraws (from his whispering in one's heart after one remembers Allâh), (4) "Who whispers in the breasts of mankind, (5) "Of jinn and men." (6)

Hadith about Ahl-Bida

Narrated Abu Umamah:

"The Prophet said: If anyone loves for Allah's sake, hates for Allah's sake, gives for Allah's sake and withholds for Allah's sake, he will have perfect faith."

Source: Sunan Abi Dawood 4681 Grade: Sahih

Narrated Abu Rafi':

The Prophet (ﷺ) said: Let me not find one of you reclining on his couch when he hears something regarding me which I have commanded or forbidden and saying: We do not know. What we found in Allah's Book we have followed.

Source: Sunan Abi Dawood 4605 Grade: Sahih

Narrated Abu Huraira:

The Prophet (ﷺ) said, "Leave me as I leave you, for the people who were before you were ruined because of their questions and their differences over their prophets. So, if I forbid you to do something, then keep away from it. And if I order you to do something, then do of it as much as you can."

Source: Sahih al-Bukhari 7288

Narrated Abu Huraira:

Allah's Messenger (ﷺ) said, "All my followers will enter Paradise except those who refuse." They said, "O Allah's Messenger (ﷺ)! Who will refuse?" He said, "Whoever obeys me will enter Paradise, and whoever disobeys me is the one who refuses (to enter it)."

Source: Sahih al-Bukhari 7280

Narrated Jabir bin `Abdullah:

Some angels came to the Prophet (ﷺ) while he was sleeping. Some of them said, "He is sleeping." Others said, "His eyes are sleeping but his heart is awake." Then they said, "There is an example for this companion of yours." One of them said, "Then set forth an example for him." Some of them said, "He is sleeping." The others said, "His eyes are sleeping but his heart is awake." Then they said, "His example is that of a man who has built a house and then offered therein a banquet and sent an inviter (messenger) to invite the people. So whoever accepted the invitation of the inviter, entered the house and ate of the banquet, and whoever did not accept the invitation of the inviter, did not enter the house, nor did he eat of the banquet." Then the angels said, "Interpret this example to him so that he may understand it." Some of them said, "He is sleeping." The others said, "His eyes are sleeping but his heart is awake." And then they said, "The houses stands for Paradise and the call maker is Muhammad; and whoever obeys Muhammad, obeys Allah; and whoever disobeys Muhammad, disobeys Allah. Muhammad separated the people (i.e., through his message, the good is distinguished from the bad, and the believers from the disbelievers).

Source: Sahih al-Bukhari 7281

It was narrated from 'Awf bin Malik that the Messenger of Allah(ﷺ) said:

"The Jews split into seventy-one sects, one of which will be in Paradise and seventy in Hell. The Christians split into seventy-two sects, seventy-one of which will be in Hell and one in Paradise. I swear by the One Whose Hand is the soul of Muhammad, my nation will split into seventy-three sects, one of which will be in Paradise and seventy-two in Hell." It was said: "O Messenger of Allah, who are they?" He said: "The Jamaa'ah."

Source: Sunan Ibn Majah 3992 Grade: Hasan

Abu `Amir al-Hawdhani said:

Mu`awiyah bin Abi Sufiyan stood among us and said: Beware! The Apostle of Allah (ﷺ) stood among us and said: Beware! The people of the Book before were split up into seventy two sects, and this community will be split into seventy three: seventy two of them will go to Hell and one of them will go to Paradise, and it is the jamaa'ah.

Ibn Yahya and `Amr added in their version : " There will appear among my community people who will be dominated by desires like rabies which penetrates its patient", `Amr's version has: "penetrates its patient. There remains no vein and no joint but it penetrates it."

Source: Sunan Abi Dawud 4597 Grade: Hasan

Narrated Abu Sa`id Al-Khudri:

The Prophet (ﷺ) said, "You will follow the ways of those nations who were before you, span by span and cubit by cubit (i.e., inch by inch) so much so that even if they entered a hole of a mastigure, you would follow them." We said, "O Allah's Messenger (ﷺ)! (Do you mean) the Jews and the Christians?" He said, "Whom else?"

Source: Sahih al-Bukhari 7320

Abdullah ibn Masud narrated that the Messenger of Allah said:

"Do you know who the most learned among the people is?"

I (Ibn Masood) said: "No doubt, Allah and His Messenger know best."

Then the Messenger of Allah said: "Verily the most learned among the people is the one who sees most the truth when the people fall in dispute over it, even though he runs short of the deed, and crawls on his hands. These who were before us disputed and were divided into seventy-two sects, only three of which were saved and the remaining (sixty nine) were destroyed. One of those three resisted the (disbelieving) kings and fought them for the sake of the religion of Jesus, son of Mary until they were killed. The second had no power to resist the kings, thereupon they lived among their people and invited them to the religion of Allah and the religion of Jesus son of Mary, thereupon they were seized by the kings, who cut them off by saws. The third had no power to resist the kings, nor to live among the people to invite them to the religion of Allah and the religion of Jesus son of Mary, thereupon they wandered in the mountains, and fled (for their religion), where they assumed monasticism. And it is those in connection with whom Allah Almighty said in Surah Hadid verse 27:

"But the Monasticism which they invented for themselves we did not prescribe for them. (We commanded) except the seeking for the good pleasure of Allah, but that they did not foster as they should have done. Yet we bestowed, on those among them who believed, their reward, but many of them are rebellious transgressors."

The believers are those who believed in me and gave trust to me, and the rebellious transgressors are those who gave lie and were ungrateful."

Source: Al Mujam Al Kabir by At Tabarani, As Saghir hadith 624, Suab Al Iman, Al Mustadrak 3790, Majma Az Zawaid 7:260 and Hilyat Al Awliya.

It was narrated from Abu 'Ubaidah that the Messenger of Allah (ﷺ) said:

"When the Children of Isral became deficient in religious commitment, a man would see his brother *committing sin and would tell him not to do it, but the next day, what he had seen him do did not prevent him from eating or drinking with him, or mixing with him. So Allah made the hearts of those who did not commit sin like the hearts of those who did, and He revealed Qur'an concerning them and said: "Those among the Children of Israel who disbelieved were cursed by the tongue of David and 'Jesus, son of Maryam" until he reached: "And had they believed in Allah, and in the Prophet and in what has been revealed to him, never would they have taken them (the disbelievers) as their friends; but many of them are disobedient (to Allah)."[5:78-81] The Messenger of Allah (ﷺ) sat up and said: "No, not until they take the hand of the wrongdoer (i.e. restrain him] and force him to follow the right way."*

Source: Sunan Ibn Majah 4006 Grade: Daif

In an authentic hadeeth collected by Imaam Ibn Hibbaan in his Saheeh (no. 276), the Messenger of Allaah said:

"Whoever seeks the Pleasure of Allaah while angering the people will have Allaah pleased with him, who shall make the people pleased with him [anyway]. Whoever seeks to please the people while

angering Allaah will have Allaah angry with him, who shall make the people angry with him [anyway]."

Narrated Hudhaifa bin Al-Yaman:

The people used to ask Allah's Messenger about the good but I used to ask him about the evil lest I should be overtaken by them. So I said, "O Allah's Messenger! We were living in ignorance and in an (extremely) worst atmosphere, then Allah brought to us this good (i.e., Islam); will there be any evil after this good?" He said, "Yes." I said, 'Will there be any good after that evil?" He replied, "Yes, but it will be tainted (not pure.)'' I asked, "What will be its taint?" He replied, "(There will be) some people who will guide others not according to my tradition? You will approve of some of their deeds and disapprove of some others." I asked, "Will there be any evil after that good?" He replied, "Yes, (there will be) some people calling at the gates of the (Hell) Fire, and whoever will respond to their call, will be thrown by them into the (Hell) Fire." I said, "O Allah s Apostle! Will you describe them to us?" He said, "They will be from our own people and will speak our language." I said, "What do you order me to do if such a state should take place in my life?" He said,

"Stick to the group of Muslims (Jamaah) and their Imam (ruler)." I said, *"If there is neither a group of Muslims (Jamaah) nor an Imam (ruler)?"* He said, *"Then turn away from all those sects even if you were to bite (eat) the roots of a tree till death overtakes you while you are in that state."*

Source: Sahih Bukhari 7084

Asim reported:

I asked Anas bin Malik whether Allah's Messenger (ﷺ) had declared Medina as sacred. He said: Yes. (the area) between so and so. He who made any innovation in it, and further said to me: It is something serious to make any innovation in it (and he who does it) there is upon him the curse of Allah, and that of the angels and of all the people, Allah will not accept from him on the Day of Resurrection either obligatory acts or the supererogatory acts. Ibn Anas said: Or he accommodates an innovator.

Source: Sahih Muslim 1366

Narrated Aisha:

Allah's Messenger (ﷺ) said, "If somebody innovates something which is not in harmony with the principles of our religion, that thing is rejected."

Sahih al-Bukhari 2697

Abdur Rahman ibn Salim narrated from his father from his grandfather:

The Messenger of Allah said: "Verily Allah chose me and He chose for me companions. Then he made from them ministers and helpers. So whoever swears at them, then the Curse of Allah is upon him and (the curse of) the angels and all of people. Allah will not accept neither obligatory nor voluntary deeds from them."

Source: As-Sunnah by Ibn Abi Asim 1034 Grade: Sahih

Narrated Anas:

The Prophet (ﷺ) said, "Some of my companions will come to me at my Lake Fount, and after I recognize them, they will then be taken away from me, whereupon I will say, 'My companions!' Then it will be said, 'You do not know what they innovated (new things) in the religion after you."

Source: Sahih al-Bukhari 6582

Abu Hazim added:

An-Nu`man bin Abi `Aiyash, on hearing me, said. "Did you hear this from Sahl?" I said, "Yes." He said, " I bear witness that I heard Abu Sa`id Al-Khudri saying the same, adding that the Prophet (ﷺ) said: 'I will say: They are of me (i.e. my followers). It will be said, 'You do not know what they innovated (new things) in the religion after you left'. I will say, 'Far removed, far removed (from mercy), those who changed (their religion) after me."

Source: Sahih al-Bukhari 6584

It was narrated that Ibn Abbas said:

"The Messenger of Allah stood up to give an admonition and he said: 'O people, you will be gathered to Allah naked."' (One of the narrators) Abu Dawud said: "Barefoot and uncircumcised." (The narrators) Waki and Wahb said: "Naked and uncircumcised: As We began the first creation, We shall repeat it. The first one to be clothed on the Day of Resurrection will be Ibrahim, peace be upon him. Then some men from among my Ummah will be brought and will be taken toward the left. I will say: 'O Lord, my companions.' It will be said: 'You do not know what they innovated after you were gone,' and I shall say what the righteous slave said: 'And I was witness over them while I dwelt amongst them, but when You took me up, You were the Watcher over them, but when You took me up, You were the Watcher over them; and You are a Witness to all things. If You punish them, they are Your slaves, and if You forgive them, verily, You, only You, are the All-Mighty, the All-Wise.' And it will be said: 'These people kept turning away since you left them.'"

Source: Sunan an-Nasa'i 2087 Grade: Sahih

It was narrated that Abu Salamah said:

"I said to Abu Sa'eed Khudri: 'Did you hear the Messenger of Allah mention anything about the Haruriyyah (a sect of Khawarij)?' He said: 'I heard him mention a people who would appear to be devoted worshippers: "Such that anyone of you would regard his own prayer and fasting as insignificant when compared to theirs. But they will pass through Islam like an arrow passing through its target, then he (the archer) picks up his arrow and looks at its iron head but does not see anything, then he looks at the shaft and does not see anything, then he looks at the band: that which is wrapped around the iron head where it is connected to the shaft, then he looks at the feather and is not sure whether he sees anything or not."

Source: Sunan Ibn Majah 169 Grade: Sahih

Abd Allah bin Mas'ud reported the Prophet (ﷺ) as saying:

"Beware! The extremists perished," saying it three times.

Source: Sunan Abi Dawud 4608 Grade: Sahih

Narrated Abdullah bin Buraidah from Yahya bin Ya'mur who said:

"The first person to speak about Al-Qadar was Ma'bad Al-Juhani." He said: "Humaid bin Abdur-Rahman Al-Himyari and I went out until we reached Al-Madinah, and we said: 'If we could only meet someone among the companions of the Prophet (ﷺ) so we could ask him about what those people have innovated." [He said:] "So we met him - meaning Abdullah bin 'Umar - while he was leaving the Masjid." [He said:] "My companion and I were on either side of him." [He said:] I thought my companion was going to leave the speaking to me so I said: "O Abu Abdur-Rahman! There is a group of people who recite the Qur'an and seek knowledge, and they claim there is no Al-Qadar, and that the affair is left to chance.' He said: "Whenever you meet those people, then tell them that I am not of them and they are not of me. By the One Whom Abdullah swears by! If one of them were to spend gold the like of Uhud (mountain) in charity, it would not be accepted from him until he believes in Al-Qadar; the good of it and the bad of it.'" He said: "Then he began to narrate, he said: "'Umar bin Al-Khattab said: "We were with the Messenger of Allah when a man came with extremely white garments, and extremely black hair. He had no appearance of traveling visible on him, yet none of us recognized him. He came until he reached the Prophet (ﷺ). He put his knees up against his knees, and then said: "O Muhammad! What is Iman?' He said 'To believe in Allah, His Angels, His, Books, His Messengers, the Day of Judgement, and Al-Qadar, the good of it and the bad of it.' He said: 'Then what is Islam?' He said: 'Testifying to La Ilaha Illallah, and that Muhammad is His servant and Messenger, establishing the Salat, giving the Zakat, performing Hajj to the House, and fasting (the month of) Ramadan.' He said: 'Then what is Ihsan?' He said 'That (is) you worship Allah as if you see Him, and although you do not see Him, He certainly sees you.' He said: 'For all of those he replied to him: 'You have told the truth.'" He said: "So we were amazed at him, he would ask, and then tell him that he is telling the truth. He said: 'Then when is the Hour?' He (ﷺ) said: 'The one being asked knows no more than the questioner.' He said: 'Then what are its signs?' He said: 'That the slave woman gives birth to her master, and that the naked, poor, and bare-footed shepherds rival each other in the height of the buildings.'" 'Umar said: 'Then the Prophet (ﷺ) met me three days after that and said: 'O 'Umar! Do you know who the questioner was? It was Jibril. He came to teach you about the matters of your religion.'"

Source: Jami` at-Tirmidhi 2610 Grade: Sahih

Narrated `Abdullah bin `Amr:

I heard the Prophet (ﷺ) saying, "Allah will not deprive you of knowledge after he has given it to you, but it will be taken away through the death of the religious learned men with their knowledge. Then there will remain ignorant people who, when consulted, will give verdicts according to their opinions whereby they will mislead others and go astray."

Source: Sahih al-Bukhari 7307

Narrated Qays ibn Abbad :

I and Ashtar went to Ali and said to him: Did the Messenger of Allah (ﷺ) give you any instruction about anything for which he did not give any instruction to the people in general?

He said: No, except what is contained in this document of mine. Musaddad said: He then took out a document. Ahmad said: A document from the sheath of his sword.

It contained: The lives of all Muslims are equal; they are one hand against others; the lowliest of them can guarantee their protection. Beware, a Muslim must not be killed for an infidel, nor must one who has been given a covenant be killed while his covenant holds. If anyone introduces an innovation, he will be responsible for it. If anyone introduces an innovation or gives shelter to a man who introduces an innovation (in religion), he is cursed by Allah, by His angels, and by all the people.

Source: Sunan Abi Dawud 4530 Grade: Sahih

Abu Huraira reported Allah's Messenger as saying:

"He who called (people) to righteousness, there would be reward (assured) for him like the rewards of those who adhered to it, without their rewards being diminished in any respect. And he who called (people) to error, he shall have to carry (the burden) of its sin, like those who committed it, without their sins being diminished in any respect."

Source: Sahih Muslim 2674

It was narrated that Jabir bin 'Abdullah said:

"In his Khutbah the Messenger of Allah (ﷺ) used to praise Allah as He deserves to be praised, then he would say: 'Whomsoever Allah guides, none can lead him astray, and whomsoever Allah sends astray, none can guide. The truest of word is the Book of Allah and best of guidance is the guidance of Muhammad. The worst of things are those that are newly invented; every newly-invented thing is an innovation and every innovation is going astray, and every going astray is in the Fire.' Then he said: 'The Hour and I have been sent like these two.' Whenever he mentioned the Hour, his cheeks would turn red, and he would raise his voice and become angry, as if he were warning of an approaching army and saying: 'An army is coming to attack you in the morning, or

in the evening!' (Then he said): 'Whoever leaves behind wealth, it is for his family, and whoever leaves behind a debt or dependents, then these are my responsibility, and I am the most entitled to take care of the believers.'"

Source: Sunan an-Nasa'i 1578 Grade: Sahih

Narrated Ibn `Umar:

A Jew and a Jewess were brought to Allah's Messenger (ﷺ) on a charge of committing an illegal sexual intercourse. The Prophet (ﷺ) asked them. "What is the legal punishment (for this sin) in your Book (Torah)?" They replied, "Our priests have innovated the punishment of blackening the faces with charcoal and Tajbiya." `Abdullah bin Salam said, "O Allah's Messenger (ﷺ), tell them to bring the Torah." The Torah was brought, and then one of the Jews put his hand over the Divine Verse of the Rajam (stoning to death) and started reading what preceded and what followed it. On that, Ibn Salam said to the Jew, "Lift up your hand." Behold! The Divine Verse of the Rajam was under his hand. So Allah's Apostle ordered that the two (sinners) be stoned to death, and so they were stoned. Ibn `Umar added: So both of them were stoned at the Balat and I saw the Jew sheltering the Jewess.

Source: Sahih al-Bukhari 6819

Narrated Irbad ibn Sariyah:

AbdurRahman ibn Amr as-Sulami and Hujr ibn Hujr said: We came to Irbad ibn Sariyah who was among those about whom the following verse was revealed: "Nor (is there blame) on those who come to thee to be provided with mounts, and when thou saidst: "I can find no mounts for you."

We greeted him and said: We have come to see you to give healing and obtain benefit from you.

Al-Irbad said: One day the Messenger of Allah (ﷺ) led us in prayer, then faced us and gave us a lengthy exhortation at which the eyes shed tears and the hearts were afraid.

A man said: Messenger of Allah! It seems as if it were a farewell exhortation, so what injunction do you give us?

He then said: I enjoin you to fear Allah, and to hear and obey even if it be an Abyssinian slave, for those of you who live after me will see great disagreement.

You must then follow my sunnah and that of the rightly-guided caliphs. Hold to it and stick fast to it. Avoid novelties, for every novelty is an innovation, and every innovation is an error.

Source: Sunan Abi Dawud 4607 Grade: Sahih

Note that this hadith specifically mentions obeying the Muslim ruler even if it is an "Abyssinian slave". In context Abyssinian meant anything of the Christian nation of Abyssinia or Ethiopia. So when people influenced with rebellious poison today say things against Muslim rulers alleging they are American slaves or Zionist slaves or slaves to the U.N. then this is no different than if they were Abyssinian slaves. The same ruling applies even if they were literally enslaved by external kafir forces, if it is your Muslim leader then that is your leader and obedience in the good is due to them without fomenting rebellion or rebellious speech or ideas. Many know the hadith without appreciating the nuance and mistakenly think that the prophet simply meant black person or former slave as if merely denouncing cultural racism but contextually it is indicated if they are a Muslim ruler who is a slave to a kafir nation whether it's Abyssinia or otherwise then the duty of good citizenship still applies. Other hadith even mention if it's an Abyssinian slave with amputated limbs, which could be a metaphor for the situation today where the limb of state sponsored jihad is seemingly absent in many nations today. Verily it is the poison of the innovated Khawarij thought fertilized with Kafir goals of instability that desire rebellion, protests and revolution in the Muslim lands. And the hadith most certainly does not say, "If your Muslim ruler is corrupt or enslaved to kafirs then leave the country and move to a non-Muslim country." So this reverse hijra trend is against the sunnah and is done typically by the ignorant and innovators and those greedy with materialistic motives. Thereby the innovators hope to expand their numbers in non-Muslim lands where they can utilize freedom to innovate and then hope to foment instability and political change in Muslim lands where they then force their innovations back into the very Muslim lands where they were expelled from for innovating in the first place. Hence non-Muslim territory is the land where bida thrives most because kuffar will actually support the bida against true Islamic teachings to corrupt generations who then become ignorant. Following that then generations later the ignorant innovators descendants eventually become non-devout and then the foolish non-devout "Muslims" begotten by innovators and the ignorant will eventually apostate and convert to kufr openly. Or if that doesn't work then they export the innovators to the non-innovating lands to spread their deviance in the hopes of distorting Islam. That's the long-term gameplan of the kafir nations who utilize bida and the soldiers of bida to weaken the affairs of the Muslims. Yet Allah has destined plots that will conquer any opposition and will perfect his religion's supremacy over all false religions of every variety regardless of how much it is hated and plotted against by its enemies.

Narrated Abu Sa`id:

*While the Prophet (ﷺ) was distributing (something, `Abdullah bin Dhil Khawaisira at-Tamimi came and* said, "Be just, O Allah's Messenger (ﷺ)!" The Prophet (ﷺ) said, "Woe to you ! Who would be just if I were not?" `Umar bin Al-Khattab said, "Allow me to cut off his neck ! " The Prophet (ﷺ) said, " Leave him, for he has companions, and if you compare your prayers with their prayers and your fasting with theirs, you will look down upon your prayers and fasting, in comparison to theirs. Yet they will go out of the religion as an arrow darts through the game's body in which case, if the Qudhadh of the arrow is examined, nothing will be found on it, and when its Nasl is examined, nothing will be found on it; and then its Nadiyi is examined, nothing will be found on it. The arrow has been too fast to be smeared by dung and blood. The sign by which these people will be recognized will be a man whose one hand (or breast) will be like the breast of a woman (or like a moving piece of flesh). These people will appear when there will be differences among the people (Muslims)." Abu Sa`id added: I testify that I heard this from the Prophet (ﷺ) and also testify that `Ali killed those people while I was with him. The man with the description given by the Prophet (ﷺ) was brought to `Ali. The following Verses were revealed in connection with that very person (i.e., `Abdullah bin

Dhil-Khawaisira at-Tarnimi): 'And among them are men who accuse you (O Muhammad) in the matter of (the distribution of) the alms.' (9.58)

Source: Sahih al-Bukhari 6933

Narrated Yusair bin `Amr:

I asked Sahl bin Hunaif, "Did you hear the Prophet (ﷺ) saying anything about Al-Khawarij?" He said, "I heard him saying while pointing his hand towards Iraq. "There will appear in it (i.e, Iraq) some people who will recite the Qur'an but it will not go beyond their throats, and they will go out from (leave) Islam as an arrow darts through the game's body.' "

Source: Sahih al-Bukhari 6934

Narrated Abu Huraira:

Allah's Messenger (ﷺ) said, "There will be afflictions (in the near future) during which a sitting person will be better than a standing one, and the standing one will be better than the walking one, and the walking one will be better than the running one, and whoever will expose himself to these afflictions, they will destroy him. So whoever can find a place of protection or refuge from them, should take shelter in it."

Source: Sahih al-Bukhari 7081

Narrated Hudhaifa bin Al-Yaman:

The people used to ask Allah's Messenger (ﷺ) about the good but I used to ask him about the evil lest I should be overtaken by them. So I said, "O Allah's Messenger (ﷺ)! We were living in ignorance and in an (extremely) worst atmosphere, then Allah brought to us this good (i.e., Islam); will there be any evil after this good?" He said, "Yes." I said, 'Will there be any good after that evil?" He replied, "Yes, but it will be tainted (not pure.)" I asked, "What will be its taint?" He replied, "(There will be) some people who will guide others not according to my tradition? You will approve of some of their deeds and disapprove of some others." I asked, "Will there be any evil after that good?" He replied, "Yes, (there will be) some people calling at the gates of the (Hell) Fire, and whoever will respond to their call, will be thrown by them into the (Hell) Fire." I said, "O Allah s Apostle! Will you describe them to us?" He said, "They will be from our own people and will speak our language." I said, "What do you order me to do if such a state should take place in my life?" He said, "Stick to the group of Muslims and their Imam (ruler)." I said, "If there is neither a group of

Muslims nor an Imam (ruler)?" He said, *"Then turn away from all those sects even if you were to bite (eat) the roots of a tree till death overtakes you while you are in that state."*

Source: Sahih al-Bukhari 7084

The roots of the tree of Islam shall never perish and Allah will revive the religion should it ever be battered or pruned or cut at the trunk. Today there are many Muslim nations and many Muslim leaders, who while they may be imperfect, the situation is nowhere near being the roots of Islam which started with just Muhammad pbuh alone being told by Angel Gabriel to read. Plus the hadith doesn't even say there will ever be a time when there are no Muslims and no Imams/leaders. That was just a theoretical if that should happen then what should be done. Yet the tree of Islamic faith will never be uprooted from the earth until the earth is nearly ready to be judged by the planter of the seeds of Islam, Allah the All-Knowing Creator.

Thauban reported that Allah's Messenger (ﷺ) said:

Allah drew the ends of the world near one another for my sake. And I have seen its eastern and western ends. And the dominion of my Ummah would reach those ends which have been drawn near me and I have been granted the red and the white treasure and I begged my Lord for my Ummah that it should not be destroyed because of famine, nor be dominated by an enemy who is not amongst them to take their lives and destroy them root and branch, and my Lord said: Muhammad, whenever I make a decision, there is none to change it. I grant you for your Ummah that it would not be destroyed by famine and it would not be dominated by an enemy who would not be amongst it and would take their lives and destroy them root and branch even if all the people from the different parts of the world join hands together (for this purpose), but it would be from amongst them, via your Ummah, that some people would kill the others or imprison the others.

Source: Sahih Muslim 2889

Narrated Abu Huraira:

Allah's Messenger (ﷺ) said, "Whoever obeys me, obeys Allah, and whoever disobeys me, disobeys

Allah, and whoever obeys the ruler I appoint, obeys me, and whoever disobeys him, disobeys me."

Source: Sahih al-Bukhari 7137

Hudhaifah narrated that the Messenger of Allah said:

"Do not be a people without a will of your own, saying: 'If people treat us well, we will treat them well; and if they do wrong, we will do wrong,' but accustom yourselves to do good if people do good, and do not behave unjustly if they do evil."

Source: Jami` at-Tirmidhi 2007 Grade: Hasan

It was narrated that 'Abdullah bin 'Abbas said:

"*The Messenger of Allah (ﷺ) said: 'Allah refuses to accept the good deeds of one who follows innovation until he gives up that innovation.'*"

Source: Sunan Ibn Majah 50 Grade: Daif

Jabir ibn Abdullah said:

The Prophet said: *"If any man is among a people in whose midst he does acts of disobedience, and, though they are able to make him change (his acts), they do not change, Allah will smite them with punishment before they die."*

Source: Sunan Abi Dawud 4339 Grade: Hasan

Abu Hurairah said, the Messenger of Allaah said:

"A person is upon the deen(religion and lifestyle) of his friend, so let each one of you look at whom he befriends."

Source: Silsilah as-Saheehah of al-Albaani (no.927)] Grade: Saheeh

It is narrated on the authority 'Abdullah bin Mas'ud that the Messenger of Allah observed:

"Never a Prophet had been sent before me by Allah towards his nation who had not among his people (his) disciples and companions who followed his ways and obeyed his command. Then there came after them their successors who said whatever they did not practice, and practiced whatever they were not commanded to do. He who strove against them with his hand was a believer: he who strove against them with his tongue was a believer, and he who strove against them with his heart was a believer and beyond that there is no faith even to the extent of a mustard seed."

Source: Sahih Muslim 50

Jabir ibn Abdullah said:

The Prophet said: "If any man is among a people in whose midst he does acts of disobedience, and, though they are able to make him change (his acts), they do not change, Allah will smite them with punishment before they die."

Source: Sunan Abi Dawud 4339 Grade: Hasan

It was narrated from Nafi' that a man came to Ibn 'Umar and said:

"So-and-so sends his Salam to you." He said: "I have heard that he has introduced innovations (into Islam). If he has indeed introduced innovations, then do not convey my Salam to him, for I heard the Messenger of Allah (ﷺ) say: 'There will be among my nation – or among this nation – transformations, the earth collapsing, and Qadhf.' That was concerning Ahlul-Qadar."

Source: Sunan Ibn Majah 4061 Grade: Hasan

Ibn 'Abdullah bin Mughaffal narrated from his father and he said:

"I have rarely seen a man for whom innovation in Islam was harder to bear than him. He heard me

reciting: 'In the Name of Allah, the Most Gracious, the Most Merciful' Bismillahir-Rahmanir-Rahim [1:1] and he said: 'O my son, beware of innovation, for I prayed with the Messenger of Allah (ﷺ), and with Abu Bakr, and with 'Umar, and with 'Uthman, and I never heard any of them saying this. When you (begin to) recite, say: 'All the praises and thanks are to Allah, the Lord of all that exists.' (Al-hamdu Lillahi Rabbil-'Alamin).'" [1:2]

Source: Sunan Ibn Majah 815 Grade: Daif

It was narrated from Aishah that:

The Messenger of Allah said: "Marriage is part of my sunnah, and whoever does not follow my sunnah has nothing to do with me. Get married, for I will boast of your great numbers before the nations. Whoever has the means, let him get married, and whoever does not, then he should fast for it will diminish his desire."

Source: Sunan Ibn Majah 1846 Grade: Hasan

Narrated Abu Sa`id Al-Khudri:

The Prophet (ﷺ) said, "There will emerge from the East some people who will recite the Qur'an but it will not exceed their throats and who will go out of (renounce) the religion (Islam) as an arrow passes through the game, and they will never come back to it unless the arrow, comes back to the middle of the bow (by itself) (i.e., impossible). The people asked, "What will their signs be?" He said, "Their sign will be the habit of shaving (of their beards and their heads).

Source: Sahih al-Bukhari 7562

Narrated Muawiya:

I heard the Prophet (ﷺ) saying, "A group of my followers will keep on following Allah's Laws strictly and they will not be harmed by those who will disbelieve them or stand against them till Allah's Order (The Hour) will come while they will be in that state."

Source: Sahih al-Bukhari 7460

It was narrated that Abu Umamah said:

"The Messenger of Allah said: 'You must acquire this knowledge before it is taken away, and its taking away means that it will be lifted up.' He joined his middle finger and the one that next to the thumb like this, and said: 'The scholar and the seeker of knowledge will share the reward, and there is no good in the rest of the people.'"

Source: Sunan Ibn Majah 228 Grade: Daif

Narrated An-Nu`man bin Bashir:

The Prophet (ﷺ) said, "The example of the person abiding by Allah's order and restrictions in comparison to those who violate them is like the example of those persons who drew lots for their seats in a boat. Some of them got seats in the upper part, and the others in the lower. When the latter needed water, they had to go up to bring water (and that troubled the others), so they said, 'Let us make a hole in our share of the ship (and get water) saving those who are above us from troubling them. So, if the people in the upper part left the others do what they had suggested, all the people of the ship would be destroyed, but if they prevented them, both parties would be safe."

Source: Sahih al-Bukhari 2493

Narrated `Aisha:

Allah's Messenger (ﷺ) recited the Verse:-- "It is He who has sent down to you the Book. In it are Verses that are entirely clear, they are the foundation of the Book, others not entirely clear. So as for those in whose hearts there is a deviation (from the Truth).

follow thereof that is not entirely clear seeking affliction and searching for its hidden meanings; but no one knows its hidden meanings but Allah. And those who are firmly grounded in knowledge say: "We believe in it (i.e. in the Qur'an) the whole of it (i.e. its clear and unclear Verses) are from our Lord. And none receive admonition except men of understanding." (3.7) Then Allah's Messenger (ﷺ) said, "If you see those who follow thereof that is not entirely clear, then they are those whom Allah has named [as having deviation (from the Truth)] 'So beware of them."

Source: Sahih al-Bukhari 4547

Narrated Abdullah ibn Umar:

The Prophet (ﷺ) said: The Qadariyyah are the Magians of this community. If they are ill, do not pay a sick visit to them, and if they die, do not attend their funerals.

Source: Sunan Abi Dawud 4691 Grade: Hasan

Abdullah ibn Hisham reported:

We were with the Messenger of Allah, peace and blessings be upon him, and he was holding the hand of Umar ibn al-Khattab. Umar said to him, "O

Messenger of Allah, you are more beloved to me than everything but myself." The Prophet said, "No, by the One in whose hand is my soul, until I am more beloved to you than yourself." Umar said, "Indeed, I swear by Allah that you are more beloved to me now than myself." The Prophet said, "Now you are right, O Umar."

Source: Sahih Bukhari 6632

Narrated Abu Dhar:

That he heard the Prophet (ﷺ) saying, "If somebody accuses another of Fusuq (by calling him 'Fasiq' i.e. a wicked person) or accuses him of Kufr, such an accusation will revert to him (i.e. the accuser) if his companion (the accused) is innocent."

Source: Sahih al-Bukhari 6045

It was narrated that Abu Al-Aliyah said:

"Ibn Abbas said: "On the morning of Al-Aqabah, while he was on his mount, the Messenger of Allah said to me: "Pick up (some pebbles) for me." So I picked up some pebbles for him that were the size of date stones or fingertips, and when I placed them in his hand he said: "Like these. And beware of going to extremes in religious matters, for those who came *before you were destroyed because of going to extremes in religious matters."*

Source: Sunan an-Nasa'i 3057 Grade: Sahih

Abu Hurairah narrated that:

the Messenger of Allah said: "The religion is An-Nasihah (sincere advice)" three times. They said: "O Messenger of Allah! For Whom?" He said : "To Allah , His books, the A'immah (leaders) of the Muslims, and their average people."

Source: Jami` at-Tirmidhi 1926 Grade: Sahih

Narrated Abu Huraira:

A man said to the Prophet (ﷺ), "Advise me! "The Prophet (ﷺ) said, "Do not become angry and furious." The man asked (the same) again and again, and the Prophet (ﷺ) said in each case, "Do not become angry and furious."

Source: Sahih al-Bukhari 6116

Statements from Scholars about Ahl-Bida

Muhammad ibn Abdur Rahman al Azrami asked a man who was speaking of innovation and calling the people towards it:

"Did the Messenger of Allah, Abu Bakr, Umar, Uthman and Ali have knowledge of it, or did they not have knowledge of it?

The man said: They did not have knowledge of it.

Muhammada ibn Abdur Rahman al Azrami said: *So something of which they had no knowledge of, you know?*

The man responded: Then I say that they did have knowledge of it!

Muhammad ibn Abdur Rahman al Azrami asked: *Was it sufficient for them that they not speak about it or call the people towards it, or was it not sufficient for them?*

The man said: Of course it was sufficient for them.

Muhammad ibn Abdur Rahman Al Azrami asked: *So something sufficient for the Messenger of Allah and his Khalifahs is not sufficient for you?*

The man refrained. Thereupon the Khalifh who overheard the debate said:

May Allah now suffice the one who is satisfied by what they found sufficient. Similarly whoever does not feel content with what was sufficient for the Messenger of Allah, his companions, those who followed them in righteousness, the Imams that came after them, and those firmly grounded in knowledge, regarding reciting the verses on Allah's attributes, reading the reports about them and leaving them the way they came, then may Allah not suffice them.

Source: Lumatul Itiqaad by Ibn Qudamah

Narrated Hammam:

Hudhaifa said, "O the Group of Al-Qurra! Follow the straight path, for then you have taken a great lead (and will be the leaders), but if you divert right or left, then you will go astray far away."

Source: Sahih al-Bukhari 7282

It is reported that ʿUmar bin Al-Khaṭṭāb said to a young man while exhorting him:

"A man might have ten qualities, nine of them good and one bad, but the nine good ones can be spoiled by the one bad quality. Beware of the slips and faults of youth."

Source: Abd Al-Razzāq Al-Ṣanʿānī, Al-Muṣannaf 8240.

Al Shatibi said:

"The real religious innovation is that which has no evidence under Shariah whether detailed or undetermined, neither in Allah's Book, nor in the Prophetic Sunnah, nor in the consensus of the Ummah, nor in the analogism that is considerable to the learned men and Scholars. That is why it has been called a religious innovation, because it is invented with no previous model to imitate, even though its inventor rejects to be described as deviating from Shariah, since he assumes his innovation to be attested by the same proofs of Shariah. Therefore his claim is not right, neither in itself nor according to what seems apparent. It is the occurrence which makes it a religious innovation. Furthermore, what seems apparent is that his evidences, if it is proven that he has taken refuge to attestation are suspicious."

Source: Kitab Itisam

Amr ibn Salamah said:

"We used to sit in front of the door of Abdullah ibn Masud before the dawn prayer. Then when he came out we would walk with him to the masjid. So Abu Musa Ashari came to us and said: 'Did Abu Abdur Rahman (Ibn Maud) come out to you yet?

We said: No not yet.

So he sat with us until he came out. Then when he came out we all got up to him. Then Abu Musa said to him: 'O Abu Abdur Rahman, earlier I verily saw something in the masjid which I did not recognize, and I did not see -by the praise of Allah- anything but good.

He (Ibn Masud) said: And what is that?

So he (Abu Musa Ashari) said: If you will live, then you will see it for yourself. In the masjid I saw people sitting in a circle waiting for the prayer, and in every circle there is a man. And in their hands are pebbles. Then he (the man) says: 'Say Allahu Akbar hundred *times', and they will say Allahu Akbar hundred times. Then he will say: 'Say La ilaha illa Allah hundred times', and they will say La ilaha illa Allah hundred times. And he says: 'Say Subhan-Allah hundred times' and they would say Subhan-Allah hundred times.'*

He (Ibn Masood) said: And what did you say to them?

He (Abu Musa Ashari) said: I did not say anything to them, waiting for your opinion or waiting for your command.

He (Ibn Masud) said: Why did you not tell them to count their sins and assure them that none of their good deeds would be lost?

Then he left and we left with him until he reached a circle from one of these circles. So he stopped at them and said: What is this I see that you are doing?

They said: O Abu Abdur-Rahman, with these we count the takbir, tahlil and tasbih.

He (Ibn Masud) said: Then count your sins. How fast did you not become destroyed? Here the companions of your Prophet are great in numbers, here are his clothes which have not yet decayed and his bowl which has not yet broken. By the One in whose Hand my soul is in, either you are upon a religion which is better in guidance than the millah of Muhammad, or you are opening the door to misguidance.

They said: By Allah, O Abu Abdur-Rahman , we only wanted to do good.

He (Ibn Masud) said: 'And how many wants to do good but do not achieve it. Verily the Messenger of Allah narrated to us that a people will read the Quran but it will not reach beyond their throats. By Allah, I do not know but perhaps most of them will be from you.'

Then he turned away from them.

We saw most of those circles attack us on the day of An-Nahrawan along with the Khaawarij."

Source: Sunan Ad Darimi 210

It is reported that Abūl-ʿĀliyah said:

"There will come upon the people a time when their hearts will be derelict of the Qurān; they will find neither sweetness nor pleasure by it. If they fall short of doing what they have been commanded to do, they *will say: Allāh is most forgiving, merciful (He will forgive us), and if they do what they have been forbidden from doing, they will say: we will be forgiven, we haven't committed any shirk with Allāh. Their affairs will all be based on [false] hope, having no truth and sincerity with it. They will wear the skins of lambs over hearts of wolves. The best of them in his religion will be someone who compromises."*

Source: Imām Aḥmad, Al-Zuhd article 1741.

Imām Al-Awzā'ī said:

"Faith (īmān) is not sound except with [correct] words. Faith and words are not sound except with [good] works. And faith, words and deeds are not sound except with [the correct] intentions in conformance to the Sunnah. Those who went before us of our Salaf did not separate faith from deeds: deeds are a part of faith, and faith is from [ones deeds]. īmān is a word that brings together these aspects of the religions [of Allāh] and is confirmed through [a person's] works.

So whoever believes in word, knows in his heart and confirms [his belief] through his works, then this is the strongest handhold that will never break. And whoever says [words of faith] but does not know [faith] in his heart nor confirms it with his works, it will never be accepted of him and he will be in the hereafter from those who suffer in loss."

Source: Ibanan Al Kubra by Ibn Battah 1097.

It is reported that ʿAbdullāh bin ʿAbbās said, "Love for Allāh and hate for Allāh, make your enmity because of Allāh and your allegiance because of Allāh; for indeed, the love and support of Allāh is not achieved save through this. And a man will never taste true faith (īmān) – though he may pray and fast much – except when he is like that. Today, the people's brotherhood is based upon worldly considerations (dunyā), but this will not do anything for them on the Day of Resurrection."

Source: Ibn Al-Mubārak, Al-Zuhd wa Al-Raqāʾiq article 353.

Ibn Taymiyyah said:

"If it were not for those whom Allah placed to repel the danger of them (meaning the innovators) the religion would have been corrupted. Their corruption is worse than the corruption caused by the conquering of the enemies at times of war. For indeed, when they conquer, they do not corrupt the *hearts or the religion found in them, except after a while. But as for these people (the innovators), then they corrupt the hearts from the very beginning."*

Source: Majmoo ul Fataawaa

Salih Fawzan said:

"Those groups that oppose the guidance of the Messenger, then indeed we abstain from them, even if they call themselves "Islamic" groups. Consideration is not given to names, it is only given to the facts. Names could be grand and magnificent but hollow and empty on the inside, not possessing anything or they could be false."

Source: Beneficial Answers to Questions on Innovated Methodologies

Al Shatibi said:

"If it is proven that the religious innovator is sinful, his sin is not the same in all cases: it indeed varies by variation of the perspectives from which it is considered. Those include whether or not the religious innovator is worthy of Ijtihad; whether he conceals or discloses his religious innovation; whether the religious innovation itself addresses the essentials of religion, is real or supplementary, clear

or abstruse, disbelief or not disbelief; and whether or not its perpetrator is persistent in it. to the end of those things according to which the sin is judge to be either significant, insignificant or close to certainty."

Source: Kitab Itisam

Uwais al Qarni said:

"No doubt enjoining right and forbidding wrong have left the believer with no friend. Whenever we enjoin right upon the people or forbid them to do wrong, they offense our honors, and find assistants from among the wicked to support them. They indeed charged me with the most hideous slanders. But by Allah, I will not cease to enjoin right upon them and forbid them to do evil."

Source: Siyar Alam An Nubala 4:19

Bindr Ibn Husain said:

"The company of religious innovators keeps one away from the truth."

Source: Siyar Alam An Nubala

Al Shatibi said:

"The religious innovator, overwhelmed by his inclination and ignorance of the Sunnah, has the false

impression that what occurs to his mind is the right way, apart from anything else, thereupon he inclines to it, and, because of which deviates from the right path. He then strays wherefrom he thinks to be on the right way. His example is like the one who, at night, passes by the way, with no guide to lead him, thereupon he is about to go astray from it and fall in loss, even though he claims to seek for it. The religious innovator similarly, from among this ummah, goes astray in the proofs of the Sunnah, which he takes by way of inclination and desire rather than by way of submission to it under the rulings and judgments of Allah Almighty. That is indeed the difference between the religious innovator and anyone else."

Source: Kitab Itisam

Yahya ibn Muath Ar Razi said:

"The difference among the people goes back ultimately to three principles, each of which has two opposite extremes, and if man leave one he then would fall in its opposite:

Monotheism and its opposite is Polytheism.

The Sunnah and its opposite is the religious innovation.

And Obedience and its opposite is disobedience."

Source: Siayar Alam Al Nubala

Ahmad ibn Abu Hawari said:

"Whoever does a deed in which he does not follow the Sunnah, his deed is void."

Source: Shatharat Ath-Thahab 2:110

Al Shatibi said:

"We say that to punish the religious innovators by sentencing them to blame, torment to be a lesson for others to learn, deportation and exile, and disapproval of their conduct, goes back to the state of the religious innovation in itself, as to whether or not it causes great mischief in the religion, and its inventor is famous and renowned for it among the people, advocates others to it, dares to transgress upon the people because of his great number of followers and acts upon it with ignorance."

Source: Kitab Itisam

Ibn Taymiyyah said:

"Violating something introduced by the Messenger of Allah, because one models on the practice of someone he believes to be a pious person, shows that this action is driven by a belief in the righteousness of that person in question. And because he is such a pious person he is not expected to violate the Shariah. Even if this is the case and that person is one of the most pious of people, such as the senior Companions and their Successors, their violations of the Book and Sunnah are unacceptable. How would it be then if the pious person in question is not even pious?"

Source: Furqan bayna Awliya Al Rahman wa Awliya Shaytan

Abu Sulaiman Ad Darani said:

"I sometimes accept no word from anyone of the people except with two just witnesses: the Book of Allah and the Sunnah of His Messenger."

Source: Siyar Alam Al Nubala

Fudayl ibn Iyad said:

"Whoever marries his beloved daughter to an innovator has cut off the ties of relationship with her."

Source: Sharus Sunnah by Al Barbaharee 137

It is reported that ʿAlī bin ʾAbī Ṭālib said:

"Do not be with the sinner (fājir), for he will beautify to you the things he does, and he will want you to be like him; and he will beautify to you the worst of his practices; and his entrance upon you and leaving from your company will cause ignominy and discredit [of you]. And do not accompany the fool (aḥmaq), for he will exhaust himself [to help you] but will not benefit you, and he may want to benefit you but end up harming you; his silence is better than his speaking, his distance is better than his closeness, and him dying is better than him living. And do not accompany the liar, for life will not benefit you with him, he will tell others what you say, and tell you what others say; and if you speak the truth, it will not be believed."

Source: Abū Bakr Al-Daynūrī, Al-Mujālasah wa Jawāhir AlʿIlm 1379.

It is reported that Al-Ḥasan Al-Baṣrī said:

"Do not sit with the people of desires (Bidʿah, heresy), even if you think you have a response [to what they say]."

Source: Al-Harawī, Dhamm Al-Kalām article 765.

Al-Khallāl records that Imām Aḥmad said about the Khawārij:

"Do not sell food or clothes to them, and do not buy from them. And he said, The Khawārij are renegades, an evil people."

Source: Al-Khallāl, Al-Sunnah 1:155

It is reported that Imām Mālik said:

"Whatever you fool around with, don't fool around with your deen (religion)."

Source: Al-Lālakā'ī, Sharḥ 'Uṣūl 'I'tiqād Ahl Al-Sunnah 1:163

It is reported that Al-Fuḍayl bin 'Ayyād said: *"How will you be if you reach a time when you will see people who do not distinguish truth from falsehood, believer from unbeliever, trustworthy from treacherous, nor ignorant from knowledgeable, and neither recognize what is right nor censure what is wrong?"*

Source: Al Ibanah Al Kubra by Ibn Battah

After reporting this report, Ibn Battah said:

"To Allāh we belong and to Him we will return! We have reached that time, we have heard this and have come to know most of it and witnessed it. If a man to whom Allāh has bestowed sound reasoning looks and thinks carefully and ponders the matter of Islām and its people and treads the rightly guided path as regards to them, it will become clear to him that most people have turned back on their heals, deviated from the correct path, and turned away from correct proof. Many people have started to like what they used to hate, allow what they used to forbid and recognize what they used to reject. And for sure this is not the [right] character of the Muslims, nor the behavior of those who have insight into this religion, and neither of those who believe in it and are certain about it."

Abu Dawood as-Sijistaanee said, "I said to Abu Abdullaah Ahmad bin Hanbal: I see a man from Ahl us-Sunnah with a man from Ahl ul-Bid'ah. Shall I leave his speaking to him? He said, 'No, inform him that the man that you saw him with is a person of innovation, so if he leaves him, then speak to him, otherwise treat him the same as him, as Ibn Ma'sood said, 'A man is like his companion'."

Source: Tabaqaat ul-Hanaabilah

Aḥmad bin Yūnus reports:

"I saw Zuhayr bin Muʿāwiyah come to Zāʾidah bin Qudāmah and speak to him to get him to narrate ḥadīth to a man, so Zāʾidah asked, Is he from Ahl Al-Sunnah? Zuhayr replied, I do not know that he has any bidʿah. Zāʾidah said, No, that is another matter! Is he from Ahl Al-Sunnah? Zuhayr said, Since when have people become like this? Zāʾidah replied, Since when did people curse Abū Bakr and ʿUmar?!"

Source: Al-Khaṭīb Al-Baghdādī, Al-Jāmiʿ li Akhlāq Al-Rāwī 754.

Imam Barbaharee said:

"From the Sunnah is that you do not obey anyone in disobedience to Allah; neither the parents nor the entire creatures. There should be no obedience to any creature in disobedience to Allah. Do not love anyone upon it (disobedience to Allah); you should hate all that for the sake of Allah."

Source: Sharus Sunnah point 169

It is reported that Ḥudhayfah said:

"How will you be (in the end times) when you open up your religion like the woman who opens her legs to expose her qubul not stopping anyone from coming to her?"

Source: Abū ʿAmr Al-Dānī, Al-Sunan Al-Wāridah fī Al-Fitan 241

It is reported that Al-Fuḍayl bin ʿAyyāḍ said:

"Do not mix except with those who have good character; for the one who has good character brings nothing but good, whilst the one who has bad character brings nothing but evil."

Source: Al-Bayhaqī, Shuʿab Al-Īmān, 87044

It is reported that Isḥāq bin Rāhuway said:

"If you ask the ignorant: 'Who are Al-Sawād Al-Aʿẓam (Main Body of the Muslims)?' they will say, 'All the people (together).' But they do not know that The Jamāʿah (Main Body) is a scholar who follows the footsteps of the Prophet and his way. So whoever is with him and follows him is [one of] The Jamāʿah, but whoever contradicts him in it leaves The Jamāʿah."

Source: Abū Nuʿaym, Ḥilyatu Al-Awliyāʾ 9:238 and 239

It is reported that Muhammad bin Sīrīn said:

"If the Dajjāl (Antichrist) appears, I believe the heretics (People of Desires, Bid'ah) will follow him."

Source: Al-Lālakā`ī, Sharh Usūl I'tiqād Ahl Al-Sunnah 1:131

It is reported that Sufyān Al-Thawrī said:

"There is nothing that corrupts a person or rectifies him more than [his] companion."

Source: Ibanah al Kubra by Ibn Battah 504

Al-Sha'bī once said: *"When these [people] report to you from Allāh's Messenger – praise and peace of Allāh be upon him, adhere to it; but when they merely opine, throw it in the trash."*

Source: Al-Dārimī, Al-Sunan 1:78.

It is reported that 'Imrān bin Husayn was once relating hadeeth amongst a group of people, when a man said:

"Leave this and give us something from the Book of Allāh. 'Imrān said, "You are a dunce (stupid). Do you find in the Book of Allāh details of prayer. Do you find in the Book of Allāh details of fasting!? This

Qur'ān prescribes those matters, and the Sunnah explains them.""

Source: Al-Harawī, Dham Al-Kalām article 244

It is reported that 'Abdullāh bin Ahmad bin Hanbal said: "I asked my father, "Who are the [real] people?" He replied, "The [real] people are none but those who say haddathanā and akhbaranā (those who report hadīth).""

Source: Abū Bakr Al-Daynūrī, Al-Mujālasah wa Jawāhir Al-'Ilm article 3438.

Imam Barbaharee said:

"The foundation upon which the Jama'ah is built is the companions of Muhammad, may Allah be pleased with them all. They are Ahl Sunnah wa Jama'ah. Therefore whoever does not take (his religion) from them has certainly gone astray and committed innovation. And every innovation is misguidance, and misguidance and its followers will be in the Fire."

Source: Sharus Sunnah point 3

It is reported that Mufaddal bin Muhalhal said: "If the heretic started mentioning his bid'ah right at *the beginning of the sitting, you would be on your guard and flee from him, but what he does is begin by mentioning ḥadīth from the Sunnah. Then, he slips his bid'ah in on you. It might then stick to your heart; but when will it leave your heart?"*

Source: Ibn Baṭṭah, Al-Ibānah Al-Kubrā, 2:444.

Imām Sa'īd bin Al-Musayyib once saw a man praying more than two rak'ah after the beginning of Fajr, making many bows and prostrations, and so he forbade him. The man said, *"O Abu Muḥammad, is Allāh going to punish me for praying?"* Sa'īd said, *"No, but He will punish you for contradicting the Sunnah."*

Source: Al-Bayhaqī, As-Sunan Al-Kubraa 2:466. graded ṣaḥīḥ by Shaykh Al-Albānī.

It is reported that Al-A'mash said:
"They (the Salaf) never used to ask about [the religious condition of] a man after knowing three things about him: where and upon whom he entered, where and with whom he walked, and the close company he kept."

Source: Ibn Baṭṭah, Al-Ibānah article 419.

'Alī bin Abī Khālid reports:

"I once said to Aḥmad, "This shaykh – referring to an older man who was with us – is my neighbor. I told him not to keep the company of a certain person, and he would like to hear what you have to say about him: I am referring to Ḥārith Al-Qaṣīr (Al-Ḥārith Al-Muḥāsibī). Many years ago, you saw me with him and told me not to sit with him nor speak with him. I have not spoken to him since that time. This shaykh, however, does sit with him. So what do you say?"

I saw Aḥmad go red with anger, his eyes bulging; I had never before seen him like this. He started to say, "Him! May Allāh do such-and-such to him! Only those well-informed of him know what he really is, only those who really know him know what he is. Al-Mughāzilī, Yaʿqūb and so-and-so sat with him, and he caused them to adopt the views of Jahm (Ibn Ṣafwān, leader of the Jahmites). They were destroyed because of him."

The old man said, "But Abū ʿAbdillāh, he reports ḥadīth, and he is mild and humble; he has done such-and-such [good works]." Abū ʿAbdillāh (Imām Aḥmad) became angry and began repeating, "Let not his humility and softness deceive you". He also said,

"Do not be fooled by his bowed head, he is an evil man; only those well-informed of him through experience know him. Do not speak to him – with all disrespect to him. Are you going to sit with everyone who narrates from Allāh's Messenger – may the praise and peace of Allāh be upon him – though he be a heretic (mubtadi')? No, with all disrespect."

Source: Ṭabaqāt Al-Ḥanābilah, article 325.

It is reported that Al-Ḥasan Al-Baṣrī said:

"One who acts without knowledge is like one who travels off the path; and the one who acts without knowledge corrupts more than he rectifies. So seek knowledge in a way that does not harm your worship, and seek to worship [Allāh] in a way that does not harm [your seeking of] knowledge. For verily, there were people (the Khawārij extremists) who sought to worship [Allāh] but abandoned knowledge until they attacked the Ummah of Muḥammad with their swords. But if they had sought knowledge, it would not have directed them to do what they did."

Source: Ibn 'Abd Al-Barr, Jāmi' Bayān Al-'Ilm wa Faḍlihi article 905.

It is reported that Muḥammad bin Sīrīn said:

"There were people who abandoned knowledge and sitting with the scholars, and [instead] took to their chambers and prayed until their skin dried [from exertion in worship]. Thereafter they began to contradict the Sunnah and thus were destroyed. By Allāh, never does a person act without knowledge, except that he spoils and corrupts more than he fixes and rectifies."

Source: Al-Aṣbahānī, Al-Targhīb wa Al-Tarhīb

It is reported from Al-'Abbās bin Al-Walīd that 'Uqbah said:

"I was once with Arṭa'ah bin Al-Mundhir when one of the people in the gathering said, "What do you say about a man who sits with the followers of the Sunnah and mixes with them, but when the followers of Bid'ah are mentioned he says, 'Spare us from mentioning them, do not talk about them?'" Arṭa'ah said, "He is one of them, do not let him confuse you about his condition." I felt this was strange, so I went to Al-Awzā'ī – and he used to clarify these matters when they came to him. He said, "Arṭa'ah is right, the matter is as he said; this person forbids talking about [Ahl Al-Bid'ah], so how can [people] be on guard against them if they are not exposed?""

Source: Ibn 'Asākir, Tārīkh Dimishq 8:15.

Umar bin Al-Khaṭṭāb said:

"Verily, the followers of opinion are the enemies of the Sunan (the teachings of Allāh's Messenger as passed down in hadith): they were unable to preserve them and their meanings escaped them, and when asked [questions] they were too embarrassed to say 'We don't know,' so they opposed the Sunan with their opinions."

Source: Ibn Abī Zamanīn, Uṣūl Al-Sunnah article 8; Al-Lālakā`ī, Sharḥ Uṣūl I'tiqād Ahl Al-Sunnah article 201

It is reported that Imām Al-Awzā'ī used to say:

"Whoever hides his heresy (bid'ah) from us, his companionship is not hidden from us."

Source: Al Ibanah al Kubra by Ibn Battah 420

It is reported that 'Abd Al-Raḥmān bin Mahdī said, following a mention of the Ṣūfīah (Sufis):

"Do not sit with them, nor with the followers of Kalām. Be with the carriers of books, for they are like mines, like those who descend: one brings up a gem and another a nugget of gold."

Source: Al Ibanah al Kubra by Ibn Battah 483

It is reported that Sufyān Al-Thawrī said:

"If you loved a man for Allāh and then he innovates in Islām and you don't hate him for it, you never [truly] loved him for Allāh."

Source: Abū Nu'aym, Hilyatu Al-Awliyā` 7:34.

Ibn Taymiyyah said:

"It is not for anyone to place an individual for the ummah, calling to his way and making allegiance and enmity based on him, except for the Prophet. And it is not permissible to put forth some speech, for which allegiance and enmity will be made, except for the speech of Allah and His Messenger, and that which the Ummah unanimously agrees on. Rather this is from the acts of the people of innovation, those who place an individual and speech for themselves, by which they cause division in the Ummah. And they make allegiance and enmity based on this speech or this ascription."

Source: Majmoo Fatawaa

Salih Fawzan was asked:

"Are we required to mention the good qualities of those whom we warn against?"

He answered: "If you mention their good qualities, then this means you have called (the people) to follow them. No, do not mention their good qualities. You are not entrusted to praise and approve of their actions – you are only entrusted with exposing the error they are upon so that they may repent from it, and so others can beware of it.

It may even be that the error that they are upon wipes away their good deeds, if it is disbelief or shirk. It could also be that this error outweighs their good deeds. And perhaps it may seem like they are good deeds in your eyes, yet they are not so in the sight of Allah."

Source: Question 10 from Beneficial Answers to Questions on Innovated Methodologies

Imam Barbaharee said:

"Know, may Allah have mercy upon you, that the religion came from Allah, the Blessed and Exalted; it was not founded upon the intellect or views of men. Rather its knowledge is with Allah and his Messenger. So do not follow anything with your desires lest you deviate from the religion and thus go out of the fold of Islam; for indeed there is no proof for you. The Messenger of Allah has certainly explained the Sunnah to his Ummah and clarified it to his Companions., and they are the Jama'ah and As Sawad al Adham. And As Sawad al Adham is the truth and its followers. Therefore, whoever opposes the companions of the Messenger of Allah in any of the matters of the religion has certainly disbelieved."

Source: Sharus Sunnah point 4

It is reported that Ayyūb Al-Sakhtiyānī said:

"Whoever loves Abū Bakr has upheld the religion, whoever loves 'Umar has made the way clear, whoever loves 'Uthmān is enlightened by the light of Allāh, and whoever loves 'Alī has taken the firmest handhold. Whoever speaks well of the Companions of Allāh's Messenger is clear of hypocrisy (nifāq), but whoever belittles any one of them or dislikes [any one of them] for something he did, then he is a heretic (mubtadi'), an opponent of the Sunnah and the Righteous Predecessors (the Salaf), and it is feared that none of his deeds will be raised to the heavens until he loves all of [the Companions] and his heart is clear towards them."

Source: Ibn Abī Zamanīn, Uṣūl Al-Sunnah article 189.

Ahmed ibn Yunus reported Zaidah said:

"If he is a rafidi then I do not pray behind him."

Source: Kitab As Sunnah by Harb Ismail al karmani

Abd Al-Raḥmān bin Mahdī reports:

"I entered upon Mālik bin Anas when a man was asking him about the Qur`ān. [Imām Mālik] said, "Perhaps you are a companion of Amr bin 'Ubayd. May Allāh curse 'Amr, for he was the one who innovated this bid'ah of Kalām. If Kalām was knowledge, the Companions and their Followers would have spoken it, like they spoke about the regulations and laws [of Islam]. But [Kalām] is falsehood that leads to falsehood.""

Source: Abul-Faḍl Al-Muqri`Al-Rāzī, Aḥādīth fī Dham Al-Kalām wa Ahlihī

It is reported that 'Umar bin Al-Khaṭṭāb said:

"We were once in a time when we did not think anyone learned the Quran seeking anything but Allāh the Exalted, but now I fear there are men who

learn it and intend the people and what they can get from them. So seek Allāh with your recitation and deeds. For verily, we used to know you when Allāh's Messenger was amongst us, when revelation would descend and Allāh would tell us about you. As for today, Allāh's Messenger has passed on, and the revelation has stopped; and I only know you as I say: whoever shows what is good, we love him for it and think good of him, and whoever shows what is evil, we hate him for it and suspect him. Your secret and private matters are between you and your Lord the Mighty and Majestic."

Source: Al-Ājurrī, Akhlāq Ḥamalat Al-Qur`ān article 26.

It is reported that:

"ʿAbdullāh bin Al-Ḥasan used to often sit with Rabīʿah. One day they were revising and studying various practices from the Sunnah when a man in the gathering said, "[But] this is not what is practiced [by the people]." ʿAbdullah said, "So if the ignorant become so numerous that they become the rulers and judges, will they then be a proof over the Sunnah?" Rabīʿah said, "I bear witness that these are the words of the sons of the Prophets.""

Source: Al-Khaṭīb Al-Baghdādī, Al-Faqīh wa Al-Mutafaqqih article 384.

Ibn Shihāb reports:

'Umar bin 'Abd Al-'Azīz, said, "The Messenger of Allāh and the authorities (leaders of the Muslims, the Caliphs) after him set certain ways and practices. To follow those ways is to believe in Allāh's Book and to complete [ones] obedience of Him, and to be strong upon the religion of Allāh. It is not for anyone to alter those ways or change them for something else, and it is not for anyone to consider the views and opinions of those who contradict them. Whoever follows what [the Prophet and his Caliphs] laid down will be guided, whoever seeks enlightenment through it will be enlightened. But whoever contradicts those ways and follows a way other than the way of the Believers, Allāh the Mighty and Majestic will leave him in the path he has chosen and land him in Jahannam (Hell); and what an evil destination that is.'"

Source: Al-Lālakā`ī, Sharḥ Uṣūl I'tiqād Ahl Al-Sunnah 1:94.

It is reported that Abū Al-Dardā` said:

"Be a scholar or a learner, or a person who loves [the scholars] or a follower [of the scholars], but do not be the fifth. Ḥumayd (one of the reporters) asked Al-Ḥasan (Al-Baṣri, who reported this from Abū Al-Dardā`), "And who is the fifth?" He replied, "A heretic (mubtadi', religious innovator}."

Source: Ibn ʿAbd Al-Barr, Jāmiʿ Bayān Al-ʿIlm 1:142.

It is reported that Al-Fuḍayl bin ʿAyyāḍ said:

"Verily, Allāh has angels who seek out the circles of remembrance [of Allāh], so be careful who you sit with; make sure it is not with an adherent of bid'ah, for Allāh does not look at them. And the sign of nifāq (hypocrisy in faith) is that a man mingles with an adherent of bid'ah."

Source: Ibn Baṭṭah, Al-Ibānah Al-Kubrā 1:460

It is reported that Bishr bin Al-Ḥārith said:

"I heard Al-Fuḍayl bin ʿAyyāḍ say, "It has reached me that Allāh has barred repentance from every adherent of bid'ah (religious innovation), and the worst of the people of bid'ah are those who hate the Companions of Allāh's Messenger." He then turned to me and said, "Make the firmest of your deeds with

Allāh your love for the Companions of His Prophet, for [then], were you to come to the standing of judgment (on the Day of Resurrection) with the likes of the Earth in sins, Allāh would forgive you; but if you come [on that Day] with even the smallest amount of hatred for them, no [good] deed will benefit you.""

Source: Abū Bakr Al-Daynūrī, Al-Mujālasah wa Jawāhir Al-'Ilm 5: 412.

It is reported that Imām Al-Awzā'ī wrote:

"O Muslims, fear Allāh and obey Him, and accept the advice of the sincere advisers and the exhortation of the exhorters, and know that this knowledge is religion, so be careful about what you do [in it] and from whom you take [it] and who you follow and who you trust your religion to. For verily, the followers of Bid'ah are all falsifiers and liars, neither are they careful nor do they fear and protect [against wrongdoing], and nor are they to be trusted to not distort what you hear. They say what they know not when criticizing and decrying or when affirming their lies. But Allāh encompasses what they do. So be on guard against them, suspect them, reject them and distance yourselves from them, for this was what

your earlier scholars and the righteous latter ones did and instructed others to do. Beware of rising against Allāh and becoming instruments in the destruction of His religion and undoing its handholds by respecting the innovators, for you know what has come down to us about respecting them. And what stronger respect and veneration can there be than taking your religion from them, following them, believing them, being close to them and helping them in alluring those they allure and attracting those they attract of the weak Muslims towards their ideas and the religion they practice? This is enough to be considered a partnership and contribution to what they do."

Source: Ibn 'Asākir, Tārīkh Dimishq 6:361 and 362.

It is reported that Al-Fuḍayl bin 'Ayyāḍ said, "*Whoever helps an adherent of bid'ah (heretic) has helped in the destruction of Islam.*"

Source: Abū Nu'aym, Ḥilyatu Al-Awliyā`

It is reported that Abū Isḥāq Al-Hamdānī and Ibrāhīm bin Maysarah said,

"*Whoever respects an adherent of bid'ah has helped in the destruction of Islam.*"

Reported from Al-Hamdānī by Al-Ājurrī, Al-Sharī'ah Volume 5 page 260; and from Ibn Maysarah by Al-Lālakā`ī, Sharḥ Usūl I'tiqād Ahl Al-Sunnah Volume 1 page 265.

It is reported ʿUmar bin Al-Khaṭṭāb said,

"Stay well away from the enemies of Allāh during their festivals."

Umar also said, *"Do not learn the speech of the non-Arabs (unbelievers) and do not enter upon the polytheists in their churches during their holidays, for the wrath [of Allāh] descends upon them then."*

It is also reported that ʿAbdullāh bin ʿAmr bin Al-ʿĀṣ said, *"Whoever takes residence in the lands of the non-Arabs (unbelievers) and takes part in their Nayrūz and their Mahrijān (two Persian festivals) and copies them until the day he dies will be resurrected and gathered with them on the Day of Resurrection."*

Source: Al-Bayhaqī, Al-Sunan Al-Kubrā volume 9 page 234.

It is reported that a man came to ʿAbdullāh bin Masʿūd and asked, *"Teach me some comprehensive and beneficial words."* He replied, *"Worship Allāh* and do not associate any partners with Him, and be with the Qur'ān wherever it is. And whoever comes to you with some truth – whether he is young or old, even if he is hated by you – then accept [that truth]. And whoever comes lying to you – even if he is beloved and close – then reject it from him."

Source: Abū Bakr Al-Kharā`iṭī, Masāwī Al-Akhlāq wa Madhmūmihā page 72

It is reported that Ibn Mas'ūd said, "Whoever wants to honor his religion and do good to it should avoid mixing with the ruler or sitting with the followers of desires (heretics, people of bid'ah), for sitting with them is more contagious than scabies."

Source: Ibn Waddāḥ, Al-Bida' page 136.

It is reported that 'Uthmān bin Ḥāḍir said, "I said to Ibn 'Abbās: 'advise me.' He replied, 'It is upon you to be upright, follow al-athar, and beware of innovating [in religion].'"

Source: Al Ibanah al Kubra by Ibn Battah

Salih Fawzan said:

"You find the followers of innovations despising authentic hadith and the Sunan (ways of guidance of

Allah's Messenger). The worst enemy to them and the most detestable of what they hear is to say: 'So and So hadith forbids or prohibits this.'

They do not want to hear the Hadith or Sunan that oppose what they are upon. This is a sign that the Sunnah and innovation cannot coexist. As for the person upon the Sunnah, if he hears a Hadith from the Messenger of Allah, he feels happy with that and adds good to his good, and more knowledge to (his) knowledge.

The one upon the Sunnah is happy with the Hadith of the Messenger of Allah whereas the follower of innovation flees from them. This is something clear regarding the innovators; they wage war against the Sunan because it suppresses what they possess of innovations. This contains discouragement from innovations; that innovations wipe out the Sunan and as well, remove the love of the Sunan from the hearts."

Source: Explanation of Sharus Sunnah by Imam Barbaharee

It is reported that Al-Musayyib bin Rāfi' Al-Asadī said, "We only follow, we do not innovate; we follow behind and do not start anything [in the *religion], and we will never stray as long as we adhere to the narrations."*

Source: Al-Harawī, Dhamm Al-Kalām wa Ahlihī

It is reported that Abul-Jawzā` said, *"I would prefer to sit with swine than to sit with the people of desires (heretics, adherents of bid'ah)."*

Source: Al-Dhahabī, Siyar A'lām Al-Nubalā`, in his biography of the Abul-Jawzā`.

It is reported that Imām Layth bin Sa'd said, *"Even if I saw a heretic (follower of bid'ah) walk on water, I would not accept him."* This was reported to Imām Shāfi'ī, and he said, *"He didn't go far enough. Rather, if I saw one walk in the air, I would not accept him."*

Source: Al-Lālakā`ī, Sharh Usūl 'I'tiqād Ahl Al-Sunnah Volume 1 page 228; Ibn Battah, Al-Ibānah Al-Kubrā Volume 2 page 175; Ibn Al-Jawzī, Talbīs Iblīs page 14 – with slightly variant wordings.

Imām Ahmad said:

"The graves of Ahl Al-Sunnah who committed major sins are gardens (from Paradise) whilst the graves of

the heretics (adherents of Bid'ah) who were ascetics are pits (from the Fire). The sinners from Ahl Al-Sunnah are the beloved (awliyā`) of Allāh, whereas the ascetics of Ahl Al-Bid'ah are the enemies of Allāh."

Source: Ibn Abī Ya'lā, Ṭabaqāt Al-Ḥanābilah Volume 1 page 182.

Al-Ḥāfidh Ibn ʿAbd Al-Barr states:

"The definition of knowledge according to the scholars is whatever a person is clear and sure about. Anyone who is certain and clear about something knows it. Therefore, whoever is not certain about something but says it blindly following someone else, does not know it. Blind following is – according to the scholars – different from following (al-ittibā'). Because following is to follow a person based on what has become clear to you of the correctness of his position, whereas blind-following is to say what he says while not understanding it or its reasoning."

Source: Jāmi' Bayān Al-'Ilm Volume 2

It is reported that ʿAbdullāh bin Mas'ūd said,

"One of the worst sins is when a man says to his brother, "Fear Allāh,' and he replies, "Worry about yourself."

Source: Abū Bakr Al-Daynūrī, Al-Mujālasah wa Jawāhir Al-'Ilm article 2619.

Imam Barbaharee said:

"Beware of little newly invented matters because small innovations will add up till it becomes big. This was the case with every innovation introduced in theis Ummah. At the beginning, it was small, looking like the truth. Then the one who entered into it was deceived by it, and then was unable to come out of it. So it became big and taken as a religion through which worship is made. So he contradicted the straight way and thus went out of the fold of Islam."

Source: Sharus Sunnah point 6

It is reported that a group of heretics (People of Bid'ah) and their devout worship was mentioned to ʿAbd Al-Raḥmān bin Mahdī. He said, *"Allāh only accepts what conforms to what has been commanded and what is in the Sunnah."* Then he recited, And a monasticism which they (Christians) innovated, We did not ordain it upon them [Al-Ḥadīd: 27]. He went on to say, *"So Allāh did not accept this from them and reprimanded them for it."* He then said, *"Stick to the way and the Sunnah."*

Source: Abū Nu'aym, Ḥilyah Al-Awliyā` Volume 4.

Ibn Mubarak said:

"Verily Allah has angels who seek out the gatherings of remembrance. So look to who your gathering is with. Do not let it be with an innovator, because Allah does not look at them. And the sign of nifaq is that a man gets up and sits down with an innovator."

Source: Ibanah Al Kubra by Ibn Battah 469

Ibn Taymiyyah said:

"Shaykh Abu 'Amar Ibn Salah said: To take the school out of the hands of Abul-Hasan al-Aamadee is better than re-capturing 'Akka (Acre) from the hands of the Crusading Christians. It is more important that we get this school (academy of learning) out of the hands of Abul-Hasan al-'Aamidee (who was an innovator, a Jahmee and Ashari). It is more important that we get this school out of his hands,

where he can mislead the Muslims and teach the children innovation than that we get the seaport of 'Akka.

Source: Majmoo Fatawa

Fudayl Ibn Iyyad said:

"I have met the best of people – all of them followers of the Sunnah – they prohibit from the innovator. And the follower of Sunnah, even if he only has little knowledge, then I hope for him. But the innovator, even if he has many deeds then Allah does not raise it (accept it)."

Source: Mukhtasar Al Hujjah fi Bayan Al Mahajjah

It is reported that Al-Awzāʿī said:

"Follow the narrations [ways] of those who have preceded (the Salaf) even if people reject you; and beware of people's opinions, even if they beautify them for you."

Source: Al-Ājurrī, Kitāb Al-Sharīʿah 1:138; Ibn ʿAbd Al-Barr, Jāmiʿ Bayān Al-ʿIlm wa Faḍlihi 3:373.

Ma'an bin ʿĪsā reports Imām Mālik said:

"I am but a man. I make mistakes sometimes and I am correct sometimes, so examine my opinions and accept anything that agrees with the Book and Sunnah; and leave anything that does not agree with the Book and Sunnah."

Source: Ibn ʿAbd Al-Barr, Jāmiʿ Bayān Al-ʿIlm wa Faḍlihi Volume 2 page 465.

Mālik bin Anas was once returning from the mosque, leaning on my arm, when a man called Abū Al-Juwayrīyah who was accused of Al-Irjāʾ caught up with him. He said: "*O Abū ʿAbdullāh, listen to something I have to say and debate with me and let me tell you my opinion.*" [Imām] Mālik said, "*And what if you overcome me?*" The man replied, "*If I defeat you, you follow me.*" Mālik asked, "*And what if another man comes and defeats us?*" He replied, "*Then we follow him.*" To this, Mālik said, "*O servant of Allāh, Allāh sent Muḥammad with a single religion, but I see you moving from religion to religion. ʿUmar bin ʿAbd Al-ʿAzīz said, 'Whoever makes his religion the object of argumentation will frequently change it.'*"

Source: Al-Ājurrī, Kitāb Al-Sharīʿah

Abdul-Awwal narrates that he heard his father Hammaad ibn Muhammad al-Ansari say:

Whoever falls into an innovation, it is said to him:

"This action of yours is an innovation".

And if he persists in this (innovation), then it is said to him:

"You are an innovator (mubtadi')."

Source: al-Majmoo' fee Tarjamatil-Muhaddith Hammaad ibn Muhammad al-Ansaaree wa Seeratuhu wa Aqwaalauhu – Volume 2, Quote Number 39, Page 482

It is reported from Al-Awzâ'î that he said:

I have been told that it used to be said, "Woe to those who study [their religion] for a purpose other than worship, and those who seek to permit what is forbidden through doubts and specious arguments."

Source: Al-Khattîb Al-Baghdâdî, Iqtdâ Al-'Ilm Al-'Amal, page 77.

O People of Scripture! Do not be extreme in your religion! [Al-Mâ`idah verse 77]

It is reported from Qatâdah that he said, commenting on this verse, "*Meaning: do not innovate in religion and do not sit with a religious innovator (mubtadi')."*

Source: Ibanah al Kubra by Ibn Battah

It is reported from Abû Qilâbah that he said:

"Do not sit with the People of Desires (Bid'ah), for I fear that they will immerse you in their misguidance or mix up and confuse what you already know."

Source: Ibanah al Kubra by Ibn Battah

It was once said to 'Abdullah bin Al-Mubârak, "O Abû 'Abd Al-Rahmân, you often sit alone at home." He said, "I am alone? I am with the Prophet and his Companions." Meaning: reading hadîth.

Source: Ibn 'Asâkir, Târîkh Dimishq

Shaqîq bin Ibrâhîm reports:

It was once said to 'Abdullah bin Al-Mubârak, "After you have prayed with us you don't sit with us?" He replied, "I go and sit with the Sahâbah and the Tâbi'în." We said, "And how can you sit with the Sahâbah and Tâbi'în (when they have all passed away)?" He replied, "I go and read the knowledge I *have collected, I find their narrations and deeds. What would I do with you? You sit around backbiting people."*

Source: Al-Dhahabî, Siyar A'lâm Al-Nubalâ` in his biography of 'Abdullah bin Al-Mubârak.

It is reported from Imâm Sufyân bin 'Uyainah that he said:

"Whoever's sin was because of [carnal] desires, hope for him (as he may repent and be forgiven); but whoever's sin was out of pride, fear for him. For indeed, Âdam sinned out of simple desire, and was forgiven; whereas Iblîs sinned out of pride, and was cursed."

Source: Al-Dhahabî, Siyar A'lâm Al-Nubalâ` in his biography of Sufyân bin 'Uyainah.

Mu'âdh bin Jabal used to say:

"Ahead of you are times of trials (fitan) in which there will be much wealth and in which the Qurân will be opened and taken (read) by believers and hypocrites, men and women, young and old and freemen and slaves. At that time it is likely that there will be people who will say, "Why aren't the people following me when I have read the Qurân? They will

not follow me until I invent something else." So, beware of everything that is innovated (in religion), for those things that are innovated are misguidance."

Source: Ibn Waḍḍāḥ, Al-Bidaʿ page 62, Al-Lālakāʾī, Sharḥ Uṣūl Iʿtiqād Ahl Al-Sunnah wa Al-Jamāʿah and others.

Imam Barbaharee said:

"Know that deviation from the Path is from two angles:

Firstly: a man who strays from the path while desiring nothing but good. He should not be followed in his error for he is destroyed.

Secondly: the one who defies the truth and disagrees with those who were before him among the pious. Such a person is going astray and will lead others astray. He is a rebellious devil in this Ummah. It is incumbent upon whoever knows him to warn people about him and explain his condition to the people so that no one will fall into his innovation and as a result, be destroyed."

Source: Sharus Sunnah point 7

It is reported ʿAbdullāh bin Masʿūd said:

"One should get used to the idea that if everyone on Earth disbelieved, you would not disbelieve. Do not be an im'ah (characterless)."

He was asked, *"And what is an im'ah?"*

He replied, *"A person who says, 'I am with the people (I do what they do).' Verily, there is to be no following examples in evil."*

Source: Al Ibanah al Kubra by Ibn Battah

Fudayl ibn Iyaad said:

"Whoever attends the funeral of an innovator, then Allah will continue to be dissatisfied with him until he returns."

Source: Ar Radd ala Al Mubtadiah 39

Sufyan ibn Uyaynah said to a man:

"From where did you come?

The man said: From the funeral prayer of fulan ibn fulan.

Sufyan ibn Uyaynah said: *"I will not narrate any hadith to you. Ask Allah for forgiveness, and do not return. You saw a man who hates the companions of the Messenger of Allah and then you attended his funeral!"

Source Mukhtasar Al Hujjah fi Bayyan Al Mahajjah 324

Muhammad ibn Bashshar said:

"I said to abdur Rahman ibn Mahdi: Should I attend the funeral of the one who swears at the companions of the Messenger of Allah?

Abdur Rahman ibn Mahdi said: If he was from my blood I would not inherit him."

Source: Ibanah As Sughra by Ibn Battah

It was said to Hasan:

Verily Fulan washed the corpse of a man from the people of desires.

So Hasan said: *"Inform him that when he dies we will not pray upon him."*

Source: Ibanah As Sughra by Ibn Battah

It is reported 'Abdullah bin Mas'ūd said:

"For every bid'ah with which Islām is plotted against, Allah has a beloved worshipper (walī) who refutes and repels it and speaks about its signs, so *take the full opportunity of attending such places, and trust in Allah."*

Source: Ibn Waddāh, Al-Bid'ah page 5.

Hasan al Basri said:

"There is no backbiting for a person of innovation or a person who openly commits sins."

Source: Al-Laalikaa'ee in Sharh-Usoolul-I'tiqaad

Ibn Taymiyyah said about the Khawārij:

"They are more evil to the Muslims than others – and there is none more wicked to the Muslims than them, not the Jews nor the Christians. They strived to kill every Muslim who did not agree with them. They made permissible the spilling of Muslim blood, and the taking of their wealth and property, and the killing of their children, declaring them to be unbelievers – they (the Khawārij) took this path as their religion due to their extreme ignorance and their misguided innovation…"

Source: Minhaj as Sunnah

Imām Ash-Shāfi'ee said:

I entered Baghdad and went to Bishr al-Mirīsī, so he accommodated me in his room. Then his mother said to me: "Why have you come to him?" I replied: "To hear from him knowledge." So she said [about her own son, Bishr]: "He is an innovating heretic."

Source: Al-Khatīb in Tārīkh Baghdād

Fitr ibn Hammad asked Mu'tamar ibn Sulayman:

"An imam of a people says: The Quran is created, should I pray behind him?

Ibn Sulayman said: "I pray behind a Muslim, it is more beloved to me."

So Fitr went to Yazid ibn Zuray and asked him:

"An imam of a people says: The Quran is created, should I pray behind him?"

Yazid ibn Zuray said: "No, and (he is shown) no respect."

Source: Kitab As Sunnah by Harb ibn Ismail al karamani

It is reported that 'Alī bin Abī Ṭalib said:

"The thing I fear for you most is following desires and having extensive hopes (about this worldly life). Following one's desires blocks you from the truth, and having extensive hopes makes you forget the hereafter. Verily, this worldly life is departing and the hereafter is approaching and each of them has its children. So be children of the hereafter, not children of this world, for today there are (opportunities to do) deeds and there is no reckoning, but tomorrow there will be reckoning and no deeds."

Reported by Abū Nu'aym, Ḥilyah Al-Awliyā, and others.

It is reported that Sufyān Al-Thawrī said:

"A person who sits with a heretic (an adherent of bid'ah) will not escape one of three things: Either he will become a trial (fitnah) for others, or some deviation will occur in his heart and he will slip and be cast into the Fire by Allah, or he will say to himself, 'By Allah, I don't care what they say, I am confident about myself;' but whoever feels secure from Allah about his religion even for the blinking of an eye, Allah will take his religion away from him."

Source: Ibn Waḍḍāḥ, Al-Bida' 125.

Al-Ḥasan Al-Baṣrī said:

"Do not sit with an adherent of bid'ah for he will cause a disease in your heart."

Source: Ibn Waddāh, Al-Bida' 124.

It is reported Abū Idrīs Al-Khawlānī said:

"I would rather hear of a fire in the masjid than hear of a bid'ah in it without there being anyone to do away with it. Never do a people innovate a bid'ah in their religion except that Allah removes a sunnah from them."

Source: Ibn Waddāh, Al-Bida' 92.

'Abdullah bin Mas'ūd said:

"Everyone speaks of good things. It is those whose words and deeds match who have acquired their share. Those whose words and deeds do not match have only reproached themselves."

Source: Ibn Al-Mubārak, Al-Zuhd wa Al-Raqā`iq

Sufyan bin Uyaynah said:

"He who utters a word against the Companions of the Messenger of Allah is a person of desires(innovation)."

Source: Sharus Sunnah by Imam Barbaharee

It is reported that 'Umar bin Al-Khattāb said:

"Do not be fooled by one who recites the Qurān. His recitation is but speech – but look to those who act according to it."

Source: Al-Khaṯīb, Iqtiḍā` Al-'Ilm Al-'Amal number 109

Imām Mālik said: "

"Knowledge is not to be taken from four types of people: a foolish person who openly acts foolish, even if he reports the most narrations; an adherent of bid'ah who calls to his desires; a person who lies, even if I don't accuse him of lying in ḥadīth; and a righteous pious worshipper who does not accurately retain what he narrates."

Source: Al-Dhahabī, Siyar A'lām Al-Nubalā` in his biography of Imām Mālik.

Al-Fuḏayl bin ʿAyyāḍ said:

"Allah accepts only those deeds which are both correct and sincere (pure). If the deed is done correctly but not sincerely, it will not be accepted. And if it is sincere but not correct, it will not be accepted." He was asked, "Abū 'Alī! What is the sincere and correct deed?" He replied, "The sincere deed is one that is done only for Allah. And the correct deed is one done according to the Sunnah."

Source: Abū Nuʻaym, Ḥilyah Al-Awliyā` Volume 8 page 95.

Imām Al-Shāfi'ī said:

"Whenever any people of desires (heretics) came to Mālik he would say to them, "As for me, I am upon clarity as regards my religion. As for you, you are a doubter, go and argue with another doubter like yourself.""

Source: Al-Dhahbī in Siyar A'lām Al-Nubalā' under the biography of Imām Mālik.

Abū 'Uthmān Sa'īd bin Ismā'īl Al-Naysābūrī said:

"Whoever governs himself by the Sunnah – in word and deed – will speak with wisdom. But whoever governs himself according to his own desires will speak heresies (bid'ah); because Allah said:

And if you obey him (the Messenger) you will be guided. [Sūrah Al-Nūr: 54]"

Source: Abū Nuʻaym in Al-Ḥilyah al Awliya

Ibn Taymiyyah said:

"It is as they said, for if a person does not follow what the Messenger came with he will act according to his own wishes. Thus he will be one who follows his desires without guidance from Allah."

Source: Minhāj Al-Sunnah Volume 5 page 117

Imam Barbaharee said:

"When you hear a man defaming the narrations without accepting them or rejecting anything from the sayings of the Messenger of Allah, consider him out of Islam; for he is a man of evil way and speech. This is because the Messenger of Allah and his companions are not to be defamed. We only know Allah, the Messenger of Allah, the Quran, good and evil, the world and the Hereafter through the narrations. And the Quran is more in need of the Sunnah than the Sunnah being in need of the Quran."

Source: Sharus Sunnah point 66

Abdullah bin 'Umar said:

"Every bid'ah (religious innovation) is misguidance, even if people think it is good."

Source: Al-Lālakā'ī in Sharh Usūl I'tiqād Ahl Al-Sunnah wa Al-Jamā'ah Volume 1 Page 134, number 111; and Ibn Battah in Al-Ibānah Al-Kubraa

Abu Muhammad asked Ali ibn Madani:

"A people say: such and such. Do you consider these to be Muslims?

So Ali ibn Madani said, *"If a man had mentioned that in front of Hammad and others than him among the mashayikh then they would have expelled him and not narrated anything to him. It is hated to narrate their words with the severest hatred."*

So Abu Muhammad asked Ali ibn Madani: *And is it hated that a man mentions the words of the people of innovation?*

Ibn Madani said: *"Yes. Because I fear that he will mention it in front of a man who is weak-hearted, and so it (the innovation) will befall in his heart."*

Source: Kitab As Sunnah by Harb ibn Ismail al Karmani

Fudayl Ibn Iyaad said:

"I eat the food of a Christian and a Jew, but I do not eat the food of an innovator."

Source: Dhamm Al Kalam 1048

Imam Ahmad said:

"The companions of the Messenger of Allah-after the four caliphs-are the best of the people, and it is not permissible for anyone to speak ill of any of them, blaming them for deficiencies and shortcomings It is indeed obligatory upon the ruler to reprimand and punish whoever does that, and he should not be pardoned."

Source: Kitaab As-Sunnah and Manaaqibul Imam Ahmad, of Ibnul Jawzee 170

Muaadh ibn Jabal said:

"O people, you must seek knowledge before it is taken away, for indeed when its people (the scholars) die, it will be taken away. And beware of bidah, innovation and sophistication and adhere to the ancient way (the way of the Prophet)."

Source: Al-Bidaayah Wannahy'anha by Ibn Waddaah

Huhayfah bin Al-Yamaan said:

"Do not perform any act of worship that was not practiced by the Companions of the Messenger of Allah, for the earlier generation did not leave any room for the latter to add anything(to the religion). Fear Allah, O readers, seekers of knowledge, and follow the path of those who came before you."

Source: Al Ibanah by Ibn Battah

Abdullah ibn Masood said:

"Whoever wants to follow an example, let him follow the example of those who have passed away, the Companions of Muhammad. They were the best of this ummah, the purest in heart, the deepest in knowledge, the least in sophistication. They were people whom Allah chose to be the Companions of his Prophet and to convey His religion, so imitate their ways and behavior, for they were following the Straight Path."

Source: Al Baghawi in Sharh as Sunnah

Haytham ibn Jameel was asked:

"A man is well learned with regards to the affairs of the Sunnah, should he debate and argue about them?"

He replied:

"No, however he should inform the people about the Sunnah, so if it is accepted from him then good and if not then he should keep silent."

Source: Jaami'u Bayaan Al-Ilmi Wa Fadhlihi

Abdullah ibn Masood said:

"Follow and do not innovate, for everything has been taken care of and you must follow the ancient way (of the salaf)."

Source: Ad-Daarimi in his Sunan

Abdullah ibn Masood said:

"The Jamaah is whatever agrees with the truth-even if you are alone."

Source: Reported in Taarekh Dimashq with an authentic chain of narration

Ishaaq ibn Raahawaih, (the teacher of Imam Bukhari) said:

"If you were to ask the ignorant people about the "Main Body" they would say, "The majority of people" they do not know that the jamaa'ah is the scholar who clings to the narrations from the Prophet

and his way. So whoever is with him(the scholar) and follows him, then he is the Jamaah."

Source: Abu Nuaym in Hilyatul Awliyaah

Fudayl Ibn Iyyad said:

"The Hand of Allah is upon the Jama'ah, and Allah does not look at the innovator."

Source: Ibanah As Sughra by Ibn Battah

Yahya ibn Maeen said:

"Defending the Sunnah is more excellent than Jihad in Allah's cause." So it was said to Yahya ibn Maeen," A man spends his wealth, tires himself out and fights in Jihad, and this one(who defends the sunnah) is more excellent than him?" He said: "Yes, by a great deal"

Source: Siyaar Alaamin Nubulaa of Adh Dhahabee

Fudayl Ibn Iyaad said:

"If Allah knows about a man that he hates an innovator, then I am hoping that Allah will forgive him. Even if his (good) deed is little. A follower of Sunnah will not support a follower of innovation *except out of hypocrisy and whoever turns his face against a follower of innovation Allah will fill his heart with Faith. And whoever rebukes a follower of innovation, Allah will make him safe on the Day of Greatest Terror. And whoever humiliates a follower of innovation Allah will raise him hundred ranks in Paradise. So never be a follower of innovation for the sake of Allah forever."*

Source: Sharus Sunnah by Imam Barbaharee

Abdullah ibn Amr ibn al-Aas said:

"No bidah is introduced but it will spread further and no Sunnah is neglected but it will diminish further."

Source: Ibn Battah in Al Ibaanah

Imam Al Awzaai said:

"You must follow the footsteps of those who came before, even if the people reject you. Beware of personal opinions even if people make them attractive. The clear way is that of the Straight Path."

Source: Al Khateeb in Sharaf Ashaab al-Hadeeth

Ayub as-Sakhtiyaani said:

"The more the innovator increases his efforts in innovation, the further away he becomes from Allah."

Source: Al Bidah Wan-Nahy'anha by Ibn Waddaah

Hassan ibn Atiyah said:

"No people introduce innovation into their religion but an equivalent amount of Sunnah will be taken away."

Source: Al-Laalkaa'i in Sharh Usool I'tiqaad Ahl as-sunnah wal-Jamaah

Ibn Abbaas said:

"Indeed the most detestable of things to Allah are the innovations."

Source: As-Sunan al Kubraa

Al Hasan al Basri said:

"Do not sit with the people of innovation and desires, nor argue with them, nor listen to them."

Source: Sunan Ad-Daarimee

Al-Fudayl ibn Iyaad said:

"I met the best of people, all of them people of the Sunnah and they used to forbid from accompanying people of innovation."

Source: Sharh Usool I'tiqaad Ahlis Sunnah wal Jamaah, number 267

Ibrahim ibn Maysarah said:

"Whoever honours an innovator has aided in the destruction of Islam."

Source: Sharh Usool I'tiqaad Ahlis-Sunnah wal Jamaah

Sufyaan Ath-Thawri said:

"Whoever listens to an innovator has left the protection of Allah and is entrusted with the innovation."

Source: Al-Hilyah by Abu Naeem

Imam al Barbahaaree said:

"the innovators are like scorpions. They bury their heads and bodies in the sand and leave their tails out. When they get the chance they sting, the same with the innovators who conceal themselves amongst the people, when they are able, they do what they desire."

Source: Tabaqaatul-Hanaabilah

Abu Haatim said:

"A sign of the people of innovation is their battling against the people of Narrations."

As-Saffaareenee said

"And we are not focusing on mentioning the virtues of the people of Hadith, for indeed their virtues are well known and their merits are many. So whoever belittles them, then he is despicable and lowly. And whoever hates them, then he is from the backward party of the Devil."

Source: Lawaa'ihul Anwaar

Abu Uthman As-Saaboonee said:

"The signs of the people of innovation are clear and obvious. The most apparent of their signs is their severe enmity for those who carry the reports of the Prophet."

Source: The Aqeedah of the (Pious) Predecessors page 101

Muhammad ibn An-Nadr Al-Haarithee said:

"Whoever listens to a person of innovation-and knows that he is a person of innovation-then protection is taken away from him, and he is left to himself."

Source: Sharh Usool I'tiqaad

Imam ash-Shaatibee mentioned:

"Linguistically bidah means "a newly invented matter". The Shariah definition of bidah as: "A newly invented way [beliefs or action] in the religion, in imitation of the Shariah, by which nearness to allah is sought, [but] not being supported by any authentic proof-neither in its foundations, nor in the manner in which it is performed."

Source: Al-I'tisaam of ash-Shaatibee

Imam Barbaharee said:

"Know that heresy never emerged except from the riffraff, the barbarous followers of every useless caller who incline towards every wind. And whoever is like this has no religion."

Source: Sharus Sunnah point 102

Ar-Rabee ibn Sulaymaan said:

"One day Ash-Shaafi narrated a hadith, and a man said to him "Do you accept that O Abu Abdullah?" He said, "If I narrate a saheeh hadeeth from the Messenger of Allah and I do not accept it, then bear witness that I have lost my mind.""

Source: Ibn Battah in Al Ibaanah

Imam Ahmad said:

"If you see anyone speaking ill of the Companions of the Messenger of Allah, doubt his Islam."

Source: Al-Laalikaa'ee in As-Sunnah, 2359

Imam Malik said:

"The Sunnah is like the ship of Noah. Whoever rides in it will be saved and whoever hangs back and does not get on board will be drowned."

Source: Miftaah al-Jannah fil-I'tisaam bis-Sunnah by As-Suyooti

Imam Ahmad ibn Hanbal said:

"The basic principles of Sunnah in our view are: adherence to the way of the Companions of the Messenger of Allah, following their example and forsaking bidah, for every bidah is a going astray."

Source: Al-Laalkaa'I in Sharh Usool Ahl as-Sunnah

Imam Malik said:

"Truly I am only a mortal: I make mistakes (sometimes) and I am correct (sometimes). Therefore, look into my opinions: all that agrees with the Book and the Sunnah, accept it, and all that does not agree with the Book and the Sunnah, ignore it."

Source: Ibn Abdul Barr in Jaami Bayaan al Ilm

Imam Abu Hanifah said:

"When I say something contradicting the Book of Allah the Exalted or what is narrated from the Messenger, then ignore my saying."

Source: Al-Fulaani in Eeqaaz Al Himam 50

Imam Ash-Shaafi said:

"The Muslims are unanimously agreed that if a sunnah of the Messenger of Allah is made clear to someone, it is not permitted for him to leave it for the saying of anyone else."

Source: I'laam by Ibn Qayyim

Imam Ahmad said:

"Do not follow my opinion; neither follow the opinion of Malik, nor Shafi, nor Awzaai, nor Thawri, but take from where they took."

Source: Ibn al Qayyim in I'laam

Muhammad Sultan al Masoomi Khajnadee said:

"None of the Imams urged to anyone to follow their Madhahib, on the other hand all of the Imams advised, "Take from where we have taken."

In other words follow the Quran and Sunnah. Many of the sayings of later religious leaders, which were inaccurate, were attributed towards Imams and their sects. If they had happened to see or hear those statements which had been referred and attached to their names, they would have not only disowned the statements but also disapproved of them strongly.

All the religious scholars of olden times who were considered to be the luminaries of Islamic knowledge, always brought evidence from the Quran and Sunnah, and to take counsel from these two sources. It is a proved fact that Imam Abu Hanifa, Imam Malik, Imam Shafii, Imam Ahmad, Sufyan Thawri, Sufyan bin Uainah, Hasan Basri, Qadi Abu Yusuf, Muhammad bin Hasan Shaibani, Imam Awzaai,

Abdullah bin Mubarak, Imam Bukhari, Imam Muslim, and other venerable religious scholars always warned the people against making innovations in religious matters. They always advised people to be careful and cautioned them against following anyone except the sinless Prophet, no one is sinless except him, however pious and God-fearing he may be. So anything which is in accordance with the Quran and Sunnah is acceptable and anything which is contrary to or inconsistent with the Quran and Sunnah will be rejected altogether. Imam Malik said: "The views and opinions of everybody may be accepted or rejected except he who is resting in this grave." While saying this, Imam Malik pointed towards the grave of the Prophet. All the religious scholars and Imams warned and prevented the people from mindless and blind imitation. Allah at many places in the Quran has rebuked such blind followers. History is witness that mindless and blind following of religious leaders and ancestors leads the people to infidelity."

Source: Hadiyyatus-Sultan ila Muslimi Biladil-Yaban

Imam Barbaharee said:

"You should know – may Allah have mercy upon you – that knowledge is not by lots of narrations and books. But the Scholar is one who acts upon knowledge and the Sunan even if he has little knowledge and few books. And whoever opposes the Quran and Sunnah is a follower of innovation even if he has much knowledge and many books."

Source: Sharus Sunnah point 104

Al Fudayl ibn Iyaad said:

"Follow the path of guidance, and do not worry about how few are the people who follow it. Beware of the paths of misguidance and do not be deceived by the large numbers of those who are doomed."

Source: Al-I'tisaam by Imam Ash-Shaatibi

Abdul Qaadir Al-Jeelaanee said:

"As for the saved sect it is Ahlu Sunnah Wal Jamaah and there is no name for Ahlu Sunnah except one, and that is the people of hadith."

Source: Al Ghunyatut Taalibeen

Ibn Abbas said:

"You will always see a man of Ahl as-Sunnah calling people to the Sunnah and forbidding bidah."

Source: Al-Laalkaa'I in Sharh Usool I'tiqaad Ahl as-Sunnah

Imam Ahmad bin Hanbal said:

"whosoever reviles the Companions of the Prophet, then we do not believe he is safe from having rejected the Religion."

Imam Ahmad was asked concerning a Rafidi neighbor who greets him, should he answer his Salaam? He replied: *"No"*

Source: Sunnah lil-Khilaal

Imam Malik said:

"The last generations of this ummah can only be reformed by that which reformed its first generations. What was not part of the religion then cannot become part of the religion now."

Source: Ash Shifa by Al Qaadi Ayaad

Ahmad ibn Harb said:

"There is nothing more beneficial to a Muslim's heart than to mix with the righteous and to watch their actions, while nothing is more harmful to the heart

than mixing with the sinners and watching their actions."

Source: Al Bayhaqi, Al Zuhd Al Kabeer

Abdul Kareem Al Jazari said:

"A pious man never debates."

Source: Ash-Shuab, 8129

Imam Barbaharee said:

"Whoever abandons the Friday and the congregational prayers in the masjid without any excuse is an innovator. Excuse such as illness which makes him unable to go to the mosque or being afraid of an oppressive leader otherwise; there is no excuse for you."

Source: Sharus Sunnah point 128

Abu Anas Hamad Al Uthman said:

"The evil of the Jews and Christians is open and clear to the common Muslims; as for the people of innovation, then their harm is not clear to every person…This is why the Scholars see that to refute the people of innovation takes precedence over refuting the Jews and Christians."

Source: Zajarul Mutahawwin

Imam Ahmad said:

"Verily a person of theological rhetoric will never succeed, ever. You will never see anyone studying theological rhetoric, except that there is a corruption in his heart."

Source: As-Sunnah page 235

Imam Ahmad also said:

"Do not sit with the people of theological rhetoric, even if they defend the sunnah."

Source: Manaaqibul Imaam Ahmad page 205

Imam Al Awzaaee said:

"Adhere to the narrations from those who have preceded, even if the people reject you, and beware of the opinions of men, even if they beautify it with speech. So indeed the affair will become clear, while you are upon a straight path regarding it."

Source: Bayhaqee in Al-Madkhal number 233

Abu Haatim Ar Raazee said:

"A sign of the people of innovation is their hatred of the people of narrations."

Source: Ibnut Tabaree in As-Sunnah

Imam Ash Shaafie said:

"Stick to the people of hadith, since they are the most correct from amongst the people."

Source: Siyar A'laamin Nubulaa

Al Hasan Al Basri said:

"Do not sit with a person of innovation, for indeed he will put a disease in your heart."

Source: Al-Itisaam of Ash Shaatibee

Imam Ahmad ibn Hanbal said:

"The prayer is not performed behind the Qadariyyah, the Muatizilah and the Jahmiyyah."

Source: Kitab As Sunnah by Ibn Ahmad bin Hanbal

Imam Zuhree said:

"The people of knowledge who came before us used to say 'Salvation lies in clinging to the sunnah'."

Source: Ad-Daarimee, number 96

Umar ibn Abdul Azeez said:

"There is no excuse for anyone, after the Sunnah, to be misguided upon error which he thought was guidance."

Source: As-Sunnah number 95 of Al-Marwazee

Awzaa'ee said, in the explanation of the hadith of the strangers:

"Islam will not disappear, it is Ahlus Sunnah that will disappear to the point that there will only remain one of them in any one country."

Source: Laalikaa'ee number 19

Yunus ibn Ubayd said:

"It has come to the point that one who knows the Sunnah will think it something strange, and stranger than this person is who finds the Sunnah something familiar."

Source: Laalikaa'ee and Ibn Battah

Bishr ibn al Harith said:

"Look at the person who has the most piety, chastity and purest earning from the people and then accompany him and do not sit with the one who will not help you upon your life in the hereafter."

Source: Ash-Shuab

Umar ibn al Khattab said:

"We used to say that this Ummah will be doomed by knowledgeable hypocrites."

Source: Al Wilaayah Alaa Al Buldan

Hubayrah said:

"Consider the people based upon their friends."

Source: Raudatul Uqalaa

Umar ibn al Khattab said:

"Whoever acts on whims and desires and sin loses out and harms no one but himself. Whoever follows the sunnah and adheres to laws and follows the right path, seeking that which is with Allah for those who obey Him, is doing the right thing and is a winner."

Source: Taareekh At Tabaree

Al Humaydee said:

"By Allah, that I should fight against those who reject the ahadeeth of Allah's Messenger is more beloved to me than that I should fight against a like number of Turks."

Source: Siyar volume 10

Imam Malik was asked about the Raafidah and said:

"Do not speak to them (the Shia), nor relate from them, for indeed they lie."

Source: Minhaaj As-Sunnah

Imam Ash Shafi'i said:

"Among the people who follow their own desires, I have not seen a group bear witness to more lies than the Rafidah."

Source: Ikhtisaar Uloom al Hadith by Ibn Katheer

Abu Ubayd al-Qaasim ibn Salaam said:

"The follower of the Sunnah is like the one who holds onto hot coals. And today in my opinion, this is better than fighting with swords in the Cause of Allah."

Source: Taareekh Baghdaad

Al Fudayl ibn Iyyad said:

"The souls are arrayed armies. So those that know one another will unite with one another, and those that don't know one another will be divided. And it is not possible for a person of the Sunnah to support a person of innovation except due to hypocrisy."

Source: Sharrh Usool Itiqaad Ahlis Sunnah wal Jamaah

Yahya ibn Yahya an Naisaboori said:

"Defending the Sunnah is more virtuous than Jihad."

Source: Naqd al Mantiq

Al Hasan al Basri said:

"A person may struggle in the way of God, without ever striking a sword even once."

Source: Tafsīr Ibn Kathīr, commentary on al-Ankabut

Umar bin Khattab said:

"Do not speak about that which does not concern you. Know your enemy and be wary of your friend, except for the trustworthy one. And no one is trustworthy, except for the person who fears Allah. Do not walk with the evildoer, lest he teaches you some of his wickedness; and do not reveal your secrets to him. And when you consult others in your affairs, consult only those who fear Allah."

Source: Sifatus-Safwah

Hudhayfah ibn al Yamaan said:

"Every act of worship that the Companions of the Messenger did not do, do not do them."

Source: Abu Dawood Grade: Sahih

Ibn Qudaamah said:

"The salaf used to forbid others from sitting with the innovators, looking into their books, and listening to their speech."

Source: Al Adaab Ash Shariah

Ibn al Jawzee said:

"A person who truly fears his Lord does not care about others and does not put himself in a position where his religion is at risk."

Source: "Sincere counsel to students of Sacred Knowledge" by Ibn al Jawzee page 72

Imam Malik said:

"It is not allowed to take as a witness the innovators and people of desires."

Source: Jaami Bayaan Al'Ilm wa Fadhlihi

Muadh ibn Muadh said:

"I prayed behind a man from Banu Sad. Then it reached me that he was a qadari, so I repeated the prayer after forty years or thirty years."

Source: Kitab As Sunnah by Ibn Ahmad bin Hanbal

Abu Shamah said:

"The order to stick to the Jamaah means sticking to the truth and its followers; even if those who stick to the truth are few and those who oppose it are many, since the truth is that which the first Jamaah from the time of the Prophet and his Companions were upon. No attention is given to the great number of the people of futility coming after them."

Source: Al Baa'ith Alal-Bidah Wal Hawaadith

Muhammad Sultan al Masoomi Khajnadee said:

"Later religious leaders and intellectuals wrote volumes over volumes and thousands of pages and *the masses took those writers as Jurists, whereas their knowledge about Islam was shallow. These so-called scholars made it incumbent on people to follow one of the four Imams and prohibited them from following another at the same time. In other words they raised up the Imams to the level of the Prophets – to whom Scriptures are revealed – and made it obligatory to obey every word of the Imam. Would that these so-called scholars had understood the preaching of the Imams. Most of them only know the name of their Imam and nothing more than that. Even more strange is that a few of the later scholars contrived some issues and attributed these issues to one of the imams, and succeeding generations too took the concocted issues as Imams' verdicts and started following them without any verification, whereas there is no relevancy between Imams' viewpoints and these innovated issues. So, Imams are free from such precepts."*

Source: Hadiyyatus-Sultan ila Muslimi Biladil-Yaban

Regarding the people of innovation, Imam Ahmad said:

"They differ concerning the Book, they are in opposition to the Book, and they all agree with each other in contradicting the Book. They use the unclear and ambiguous texts as proof for their views and they misguide the people because of what they have difficulty understanding."

Source: Majmoo ar-Rasaail Al Kubra

Ibn al Qayyim said:

"Whoever obtains an authentic hadith from Allah's Messenger if he wants to turn away from it let him know that the Prophet is the one who is addressing you."

Source: Madaarij Us-Salikeen

Umar ibn abdul Aziz said:

"Whoever acts without knowledge harms more than benefits."

Source: Musannaf of Ibn Abi Shaybah

Ali ibn Abi Talib said:

"Serious matters are the best, and newly invented matters are the worst. Every newly invented matter is an innovation, and everyone who introduces something new is an innovator. The one who innovates is misled, and no innovator introduces an innovation but he has forsaken a Sunnah."

Source: Al Bidaayah Wan-Nihaayah,

Ibn Hibban said:

"The best brothers are those who wish the most well for one. It is better to be hit by a person who wishes well for you than to be greeted by a bad one."

Source: Ar-Rawdhah

Ibn Hibban also said:

"The noble does not hurt the wise, he does not joke with the stupid and he does not mingle with the sinner."

Source: Ar-Rawdah page 173

Umar ibn khattab said to Ziyad:

"Do you know what (things) destroy Islam? They are the death of a scholar, the Munafiq(hypocrite) who argues using the Quran, and the Imams who lead the people astray."

Source: Ad-Daarimee

Hasan al Basri said:

"The Sunnah is - by Him besides whom none has the right to be worshipped – between those who exceed the limits and those who fall short. So be patient upon it, may Allah have mercy upon you. For indeed the Ahlus-Sunnah were a minority from those who preceded and shall be a minority from those to come. They did not accompany the people who are excessive when they exceeded the limits, nor the people of innovation when they innovated. Rather, they persevered upon the Sunnah, until they met their Lord."

Source: Sunan ad-Darimi

Ibn al Qayyim said:

"The one who remains silent in the face of falsehood is a tongueless devil."

Source: Ad Da'u wad-Dawaa

Sa'eed ibn Jubayr said:

"For my son to accompany a wicked sinner is more beloved to me than for him to accompany an innovator who performs great worship."

Source: Ash-Sharh Wal-Ibaanah

Matr Al-Warraq said:

"A few deeds from the sunnah is better than many deeds of bidah. Whoever performs a deed from the sunnah, Allah will aaccept it from him. And whoever performs an act of bidah, Allah will reject his bidah."

Source: Hilyah al Awliya

Hishaam bin Urwa used to say:

"Do not question the people about what they have innovated today because they have prepared answers for it, rather ask them about the sunnah because they do not know it."

Source: Imam Aloosi in Ghayatul Amaanee Fi Radd Alan-Nabahaanee

Ali ibn abi Talib also said:

"I would not forsake the Sunnah of the Prophet for the opinion of anyone."

Source: Fath Al Baari

Al Bayhaqi said:

"As for wiping the face with the hands after concluding the supplication, I do not know that any of the Salaf did it."

Source: As-Sunan

Imam Ash Shafie said:

"Muslims have a consensus that when a sunnah from Allah's Messenger becomes clear to a person, it is not permissible for him to leave it for anybody's opinion."

Source: Ar-Risaalah

Salih Fawzan said:

"As for the difference of opinion in juristic issues that are based on legal deductions to which the evidences may point, such will have no (negative) effect on the Muslim Ummah; it will not bring about division and enmity because such deductions are within latitude. However, the differences concerning the Aqidah (Creed) is unacceptable; the differing parties will never be united upon it. People who differ in Aqidah will never be united, no matter the attempt of whoever attempts (to unite them), because he want to bring opposing things together; and it is impossible to bring opposing or contradicting things together.

If they want the unity of the Muslims, then they must first correct their Aqidah, the creed which the messengers of Allah from the first to the last of them paid attention to and started calling unto; they must first profess it. So if they profess one sound Creed, the Ummah will be united. That is if they are serious and truthful in their call.

However they mock those who talk and invite (others) to the sound Aqidah saying, 'This person declares people as disbelievers and desires to cause division among Muslims; he desires such and such' etc.

We say to them, 'you can never bring the Muslims together upon other than the Sound Creed'. Therefore if the Aqidah is professed as one (by all Muslims) then they will be easily united."

Source: Explanation of Sharus Sunnah by Imam Barbaharee

Muhammad Sultan Masoomi Khajnadee said:

"Many changes and alterations were brought against the religion of Islam, among these innovations was a requirement to follow a particular Madhhab and to support it fanatically. These Madhahib developed in Islam after a lapse of three generations. Every new thing introduced in the religion was considered as a good thing and deserving reward on the Day of Resurrection. In reality, this is nothing but deviation and heresy. Righteous and pious Muslims of the early

period always depended upon the Noble Quran, Sunnah and the Ijma (consensus). They were devoted faithful and steadfast in the practice of pure Islam.

When heresy was born in religion many evils and wrong-doings started. An atmosphere of disunity, accusing and blaming each other prevailed all over the Ummah. Every sect accused the other of straying from the right path of Islam. Even it was announced, and such a base verdict was issued, that no Hanafi could offer his obligatory prayer under the leadership of Imam Shafi'i or his followers. Some claimed that only four Madhahib are Ahlus Sunnah or Sunni. As a consequence of this heresy, four different places were fixed for the Salat of four Madahib at the sacred Kabah; and instead of one congregational prayer four congregational prayers were offered at the Kabah itself. Followers of every Madhhab would wait for their Imam to come and lead the prayer. By giving rise to heresy, apostasy and innovations in religion, Satan achieved his main purpose of creating disunity in the ranks of the faithful and dividing the Muslim Ummah into different sects."

Source: Hadiyyatus-Sultan ila Muslimi Biladil-Yaban

Dirar bin Murrah said:

"Iblis (satan) said, "If I win three things from the son of Adam, I will have earned what I wanted from him: if he forgets his sins, thinks high of his actions, and becomes fond of his opinion.""

Source: Sifatus-Safwah

Ibn Taymiyyah said:

"The sign of the people of bid'ah is that they do not follow the salaf."

Source: Majmoo' al-Fatawa

Ibn Qayyim said:

"If bid'ah only consisted of Lies, then it would not have been accepted and everybody would even hurry to condemn it and refute it. And if it only consisted of Haqq (truth), then it would not have been a Bid'ah, rather, in agreement with the Sunnah, but it (Bid'ah) consist of both truth and lies in which the truth is clothed with lies."

Source: as-Sawaa'iq al-Mursalah

Imam al-Barbahaaree said:

"Beware of small innovations, because they grow and become large. This was the case with every innovation introduced into this Ummah. It started as something small, bearing a resemblance to the truth, which is why those who entered into it were misled, and then were unable to leave it. So it grew and it became the religion which they followed, so they deviated from the Straight Path and thus left Islaam. May Allaah have mercy upon you! Examine carefully the speech of everyone you hear from, in your time particularly. So do not act in haste, nor enter into anything from it, until you ask and see: Did any of the Companions of the Prophet sallallaahu 'alayhi wa sallam speak about it, or any of the (early) Scholars? So if you find a narration from them about it, cling to it and do not go beyond it for anything, nor give precedence to anything over it and thus fall into the Fire."

Source: Sharh us-Sunnah (number 8) of Imam al-Barbahaaree

Ali bin Abi Talib said:

"No one prefers me over Abu Bakr and Umar except that I whip him with the punishment of the inventor of lies."

Source: Kitab As Sunnah by Ibn Ahmad bin Hanbal

Ali also said:

"My example in this Ummah is like the example of Jesus son of Maryam. A group of people loved him and were excessive in the love for him, so they were destroyed. And a group hated him and were excessive in the hate for him, so they were destroyed. And a group loved him and were moderate in their love for him, so they were saved."

Source: Kitab As Sunnah by Ibn Ahmad bin Hanbal

Ibn Taymiyyah said:

"The Imaams of the Sunnah and the Jamaa'ah, and the people of knowledge and eemaan (faith) have in them 'adl (justice), 'ilm (knowledge) and rahmah (mercy), and they know the truth which conforms to the Sunnah and which is free from innovations. They do justice to those who depart from the Sunnah and the Jamaa'ah, even if they have been wronged, just as Allaah – the Most High – said: "O you who believe!! Stand out firmly for Allaah and be witnesses, and do not let the hatred of others swerve you away from *doing justice. But be just! That is closer to taqwaa (piety)."* [Soorah al-Maa'idah 5:8]. *Likewise, they are merciful to the creation; desiring for them goodness guidance and knowledge. They never intend for them any harm or evil. Rather, when they criticize them and explain to them their error, ignorance or wrongdoing, then their purpose in doing so is only to clarify the truth, and to be merciful to the creation, to enjoin the good and forbid the evil, and to make the word of Allaah uppermost so that the way of life becomes purely for Allaah."*

Source: Radd 'alal-Bakree

Abu Amr al-Awzaa'i said:

"If innovations appear, and the People of Knowledge do not denounce [and reject] it, it will soon become a Sunnah!"

Source: Sharaf Ashaab Al-Hadeeth by al-Khateeb al-Baghdadi

Hasan al Basri said:

"When a fitnah first approaches, every scholar recognizes it, and only when it dies away does every ignorant come to know of it."

Source: "The way out of Tribulations" by Muhammad Ismail al Muqaddam page 11

Abdullaah ibn Masud said:

"Beware of the innovations which the people invent, since the Deen does not pass out of the hearts all at once – rather Shaitaan introduces innovations for him until he expels Faith from the heart; and it will soon happen that the people will abandon the obligatory duties which Allaah has made binding upon them - the Prayer, the Fast, the lawful and the prohibited, and speak about their Lord - the Mighty and Majestic. So who ever reaches that time then let him flee." It was said: O Abu Abdur-Rahman, to where? He said: "Not to anywhere, he should flee with his heart and his Deen and not sit with anyone of the people of innovation."

Source: Sharh Usool ul-I'tiqaad

Mu'aadh bin Jabal used to say, whenever he sat in a circle of knowledge:

"and I warn you of what is innovated, for all that is innovated is misguidance"

Source: ash-Sharee'ah, from also Abu Dawood with similar wording

Abdullaah ibn Mas'ud said:

"follow the sunnah of Muhammad and do not innovate, for what you have been commanded is enough for you."

Source: ad-Daarimee

Abdullaah ibn Abbaas said:

"do not sit with the people of innovation, for verily their sittings are a sickness for the hearts"

Source: ash-Sharee'ah of al-Aajurree

Ibn Abbaas said:

"Indeed the most detestable of things to Allaah are the innovations."

Source: al-Bayhaqee in as-Sunan al-Kubraa

Abdullaah ibn as-Sariyy said:

"It is not the Sunnah with us, that the People of Desires should be argued with but the Sunnah with us, is that we do not talk to a single one of them."

Source: Al-Ibanah

Al-Hasan al-Basri said:

"Do not sit with the people of innovation and desires, nor argue with them, nor listen to them."

Source: ad-Daarimee in his Sunan

Imaam Maalik said:

"How evil are the people of innovation, we do not give them salaam."

Source: al-Baghawee in Sharh us-Sunnah

Imam ash-Shaafi'i said:

"That a person meets Allaah with every sin except Shirk is better than meeting Him upon any one of the innovated beliefs."

Source: al-Bayhaqee in al-I'tiqaad

Al-Fudayl bin 'Iyaad said:

"Whoever sits with a person of innovation, then beware of him and whoever sits with a person of innovation has not been given wisdom. I love that there was fort of iron between me and a person of innovation. That I eat with a Jew and a Christian is more beloved to me than that I eat with a person of innovation."

Source: al-Laalikaa'ee 1149

Al-Fudayl bin 'Iyaad said:

"If a man comes to a person to consult him and he directs him to an innovator, then he has made a deception of Islaam. Beware of going to a person of innovation for they divert [people] from the truth."

Source: Sharh Usool ul-I'tiqaad of al-Laalikaa'ee 261

Sallam ibn Abi Muti said:

"The Jahmiyyah are kuffar. One does not pray behind them."

Source: Kitab As Sunnah by Ibn Ahmad bin Hanbal

Al-Fudayl ibn 'Iyaad said:

"Do not sit with a person of innovation. Allaah has rendered his actions futile and has taken the light of Islaam from his heart."

Source: Sharh Usool ul-I'tiqaad of al-Laalikaa'ee

Ubayd Al Jabiree said:

"If you are able to stay away from the innovators so that you do not share with them in any activity, religious or worldly then do so.

As for religious activities, they are referred to as Dawah based activities; then do not accommodate them and do not help them in building Masaajid by which innovation is spread, nor schools by which innovation is spread, nor in printing books in which innovation is spread; never. Because he who helps them while he knows their condition, then he is like them, whether intentionally or unintentionally."

Source: Collection of Books of how to Deal with the People of Bida by Ubayd al Jabiree

Aboo 'Uthmaan as-Saaboonee said describing Ahlus Sunnah:

"And they avoid the People of Innovation and Misguidance, having enmity for the People of Desires and Ignorance. They hate the People of Innovation who introduce into the Deen that which is not from it. They do not love them, they do not accompany them, they do not listen to their words, nor sit with them or argue or dispute with them regarding the Deen. And they protect their ears from listening to their falsehoods, which if they pass by the ears and settle in the hearts, harm the hearts and bring corrupt ideas and whisperings upon them."

Source: Aqeedatus-Salaf wa Ashaabil-Hadeeth

Abu Moosaa said:

"That I live next to a Jew and a Christian, and monkeys and pigs, is more beloved to me than that if I were to live next to a follower of desires (i.e. deviant), who will spread disease to my heart."

Source: Lamm Ad-Darr-ul-Manthoor

Yoonus bin 'Ubaid said to his son:

"I forbid you from fornicating, stealing and drinking alcohol. But if you were to meet Allaah having committed these (sins), that would be more beloved (to me) than if you were to meet Him with the views of 'Amr bin 'Ubaid or the followers of 'Amr."

Source: Lamm Ad-Darr-ul-Manthoor

Abul-Jawzaa said:

"If the apes and the swine were to live with me in a house, that would be more beloved to me than if a person from Ahlul-Ahwaa (deviants) were to live with me. They have entered into the ayah: 'And when they meet you they say: We believe. But when they are alone, they bite the tips of their fingers at you in rage. Say: Perish in your rage. Allaah knows what is in the hearts.' [Surah Imraan: 119]

Source: Lamm Ad-Darr-ul-Manthoor

Al-'Awwaam bin Hawshab said about his son 'Eesaa:

"By Allaah, if I saw 'Eesaa gathering with the people of musical instruments, alcohol and falsehood, that would be more beloved to me than if I were to see him sitting with the people of argumentation – the innovators."

Source: Lamm Ad-Darr-ul-Manthoor

Ibn Qudamah said:

"And from the Sunnah is: Making Hijrah from the people of Innovations and separating oneself from them, abandoning argument and dispute in the religion and not looking into the books of the innovators and giving attention to their speech; and every newly invented matter in religion is an innovation."

Source: Lumatul Itiqaad by Ibn Qudamah

Ahmad ibn Sinan said:

"If a man lives in the neighborhood of an innovator, I believe that he should sell his house, if it is possible *for him, and move to another place, or else his child and neighbors will be destroyed."*

Source: Al Ibanah Al Kubra by Ibn Battah

Abu Bakr Muhammad ibn Husain Ajurri said:

"Everyone who adheres to what we have written in this book of ours should boycott all of the people of desires from the Khawarij, Qadariyyah, Murjiah and the Jahmiyyah. And everyone who ascribes to the Mutazilah. And all of the Rawafid, all of the Nawasib and everyone whom the leaders of the Muslims have referred to as an innovator of an innovation of misguidance, while this is correctly narrated from him. This person should not be spoken to, not greeted, he should not be sat with or prayed behind, he should not be married nor given to in marriage by those who know him, he should not be taken as a partner, worked with, debated with, or disputed with. Rather he (the Sunni) should humiliate him by degrading him. And if you meet him on the street on one path, then if you are capable you take another (path).

Source: Ash Shariah by Ajurri

Yahyaa bin 'Ubaid said:

"A man from the Mu'atazilah encountered me (one day), so I got up and said: "Either you pass on or I will pass on, for indeed if I were to walk with a Christian, that would be more loved to me than if I were to walk with you."

Source: Lamm Ad-Darr-ul-Manthoor

Arta' Ibn al-Mundir said:

"If my son were one of the sinful wicked people, that would be more beloved to me than if he were a Follower of Desires (i.e. a deviant)."

Source: Lamm Ad-Darr-ul-Manthoor

Sa'eed bin Jubair said:

"If my son were to keep the company of a sinning scoundrel upon the Sunnah that would be more beloved to me than if he were to accompany a worshipping innovator."

Source: Lamm Ad-Darr-ul-Manthoor

It was once said to Maalik bin Mughawal:

"We saw your son playing with the birds." So he responded: "How wonderful that it preoccupies him from accompanying an innovator."

Source: Lamm Ad-Darr-ul-Manthoor

Al-Barbahaaree said:

"If you see a person whose manner and opinion is despicable, he is wicked, sinful, and oppressive, yet he is a person of the Sunnah, accompany him and sit with him, since his sin will not harm you. And if you see a man who strives hard and long in worship, is abstemious, being continual in worship, except that he is a person of innovation, do not sit with him, do not listen to his words, and do not walk along with him, since I do not feel safe that you will not eventually come to be pleased with his way and go to destruction along with him."

Source: Sharh Us-Sunnah

Abu Haatim said:

"I heard Ahmad bin Sinaan say: "That a Tanboor player were to live next to me is more beloved to me than if an innovator were to live next to me. This is since I can forbid the Tanboor player and I can break the tanboor (a mandolin-like instrument). But as for the innovator, he corrupts the people, the neighbors and the youth."

Source: Lamm Ad-Darr-ul-Manthoor

Abul-Fadl al-Hamdaanee said:

"The fabricator of ahaadeeth, and the innovator in Islaam are worse than the atheists from outside."

Source: quoted by Shaikh Ubaid al-Jabiree

Muhammad ibn an-Nadr al-Haarithee said:

"Whoever listens to a person of innovation- and knows that he is a person of innovation - then protection is taken away from him, and he is left to himself."

Source: Sharh Usool ul-I'tiqaad]

Al-Hasan Al-Basri used to say:

"Do not sit with the people of innovated beliefs, do not debate with them and do not listen to them."

Source: Sharh Usool ul-I'tiqaad

Sa'eed ibn 'Aamir said: I heard Ismaa'eel [Ibn Khaarijah] narrate, saying:

Two men from the people of the innovated sects came to Muhammad Ibn Seereen and said:

"O Aboo Bakr we want to narrate something to you." He said: *"No."* They said: *"Then may we recite an Aayah from Allaah's book to you?"* He said:

"No." He said: *"Either you two get up and leave or I will get up."* So the two men stood up and left. So one of the people said: *"What harm would it do to you for him to recite an Aayah?"* He said: *"I hated that he should recite an Aayah and that they would distort it and then it would enter my heart."*

Source: Sharh Usool ul-I'tiqaad]

Abu Qulabah said:

"Do not sit with them and do not mix with them for I do not feel safe that they will not drown you in their misguidance and confuse you about much that you used to know."

Source: Sharh Usool ul-I'tiqaad

Ayyoob as-Sakhtiyaanee said: Abu Qulabah said to me:

"O Ayyoob, memorize four things from me: Do not speak about the Quraan from your opinion, and beware of Qadr, and if the companions of Muhammad are mentioned then withhold, and do not let the people of innovation gain access to your hearing."

Source: Sharh Usool ul-I'tiqaad

Harb ibn Surayj asked Abu Jafar:

"We verily have an imam (in prayer) who is qadari?

Abu Jafar replied, "Repeat every prayer which you have prayed behind him."

Source: Kitab As-Sunnah by Harb ibn Ismail al Karmani

Umar bin Abdul Aziz said about the Qadariyyah:

"If they take that as their religion, then they are deserving of their tongues being pulled from their mouths.

Those who reject Qadar should be asked to repent. Then they either repent or they are banished from the lands of the Muslims."

Source: Kitab As-Sunnah by Harb ibn Ismail Al Karmani

Sufyan Thawri was asked:

"A man rejects the Qadar, can I pray behind him?

Sufyan said: 'Do not put him forth as an imam.'

Source: Kitab As Sunnah by Harb ibn Ismail al Karmani

Marwan asked Imam Malik:

"Does one pray behind a qadari?

Imam Malik said: 'No.'"

Source: Kitab As Sunnah by Harb ibn Ismail al Karmani

Ma'mar said: Ibn - Taawoos was sitting when one of the Mu'tazilah came and began speaking, so ibn Taawoos entered his fingers into his ears and said to his son:

"O My son put your fingers into your ears and press tightly so you do not hear any of his speech."

Source: Sharh Usool ul-I'tiqaad

Yahyaa ibn Abee Katheer said:

"If you see a person of innovation upon a certain road then take a different one."

Source: Sharh Usool ul-I'tiqaad

Al-Fudayl said:

"Do not sit with an innovator for I fear that curses will descend upon you."

Source: Sharh Usool ul-I'tiqaad

Al-Fudayl said:

"Do not trust the innovator concerning your Deen, and do not seek his advice in your affairs, and do not sit with him since whoever sits with an innovator - Allah will cause him to become blind."

Source: Sharh Usool ul-I'tiqaad

'Abdullaah ibn 'Umar as-Sarkhusee - the scholar of al-Khazar said:

"I ate a single meal with an innovator and Ibn al-Mubaarak heard of it so he said : "I will not speak to him for thirty days."

Source: Sharh Usool ul-I'tiqaad]

Salaam said: A person of the innovated sects said to Ayyoob :

"I want ask you about a word." He turned away and said: *" No, nor even a half a word."*

Source: Sharh Usool ul-I'tiqaad

Yahyaa ibn Katheer said:

"If you meet a person of innovation along the path, then take a path other than it."

Source: Sharh Usoolil-I'tiqaad of al-Laalikaa'ee

Al-Baghawi said:

"And the Prophet has informed about the splitting of this Ummah and the appearance of desires and innovations within it. And he ruled that deliverance would be for the one who followed his Sunnah and the Sunnah of his Companions.

Therefore, it is necessary for the Muslim when he sees a man engaging himself with anything from the desires and innovations, believing in them, or belittling anything from the Sunnah, that he flees from him, disowns him and leaves him — dead or alive.

So he does not give salaam to him when he meets him and nor does he respond to him if he salutes first (and he should continue doing this) until this person abandons his innovation and returns to the truth."

Source: Sharhus-Sunnah

Ibn Haanee an-Neesaabooree said:

"I witnessed Abu 'Abdullah, meaning Imam Ahmad, on his way to the mosque and a man from the skeptics (innovators) gave him salaam. He did not return salaam to him and the man gave him salaam again.

Imam Ahmad pushed him away and did not return salaam to him."

Source: Masaa'il Imaam Ahmad of Ibn Haanee an-Neesaabooree

Ibn Masud said:

"Indeed a person walks alongside and accompanies the one whom he loves and who is like him."

Source: Al-Ibaanah

Abu ad-Dardaa said:

"It is from the fiqh (understanding of a person) that he [chooses] those whom he walks with, whom he enters upon (visits) and whom he sits with."

Source: Al-Ibaanah

Yahyaa bin Katheer said:

"Sulaimaan bin Daawood – alaihis salaam –said: Do not pass a judgement over anyone with anything until you see whom he befriends."

Source: Al-Ibaanah

Musa bin Uqbah the Syrian approached Baghdad and this was mentioned to Imam Ahmad. So it was said:

"Look at whose residence he goes to and with whom he resides and finds shelter."

Source: Al-Ibaanah

Muhammad bin Ubaid al-Ghulaabee said:

"The Ahl ul-Ahwaa (People of Desires) hide everything except their intimate friendship and companionship."

Source: Al-Ibaanah

Mu'aadh bin Mu'aadh said to Yahyaa bin Sa'eed:

"O Abu Sa'eed! A person may hide his viewpoint from us, but he will not be able to hide that in his son, or his friend or in the one whom he sits with."

Source: Al Ibanah

Ibn 'Awn said:

"Those who sit with the People of Innovation are more severe upon us than the People of Innovation themselves."

Source: Al Ibanah

Yahyaa bin Sa'eed al-Qattaan said:

"When Sufyaan ath-Thawri came to Basrah he began to look into the affair of ar-Rabee' bin Subaih and the people's estimation of him. He asked them, 'What is his madhhab?', and they said, 'His madhhab is but the Sunnah'. He then asked, 'Who is his companionship?' and they replied, 'The people of Qadr' so he replied, 'In that case he is a Qadari'."

Source: Al-Ibaanah

Shaikh Ibn Baaz was asked:

"The one who praises Ahl ul-Bid'ah, is he to be counted amongst them?"

So Ibn Baaz replied, "Yes, there is no doubt about this, the one who praises them is one who actually calls to them".

Source: Aqwaal ul-Ulamaa Fee Sayyid Qutb

Ibn Taymiyyah said:

"It is obligatory to punish everyone who ascribes himself to them – the people of innovation – or who defends them, or who praises them, or who reveres their books, or who detests that they should be talked about, or who begins to make excuses for them by saying he does not understand what these words *mean or by saying that this person also authored another book and what is similar to these types of excuses, which are not made except by an ignoramus or a hypocrite. Rather, it is obligatory to punish everyone who knows of their condition and did not assist in repelling their evil, for repelling their evil is one of the greatest of obligations."*

Source: Majmoo' ul-Fataawaa

Shaikh Rabee' Ibn Hadee al-Madkhali wrote,

"Those whom it is permissible to criticize, disparage and warn the people against their harm:

First: The People of Innovation

It is permissible – rather obligatory – to speak about the people of innovation and warn against them and their fabrications, whether individually or as groups and whether they are absent or present. They include those among the Khawaarij, the Rawaafid, the Jahmiyyah, the Murji'ah, the Karaamiyyah and the people of Rhetoric – those whose knowledge of Kalaam (rhetoric) has brought them to corrupted and deviant beliefs, (Shaikh-ul-Islaam Ibn Taimiyyah has stated that there is a unanimous agreement amongst the Muslims on this) such as the rejection of all or some of Allaah's Attributes. So it is an obligation to warn against these types of people, their books and their misguided ways. And how great in number they are!

Likewise, the same applies to those who follow their methodology from the sects [and groups] of our time, such as those who separate themselves away from the people of Tawheed and Sunnah, oppose them and remain far away from their aspects of the methodology. In fact, they wage war against these aspects of the methodology and chase others away from it and its adherents (i.e. the scholars). The likes of these individuals are followed by those who support and defend them. And these followers of theirs mention their good qualities and praise them for it, praising their personalities and leaders. And they have preferred their (innovated) methodologies over the methodology of the people of Tawheed, the Sunnah and the Jamaa'ah!"

Source: Guidelines with regard to Criticizing Individuals and Groups]

Shaikh Salih al-Fawzan was asked:

"Is it obligatory to warn against the methodologies that oppose the methodology of the Salaf?

Salih Fawzan replied:

"Yes, it is obligatory to warn against the methodologies in opposition to that of the Salaf. This is from the nasihah(sincerity of purpose) that is due to Allaah, His Book, His Messenger, the leaders of the Muslims and the general folk. We caution against the people of evil and we warn against the methodologies in opposition to the methodology of Islaam and we explain the harmful effects of these matters to the people. We also encourage them to remain steadfast upon the Book and the Sunnah. All of this is obligatory."

Source: Al-Ajwibah al-Mufidah of Jamal bin Farihan al-Harithi (translated by Abu Iyaad)

Ibn Qudaamah said:

"The Salaf used to forbid sitting with the People of Innovations, looking into their books and listening to their words."

Source: Al-Aadaabus-Shareah

Imam Ahmed said concerning the rulers:

"And the killing of the one in power is not lawful, and nor is it permissible for anyone amongst the

people to revolt against him. Whoever does that is an innovator, (and is) upon other than the Sunnah and the (correct) path."

Source: Usool us-Sunnah

Aboo Dardaa said,

"Verily, the first (appearance) is the hypocrisy of a man is his censure and rebuke of his Ruler (Imaam)."

Source: At-Tamheed

Zaa'idah ibn Qudaamah who said:

"I said to Mansoor ibn ah-Mu'tamir, When I am fasting can I revile the Ruler (Sultaan)?' He said, 'No.' I then said, 'Then can I revile the People of Desires (i.e. Innovators)?' He said, 'Yes."

Source: Al-Hilyah of Abu Nu'aeem

Aboo Uthmaan as-Saaboonee said:

"And one of the distinguishing signs of Ahlus-Sunnah is their love for the Imaams of the Sunnah, its Scholars, its helpers, and its close allies, and their hatred for the leaders of innovation who call to the Hell- Fire and who direct their associates and companions to the home of torment destruction. Allaah, the Sublime, has adorned the hearts of Ahlus-

Sunnah, and the light of their hearts with love for the Scholars of the Sunna, as a bounty from Him, Whose Magnificence is perfect and Sublime.

Source: Aqeedatus-Salaf wa Ashaabul-Hadeeh

Abu Uthman As-Saaboonee also said:

"Let not my brothers, may Allaah protect them, be deceived by the abundance of the Ahlul-Bid'ah (the People of Innovation) and their large numbers (for verily, the abundance of the people of falsehood and the small number of the people of truth is a sign of the approach of the Day of Truth), since the Chosen Messenger said, "Indeed, amongst the signs of the Hour and its being close at hand, is that knowledge will diminish and ignorance will be widespread." (Bukhari, Muslim, Ahmed) And knowledge is the Sunnah and ignorance is bid'ah. And said, "Verily, faith will retreat to Madinah as a snake retreats into its burrow."

Source: Aqeedatus-Salaf wa Ashaabul-Hadeeh

Utbah al-Ghulaam said (regarding Ahlus Sunnah):

"*Whoever is not with us, then he is against us*".

Source: Al-Ibaanah

Ubayd al Jabiree said:

"Boycotting the people of innovations and boycotting the people of disobedience is the basic principle, until the one who is boycotted returns to uprightness and returns to the truth.

However, if this person who calls for boycotting is not obeyed and the people sway, due to what is with the innovators, then in this case boycotting them is not called to or commanded with. But it is for the individual who is harmed by the innovator to boycott him himself and beware of him. If you are asked then say: 'I don't feel safe from him regarding my religion. I don't feel safe from him for myself.'

If the benefit is greater to boycott the innovator, rebuke him, and warn against him, then they boycott him, rebuke him, and warn against him. If the harm is greater and the people are rallied together against Ahlus-Sunnah, then they do not boycott him. Rather they suffice with knowledge-based refutations.

Due to this I say to you, O weak ones from Ahlus-Sunnah: Hold fast to the Sunnah and do not argue with these people and do not dispute with them. Turn away from him."

Source: A collection of books of how to deal with the people of Bida by Ubayd Jabiree

Ibn Wahb reported Abdullah ibn Masud said:

"Acquire the knowledge before it is taken away and its being taken away is by the taking away of its people. Learn, for none of you knows when he will be in need of what he knows. You shall find some people who will think that they are inviting to the Book of Allah but they have actually thrown it behind their backs. So, acquire knowledge and beware of innovation, being unnecessarily stringent and delving. Take to what had earlier been established for you."

Source: Musannaf Abdir-Razzaq and Sunan Ad Daarimee

Waliullah Dahlawee said:

"For the first two centuries of the Hijra era people were not aware of any Madhhab, as fact of the matter, no Madhhab existed at all during that time. For that reason nobody knew any Madhhab and did not follow anyone except Allah's Messenger. Sahabah, Tabiun and the succeeding generation of the Tabiu followed their consensus and did not follow any individual. So anybody who ignores this consensus and opts all the sayings, verdicts and views of any one Imam and does not try to search and confirm it from the two basic sources, the Quran and Sunnah, is acting against the tenets of faith."

Source: Insaf fi Bayan Asbab al Ikhtilaf

Ahmad ibn Isaam reported that Zuhair ibn Nuaim said:

"This religion will not be established without 2 things: Patience and Certainty. It will not be established only with certainty; neither will it be established with patience only. In fact, Abu ad-Darda has given an example for them and said: The likeness of patience and certainty is as the likeness of two farmers who dig up the soil, if one sits down, the other sits down too."

Source: Sifatus Safwah by ibn al jawzi

Abu Amr Al-Awzai said:

"We go with the Sunnah, wherever it goes."

Source: Tareekh Ibn 'Asaakir

Sulaiman Taymi was crying before his death. Someone asked the reason for his crying and he replied:

"I am crying because of a sin I committed."

He was asked about the sin and he said:

"I passed by a Qadari and I greeted him; thus I fear that my Lord will hold me accountable for this action."

Source: Lumatul Itiqaad by Ibn Qudamah

Ibn Kathīr said:,

"As for Ahlus-Sunnah wal-Jamā'ah, then they say about every action and saying that is not established from the Sahābah that it is an innovation (bid'ah). That is because if it had been something good, they would have preceded us with it due to the fact that there is not a single trait from the traits of goodness except that they hastened to it."

Source: Tafsir Ibn Kathir 7278

Ibn Abdil Hadi said:

"And it is not allowed to innovate an interpretation of a verse or a sunnah which did not exist in the time

of the Salaf, nor did they know about it or clarify it for the Ummah. For verily this includes that they were ignorant about the truth in this, and they forgot about it and then this latecoming opposer was guided to it (while they were not)."

Source: As Sarim Al Munki 318

Sa'eed Ibn Jubayr said:

"That my son should accompany a sinful highway robber who is a Sunni is more beloved to me than him taking as his companion a worshipping innovator."

Source: "Al-Ibaanatus-Sughraa", by Ibn Battah in number 132.

Ibn Taymiyyah said:

"Accordance to the Sunnah and Ijmaa' (consensus), Ahlul-Bid'ah are worse than the people of sinful desires and lusts. The sins of the people of disobedience involves doing that which is forbidden such as stealing or fornicating or drinking wine or consuming wealth falsely. The sins of the people of innovation involves abandoning that which Allaah has commanded which is following of the Sunnah and the Jamaa'ah of the believers."

Source: "Majmoo al-Fataawaa"

Ibn Taymiyyah also said:

"And every statement in the religion of Islam that opposes what the Sahabah and Tabiun went forth upon (of religion), and none of them said it, rather, they said the opposite, then it is verily a statement of falsehood."

Source: Minhaj At-Tasis

Al-Imām Abu Muhammad Ibn Tamīm Al-Hanbalī said describing Imām Ahmad:

"He was harsh against ahlul-bid'ah and against the one who drew close to them if he did not abandon them, even if his 'aqīdah was correct."

Source: Tabaqāt al-Hanābilah of Abu Ya'lā

Ibn Qayyim said:

"Verily all of the people deviated during the time of Ahmad ibn Hanbal except a small group of people, and so they were the Jama'ah. And the judges, those who give fatwa, the Khalifah and his followers had all deviated, and Imam Ahmad alone was the Jama'ah. And when the minds of the people could not understand this they said to the Khalifah: 'O Amir al-Muminin, are you, your judges, your governors, the scholar and those who give fatwa all upon falsehood, and Ahmad alone is upon the truth?"

Source: Alam Al Muwaqqin

Abul-Ḥārith Aḥmad bin Muḥammad Al-Ṣā`igh, the close friend of Imām Aḥmad, reports:

"I asked Abū 'Abdillāh (Imām Aḥmad) about something that had occurred in Baghdād, and [because of which] some people were considering revolting [against the ruler]. I said, "O Abū 'Abdillāh, what do you say about taking part in the revolt with these people?" He decried it and started saying, "Subḥānallāh! The blood [of the people], the blood [of the people]! I do not believe in this and I do not tell others to do it. For us to suffer our situation in patience is better than the fitnah (tribulation) in which blood is spilt, property is taken, and the prohibited are violated (e.g. the honor of women). Do you not know what happened to the people (in the days of the previous fitnah)?" I said, "And the people today, Abū 'Abdillāh, are they not in fitnah [because of the ruler]?" He replied, "If so, it is a limited fitnah, but if the sword is raised, the fitnah will engulf everything and there will be no way to escape. To *suffer patiently this [current difficulty], where Allāh keeps your religion safe for you is better for you." I saw him decry revolting against the leaders, and say, "[Do not spill the people's] blood. I do not believe in this and I do not command it.""*

Source: Abū Bakr Al-Khallāl, Al-Sunnah 89.

Imam Ahmad said:

"And whoever rebels against a leader among the leaders of the Muslim, while the people have united behind him and they have acknowledged the Khilafah for him – no matter in what way, either being pleased with him or by force – then this rebel has divided the unity of the Muslims and he has opposed the narrations from the Messenger of Allah. So if the one who rebels against him (the leader) dies, then he dies the death of jahiliyyah. And it is not allowed for anyone among the people to fight against the leader, nor to rebel against him. So whoever does this, then he is an innovator who is not upon the Sunnah and the (straight) path."

Source: Usul as Sunnah by Imam Ahmad

Imam Malik said:

"The narrations never become few among a people, except that the desires (innovations) among them become plenty. And when the scholars become few, then the useless will emerge among the people."

Source Al Faqih wal Mutafaqqih

Muhammad Sultan Masoomi Khajnadee said:

"It is our foremost duty to avoid stubbornly following one particular Imam and his Madhhab. Concerning various religious matters, if anyone follows strictly one particular Madhhab, sect or person, surely he will not act upon many Hadith, rather there is possibility of going against many of the Hadith of the Prophet. Going against Hadith is infidelity and faithlessness."

Source: Hadiyyatus-Sultan ila Muslimi Biladil-Yaban

Abdullah ibn Abdur Rahman Abu Butyn said:

"And altogether then it is obligatory upon the one who wants good for himself not to speak about this issue, except with knowledge and clear proof from Allah. And he should be careful not to exit a man from Islam merely by his own understanding and what his intellect finds preferable. For verily, exiting

a man from Islam, or entering him therein is from the mightiest of affairs in the religion. And this issue has verily been explained sufficiently for us, just as other (issues) than it. Rather, the judgment of it in general is from the clearest of judgments in the religion. So the obligatory upon us is: Following, and leaving the innovating, (of new issues), just as Ibn Masud said: 'Follow and do not innovate, for you have verily been given sufficient...'

And verily did the Shaytan cause most of the people to err in this issue. So he made a group to become negligent, and they judged with Islam upon the one whom the texts of the Book, the Sunnah and the ijma all have pointed out his kufr. And he made others to go into the extreme, so they declared takfir upon the one whom the Book, the sunnah and the ijma all judged that he is a Muslim."

Source: Ad-Durar As-Saniyyah

Ibn Qayyim said there are three forbidden types of Taqlid:

"First, to turn away from what Allah has revealed and not resort to it, sufficing instead with following one's forefathers.

Second, doing taqlid of someone, not knowing if they are qualified so that they can be authoritatively followed.

Third, doing taqlid in the face of the proof being established, and it is clear that the proof opposes the authority being followed."

Source: I'lam al Muwaqqi'in

Muhammad Sultan Masoomi Khajnadee said:

"If we follow a specific Madhhab or a person, leaving aside a Hadith of the Prophet whose following is obligatory, who will be more misguided and unwise than us?

Regarding following a Madhhab, the last thing which can be said is only illiterate and unschooled individuals may follow an Imam without fixation of anyone in particular. An individual who loves all Imams equally and benefits from all of theme in various religious matters and acts upon the view which is more near to the Quran and Sunnah, this act of his is appreciable and is in accordance with the way of the faithful. He who deviates from the right way of Tabiun and sticks to one specific Imam and is prejudiced in his favor, is similar to one who leaves aside all Companions of the Prophet and follows one only, as the Shia and Khawarij do. This is the way of heretics and apostates. Quran, Hadith and Ijma denounces them."

Source: Hadiyyatus-Sultan ila Muslimi Biladil-Yaban

Abu Abbas al Khattab said:

"If you go out of your house and an innovator meets you, then return (home). For verily, the shaytan are surrounding him."

Source: Ibanah As Sughra by Ibn Battah

Abu Bakr Ajurri said:

"The people in previous and later times did not disagree regarding, that the Khawarij are evil people who are disobedient to Allah and His Messenger. And even if they pray, fast and strive in worship then this will not benefit them. They show that they command to the good and forbid the evil, but this will (also) not benefit them. Because they are a people who interpret the Quran according to what they desire and they disguise (falsehood) for the Muslims. And Allah verily warned us against them, and the Prophet warned us against them and the rightly guided

Caliphs after him warned us against them, and (so did) the Sahabah and those who followed them in goodness."

Source: Ash-Shariah

Musab ibn Sad ibn Abi Waqqas said:

"Do not sit with someone who is afflicted (in his religion) for he will verily do you wrong in one of two (things):

Either he will afflict you and you will follow him, or he will harm you before you leave him."

Source Dham Al Kalam 739

Imam Shafi'i said:

"So whoever judges upon the people with something other than what is apparent upon them, with the argumentation that what they show contains the possibility of something other than what they (actually) show-either with an evidence from them or without an evidence- for me he is not free from opposing the revelation and the Sunnah.

The judgments of Allah and His Messenger proves what I have described of (the fact that) it is not allowed for a judge to judge based upon assumption, even if he has an indication towards it that is close. So he should only judge how Allah has commanded him according to the clear proof which is established against the defendant or an acknowledgement from him in the clear issue. And just as Allah judged that whatever is apparent will get the (corresponding) judgment for it, then likewise He judged that whatever is apparent then it will get the judgment against it. Because He allowed the blood (of a person) based upon kufr even if it would be a statement. So it is not allowed in anything from the judgments between the slaves that he (the judge) judges therein according to anything other than the apparent and not (merely) indications."

Source: Al-Umm

Harb al Karmani said

"I said to Ahmad ibn Hanbal: 'Should a man sell his slave boy to the khawarij?

Ahmed ibn Hanbal said: No.

I said: Should he then sell foods and clothes to them?

Ahmed ibn Hanbal said: No.

I said: What if they force him? Can he then buy from them?

Ahmed ibn Hanbal said: He should not buy nor sell."

Source: As-Sunnah by Al Khallal

Salih Fawzan said:

"Do not side with the people of Fitnah, nor support them, aid them, or defend them because you will be their associate. If you defend them and consider their opinion correct, even if you did not go out with them, you will share the sin, aggression and transgression with them. Nowadays, there are those who support terrorists and vandalism, calling it Jihad in Allah's way. They killed the Muslims and those under treaty, destroying and terrorizing the Muslims saying or the one who supports them will say: 'This is Jihad in Allah's way' by way of defending them.

These people are similar to them in ruling- and Allah's refuge is sought- because they support them and consider their view to be correct. There is a great danger in this issue. You are partner with them (in sin) even if you did not carry weapon along with them, because you strengthen them and validate their opinion."

Source: Explanation of Sharus Sunnah by Imam Barbaharee

Al Hasan said:

"By Allah. Allah will never accept any deed that the innovator seeks nearness to Him with. Not the prayer, the fasting, the zakah, the Hajj, the Jihad, the Umrah or the Sadaqah.

Verily, the example of one of them is like a man who wants to travel here. Then he begins from here(the wrong place). So does that increase him in what he actually wanted except farness (from his goal)?!

Equal is the innovator because he does not increase by what he seeks nearness to Allah with, except in farness (from Allah)."

Source: Dhamm Al Kalam 605

Abu Mudhaffar As Samani said:

"Did the one who deviated deviate, and the one who was destroyed become destroyed, and the one who disbelieved disbelieve due to anything other than returning to thoughts and logical arguments, and following opinions from early and later times? And was the saved one saved by anything other than

following the Sunan of the messengers and the guiding leaders from the previous generations? And if this type of knowledge is for seeking something additional in the religion, then are there any additions after completion, except imperfections that returns to what is complete, just as the addition of limbs and fingers to two hands and two feet?

So let a person fear his Lord and he should verily not introduce into his religion what is not from it. And let him grab hold of the narration of the Salaf and the acceptable leaders, let him be upon their guidance and path. And let him bite down upon this with his molar teeth. And he should verily not cause himself to fall into a destruction by which he becomes misguided in the religion, and the truth becomes unclear for him. Allah will hold the leaders of misguidance and the callers to Hellfire to account, and on the Day of Resurrection they will not be helped."

Source: Al-Intisar li Ashab Al-Hadith

Muhammad ibn Abdul Wahhab said:

"Whoever shows Islam (outwardly) and we think that he has performed a naqid (nullifier of Islam), then we do not declare takfir upon him due to assumption, because yaqin (that which is certain) cannot be uplifted by assumption. And likewise we do not declare takfir upon the one whom we do not know any kufr from, due to a naqid which has been mentioned about him, while we did not confirm this."

Source: Muallafat Ash-Shaykh Imam Muhammad ibn Abdil Wahhab

Ibn Qayyim said:

"Whoever lays down a principle that has not been laid down by Allah and His Messenger, then this inevitably will lead him to rejecting the Sunnah or distorting it from its true place. And therefore the party of Allah and His Messenger have never laid down any principle other than what the Messenger came with. Because this is their fundamental principle upon which they rely, and it is the bond which they return to."

Source: Shafa Al-Alil

Abu Al-Aliyyah used to say:

"Learn Islam, and then when you have learned Islam, then learn the Quran. Then when you have learned the Quran, then learn the Sunnah. For verily the Sunnah of your Prophet is a Straight Path. And beware of deviating from the path left and right. And beware of these harmful desires (innovations) which cause enmity between the people."

Source Dham Al Kalam by al Harawi 806

Ibn Taymiyyah said:

"If an individual follows only one from the four Imams – Imam Abu Hanifah, Imam Shafii, Imam Malik, and Imam Ahmad bin Hanbal – and in connection with certain issue he finds a more positive and stronger argument than that of his own Shaikh or Imam, and leaves the weaker argument and embraces the strong one, this act of his is estimable. All religious scholars thought that it made no difference to the faith of the follower; on the other hand, it is said that he is dearer to the Prophet and nearer to the truth than a person who follows only one Imam eagerly and blindly and pays less heed to the Sunnah of the Prophet. He who follows Imam Abu Hanifah and thinks his Imam is always correct in every religious matter and everyone should follow him, and all other Imams who differ with him are not reliable, is certainly ignorant; such thinking may lead him to blasphemy and infidelity. We seek refuge with Allah from this evil."

Source: Fatawa Misriyah

Imam Ahmad said:

"The testimony of the Qadariyyah, Rafidah and everyone who invites to an innovation and argues for it, is not permissible."

Source: Turuq al Hukmiyyah 254

Talhah ibn Amr said:

"Do not sit with the people of desires, for verily they have an itch like the itch of scabies."

Source: Dham Al Kalam by Al harawi 1040

Harb said I heard Ahmad saying:

"If a man is an innovator and this is obvious or he announces this openly, then there is no backbiting of him. (speaking bad behind him behind his back is not considered backbiting)"

Source: Adab Ash Shariyyah by al Khallal

Muhammad ibn Juhadah said:

"Verily Amir Ash-Shabi was asked about something, but he did not have anything(evidences) regarding it. So it was said to him: 'Say your opinion.' He said: "And what can you do with my opinion?! Urinate on my opinion."

Source: Tabaqat al Kubra

Hammad ibn Zayd said: Yunus said to me:

"O Hammad, I verily see a young boy in all sorts of evil situations (of sins and disobedience), but I do not lose hope in his goodness. Until I see him accompany an innovator. At that point I know that he is destroyed."

Source: Ar Radd ala al Mubtadiah by Ibn al Banna 49

Ibn Awn said:

"A man does not innovate an innovation except that Allah takes shyness away from him, and installs harshness in him."

Source: Ibanah as Sughra by Ibn Battah

Said ibn Anbasah said:

"A man does not innovate an innovation, except that his chest is filled with hatred against the Muslims and his trustworthiness is taken away from him."

Source: Dhamm al Kalam 933

Imam Barbaharee said:

"Enjoining good and forbidding evil is with the hand, tongue and heart without the sword."

Source: Sharus Sunnah point 130

Al Hasan said:

"No innovator increases in worship, except that he increases in farness from Allah the exalted."

Source: Al Bida by Ibn Waddah 66

Bishr ibn Harith said:

"If your way is passing by an innovator then close your eyes before you reach to him."

Source: Ibanah As Sughra by Ibn Battah

When Abu Bakr ibn Ayyash was asked about the one who says the Quran is created, he said:

"Kafir. And whoever does not say that he is a kafir then he is also a kafir."

Then he said: "Does one doubt that the Jew and the Christian both are disbelievers? So whoever doubts regarding these that they are kuffar, then he (himself) is a kafir. And the one who says that the Quran is created is like them (the Jew and the Christian)."

Source: As Sunnah by Al Karmani

Imam Shafi'i said:

"Whoever speaks some words regarding the religion, or regarding something of these desires (bida) and he does not have an imam (leader) who said this before him from the Prophet and his Companions, then he has verily invented something new in Islam."

Source: Al Intisar li-Ashab al Hadith by Abu Al Mudhaffar As Sam'ani

Ibn Taymiyyah said:

"Anyone who makes it obligatory to follow a specific Imam should be asked to repent and give up following and if he is not prepared for it, he should be executed, since this is associating partners with Allah in setting down Shariah, which is one of the unique rights of the Lord."

Source: Kitab Al Qada of Insaf

Ibn Battah said:

"Know that from the characteristics of the believers among the people of truth is to believe in the correct narrations, receiving them with acceptance and to refrain from opposing them with analogy and forming a view based upon opinions and desires. For verily is belief to accept and the believer is the one who accepts. Allah said: 'But no, by your Lord, they can have no Faith, until they make you (O Muhammad) judge in all disputes between them, and find in themselves no resistance against your decisions, and accept with full submission.' (4:65) So from the signs of the believers is that they describe Allah with what He has described Himself with and with what His Messenger has described Him with from that which the scholars have conveyed, and what the trustworthy people of narration have narrated; those who are the hujjah (argument) in what they narrated of halal, haram, the sunan and the athar. And regarding that which has been correctly narrated from the Messenger of Allah it is not said 'How?' nor 'Why?', rather they follow and do not innovate, and they submit themselves and do not oppose, and they believe with certainty and they do not doubt nor are they skeptical."

Source: Ibn Battah in Ibanah Al Kubra

Ibn Mandah said:

"And likewise we say regarding what has gone forth of these narrations regarding the Attributes in this book of ours; we narrate them without tamthil (giving examples), tashbih (comparing), takyif (explaining), qiyas (analogy), and tawil (interpretation), according to what the truthful Salaf conveyed from the pure Sahabah from Mustafa. And we declare as ignorant whoever speaks about them except with a clear proof from the Messenger or a narration from a Sahabi who was present at (the time of) the revelation."

Source: Kitab At-Tawhid by Ibn Mandah

Imam Malik said:

"Whoever invents anything in this Ummah which our Salaf was not upon, then he has verily claimed that the Messenger of Allah has betrayed the religion. Because Allah says: 'Today I have fulfilled for you your religion.'(5:3) So whatever was not from the religion at that time will never be from the religion today."

Source: Kitab al Itisam by Ash-Shatibi

Imam Shafi'i said:

"My verdict upon the people of kalam is that they are hit with palm-branches and circulated through the tribes while it is called out regarding them: 'This is the punishment for the one who leaves the Book and the Sunnah and turns to kalam.'"

Source: Diyar A'lam An-Nubala by Dhahabi

Imam Ahmad said:

"It is upon you (to follow) the Sunnah, the hadith and that through which Allah benefits you. And be aware of engaging (in discussions), disputing and arguing. Because verily the one who loves the kalam (philosophy) will not succeed, and everyone who invents some kalam then his affairs in the end will be nothing but innovation, because the kalam does not invite to goodness."

Source: Al Ibanah by Ibn Battah

Imam Ahmad said:

"The fundamental principles of Sunnah for us are: Adhering to that which the Companions of Messenger of Allah were upon. And leaving innovations. And every innovation is misguidance. And leaving (both) the disputes (with the people of desires) and sitting with the people of desires (innovation). And leaving arguing, discussing and disputes in the religion."

Source: Usul As-Sunnah by Imam Ahmad

Imam Barbaharee said:

"If you see a man sitting with the followers of desires, warn him and educate him. But if he sits with him after having known, stay away from him because he is (equally) a follower of desires."

Source: Sharus Sunnah point 145

Salih Fulani said:

"There is a difference between a blind follower and a follower of evidence. A blind follower never enquires about the orders of Allah and His Prophet, he is always interested to discern the views of his Imam. Even if he finds that the views of his Imam are contrary to the Quran and Sunnah, he sticks to them. However a follower of evidence is not primarily interested to know the point of view of a particular Imam, but his query is more towards the understanding of the orders of Allah and the Prophet. A follower of evidence reaps benefit from all fields, where a blind follower sticks to one. This is the principal difference between the blind followers of later period and former righteous believers. One goes

after an Imam and his views, whereas the other picks up a right thing from wheresoever he finds."

Source Iqaz Hamam Ulul Absar

Abu Al Qasim al Lalakai said:

"I use as evidence for the madhahib of Ahlus Sunnah that which is mentioned in the Book of Allah regarding it and that which is narrated from the Messenger of Allah. So if I find something in both of them, then I mention it all. And if I find something in only one of them without the other, then I mention that. And if I don't find anything regarding it except from the Sahabah, those whom Allah and His Messenger has ordered to take as an example, and to follow their words, and to seek light from their lights, due to them testifying the revelation and their knowledge regarding the meaning of the interpretations, then I use that as evidence. But if there is no narration regarding it from a companion, then from those who followed them in goodness; those in whose words there is a cure and guidance. And worshipping Allah with their opinion is nearness to Allah and closeness (to Him). So if we see that they agreed upon something then we rely on it. And whoever's opinion they criticized, or they refuted his

bidah (innovation) or they declared takfir upon him, then we will judge with that and believe in it. And there continue to be, from the Messenger of Allah until this day of ours a people who protect this way and take it as their religion. And verily is the person destroyed who turns away from this path, due to his ignorance regarding the path of following (the narrations)."

Source: Usul Itiqad Ahlus Sunnah by Al Lalakai

Abu Said Ad-Darimi said:

"Allah praised the tabiun in His Book, when He said: 'And the first forerunners (in faith) among the Muhajirin and the Ansar and those who followed them in goodness. Allah is pleased with them.' So He testified to their following of the Sahabah, and them deserving the Pleasure of Allah due to their following of the Companions of Muhammad. And the word is united among all the Muslims that they were called At-Tabiun and they continue to narrate from them with the chains of narration, just as they narrated from the Sahabah. And they use them as an argument in the affairs of their religion, and they consider their opinion more binding than the opinion of those who came after them, due to the name which they deserved *from Allah and from the Jama'ah of the Muslims, who called them the followers of the Companions of Muhammad."*

Source: An-Naqd by Ad-Darimi

Al Awzai said:

"And I advise you to one thing, which verily will remove the doubt from you, and by holding on to it you will achieve the Straight Path, if Allah wills: You look into what the Companions of the Messenger of Allah were upon in this issue. Then if they differed in it, then take whatever agrees with you from their sayings. In that case you will be at ease in the issue. And if they agreed in the issue upon one opinion, and no-one among them deviated from it, then to where is the madhhab that opposes them? Because verily the destruction lies in disagreeing with them. Because they have verily never agreed upon one issue, and then the guidance (truth) has been in something else than it. And verily did Allah praise those who followed their example, when He said: 'And those who followed them in goodness.' (9:100) And be aware of everyone who interprets the Quran to something else than what they were upon."

Source: Ibn Battah in Ibanah al Kubra

Muhammad sultan masoomi khajnadee said:

"Different Madhahib are personal and private opinions, judgments and interpretations of legal points according to religious scholars and jurists. Allah and his prophet have not ordered us to follow these opinions and interpretations. There is a possibility of being correct or incorrect in their opinions and interpretations. There are many issues on which Imams had different views and they explained them according to their own reasons and speculations. But when the truth came to their knowledge, they reconsidered their own opinion and accepted the truth. They never stuck to their opinion when a true Hadith came to their knowledge.

If anyone accepts Islam he has only to testify that there is no god but Allah and Muhammad is His Messenger, to perform the prayers five times a day, to pay Zakat, to fast in the month of Ramadan and to make the pilgrimage to the House of Allah if he is able to do so. It is certainly not necessary for him to follow any Madhhab, Hanafi, Shafi'i, Maliki or Hanbali. If he does so, in the eyes of Islamic law, he will be considered a wrongdoer, prejudiced and sinful person, and will be treated among those who divided the religion of Islam into different sects."

Source: Hadiyyatus-Sultan ila Muslimi Biladil-Yaban

Ahmad ibn Hanbal said:

"From the narrow-mindedness in a man's knowledge is that he blindly follows men in his creed."

Source: Talbis Iblis

Al Baghawi said:

"Verily have the Sahabah, the Tabiun and their followers passed by upon this, (all) having consensus and agreeing upon having enmity for the people of innovation and boycotting them."

Source: Sharh us Sunnah by Al Baghawi

Al Shatibi said:

"If you debate the religious innovators and men of inclinations who speak in Sunnah, and attest your argument with Hadiths or traditions, they would claim that this disagrees with the consensus. That is because they transmit only from some jurisprudents of Medina or Kufah, for instance, and claim consensus, depending only on their lacking knowledge of the statement of the Scholars, and daring to refute the acts of Sunnah with their

opinions. Whenever the authentic Hadiths in support of some rulings and judgments are related to anyone of them he would have no way out except to claim that no one among the scholars has adopted it. That is because he lacks sufficient knowledge, which enables him to learn that so many others than those scholars upon whom he depends, have adopted it, even among the Companions, the Tabi'is and their followers."

Source: Kitab Itisam

Muhammad bin AbdurRahmaan Ibn Abi Dhib read a Hadeeth and it was said to him:

'Do you take this opinion?'

"So he hit the man's chest and screamed. And he said: 'I narrate to you from the Messenger of Allaah, and you say that should I accept this? Yes I take this, and that is obligatory for me, and upon everyone who hears it. Indeed Allaah chose Muhammad from the people and guided them by him, and upon his hands, so it is upon the creation to follow him, the obedient ones or the disobedient ones, there is no exit for the Muslim from this."

Source: Siyaar 'Alaam an-Nubala

Jafar bin Ahmed bin Sinan said: 'I heard my father saying:

'There is not a Mubtadi' (innovator) except that he hates the companions of Hadeeth. And if a man innovates a Bida then the sweetness of the Hadeeth is torn out from his heart.'

Source: Siyaar 'Alaam an-Nubala

ar-Rabeeya' bin Sulayman said:

A man asked ash- Shaafi'ee about a Hadeeth of the Prophet then the man said to him: 'And what is your opinion?'

Imam ash- Shaafi'ee trembled, shuddered and said: Which sky will shade me and which earth will carry me if I narrate a Hadeeth from the Messenger of Allaah and say an opinion other than that of the Hadeeth.' And he said: 'If you find a Sunnah of the Messenger of Allaah then follow it and do not turn to the saying of anyone.'

Source: Hilyatul Awliya

Abdullah bin Zayd Al-Numayrī reports that Al-Ḥasan Al-Baṣrī said:

"They (the heretics) were destroyed by their inability in Arabic (al-'ujmah)."

Source: Al-Bukhārī Al-Tārīkh Al-Kabīr

Al Shatibi said:

"The masters of practical religious innovations for the most part, do not like to debate anyone, nor argue with any Scholar about what they seek to achieve, for fear of scandal that they would find no Shariah support for their opinions. It is always their habit that whenever they find a strong Scholar, they would adulate and flatter him, and whenever they find an ignorant layman they would baffle him with problems in Shariah to shake his beliefs and put him to confusion as regard the religion. Once the signs of confusion appear on him, they would soon throw on him their religious innovations by degrees, one by one, and accuse the men endued with knowledge of being devotees of this world, who dedicate themselves to it, versus those (religious innovators) who are the devotees of Allah selected by Him apart from others. Furthermore they may present to him some statements belonging to the extremist Sufis as witnesses to what they claim, until they lead him to the fire of Hell. But by no means would they come to the matter in the right way, and debate with the Scholars endued with knowledge over it."

Source: Kitab Itisam

Ata al Khurasani said:

"Allah barely allows for the innovator to repent."

Source: Dhamm Al kalam 794

Imaam Ibn Qayyim said:

"From the conditions of repentance (tawbah) of the caller to bid'ah is that he makes clear that which he used to call to from innovation and misguidance, and that guidance is its opposite, just as Allaah has laid down the conditions of repentance for the People of the Book who's sin was concealing that which Allaah had revealed of clarification and guidance so as to misguide the people with that. So they had to rectify the deeds in themselves, and to clarify to the people that which they concealed from them, so Allaah said:

"Indeed, those who conceal what We sent down of clear proofs and guidance after We made it clear for the people in the Scripture – those are cursed by Allah and cursed by those who curse – except for those who repent and correct themselves and make evident [what they concealed]. Those, I will accept their repentance, and I am the Accepting of repentance, the Merciful." [al-Baqarah: 159-160]"

"Just as Allaah laid down the conditions of the repentance of the hypocrites whose sin was that they [tried] corrupting the hearts of the weak believers whilst they showed bias in favor and adherence to the Yahood and the polytheists who had enmity to the Messenger– and with that they made themselves seem apparently as Muslims, only as a show, to be seen and heard. So upon them was to rectify in replacement of their corruption, and to hold fast to Allaah in replacement of holding fast to the unbelievers from the People of the Book and the polytheists, and to make their Religion sincerely for Allaah rather than just to show and be heard by the people – so this is how the conditions of repentance and its reality is understood, and Allaah's Aid is sought."

Source: Uddatus Sabireen

Abu Talib al Mishkani said:

It was mentioned to Imam Ahmad bin Hanbal that al Karabisi mentioned the saying of Allah in the Quran surah 5 verse 3:

"Today I have perfected for you all of your religion."

And Karabisi said: "Had our religion been perfected for us there would not have been these differences of opinion!"

So Ahmad bin Hanbal said: This is clear disbelief(kufr)!

Source: Al Maqsid Arshad

It was mentioned to Ahmad Ibn Hanbal that a man from the people of knowledge made a mistake and erred, and that he had repented from his mistake. So Imām Ahmad said:

"Allāh will not accept that from him until repentance and recantation from his [erroneous] saying is made apparent — and he announces that he said such-and-such, and that he has repented to Allāh, the most High, for his saying and has recanted from it. If he makes that apparent, then his repentance is accepted."

Then Ahmad Ibn Hanbal recited:

"Except for those who repent and make right their mistake and openly declare [the truth which they concealed]." Quran 2 verse 160

Source: Ibn Rajab in Dhayl 'Alā Tabaqāt Al-Hanābilah

Imām Ash-Shāfi'i said:

"I never debated anyone whom I knew to be established upon innovation."

Al-Bayhaqi commented upon this statement and said:

"That is because the one who established upon innovation very rarely returns from his bid'ah. Indeed debating is with the one who is hoped will return to the truth when the truth is made clear to him."

Source: Manāqib ash-Shāfi'i

Ibn Muflih said:

"As for innovation, then repentance from it is by affirming it, and to recant from it, and to believe in the opposite of what he believed previously…" Then he said: "It has been narrated from Al-Marrūdhī that Ahmad Ibn Hanbal said: "When a innovator repents, then leave him in that state for a year until his repentance is verified to be correct."

He used as a proof the narration of Ibrāhīm At-Taymī when the people differed with him concerning Sabīgh Ibn 'Asal (the innovator) when he warned from sitting with him. So after a year had passed, he said, *"Now you may sit with him but be cautious of him."*

Source: Al-Ādāb Ash-Sharī'ah

Hasan ibn Shaqiq said:

"We were with Ibn Mubarak when a man came to him. So he (Ibn Mubarak) said to him: 'Are you that Jahmi?' He said: Yes.

He (Ibn Mubarak) said: When you go out from here, then never come back to me.

The man said: But I am repenting. He (Ibn Mubarak) said: No. Not until you show from your repentance the same as what you showed from your innovation."

Source: Ibanah As Sughra by Ibn Battah

Sufyaan Ath-Thawri said:

"Innovation is more beloved to Iblis than sin, since a sin may be repented from but innovation is not repented from."

Source: Sharh Usool I'tiqaad Ahlis-Sunnah wal-Jamaah 238

It was said to imam Ahmad bin Hanbal:

"A man fasts, prays and stays in seclusion at the masjid, is that more beloved to you or if he speaks against the people of bida?"

He replied:

"If he fasts, prays and stays in seclusion he benefits only himself, but if he speaks against the people of innovation, that benefits all the Muslims so that is better."

Source: Majmoo Al-Fatawa

Ibn Abbas said:

"No year comes upon the people without making a religious innovation and causing an act of Sunnah to die, until (a time will come) the religious innovations will survive and the acts of Sunnah will die."

Source: Kitab Al Bida by Ibn Waddah

Muhammad Ibn Fadl Al Balkhi said:

"Islam disappears for four reasons: not to act upon what they know, to act upon what they know not, not to learn, and to prevent the people from learning."

Source: Siyar Alam An-Nubala

Mansur Ibn Al Mu'tamar said:

"Allah sent Adam with the Shariah. So the people were upon the Shariah of Adam until zandaqah(hypocrisy and innovations) emerged. Then the Shariah of Adam disappeared. Then Allah sent Noah with the Shariah. Then the people were upon the Shariah of Noah, and nothing made it disappear except zandaqah. Then Allah sent Abraham and the people were upon the Shariah of Abraham until zandaqah emerged. Then the Shariah of Abraham disappeared. Then Allah sent Moses and the people were upon the Shariah of Moses until zandaqah emerged. Then the Shariah of Moses disappeared. Then Allah sent Jesus and the people were upon the Shariah of Jesus until zandaqah emerged. Then the Shariah of Jesus disappeared. Then Allah sent Muhammad with the Shariah. So it is not feared that this religion will disappear, except due to zandaqah."

Source: Ibanah As Sughra by Ibn Battah

adh-Dhufayri said:

"And it is for this reason that the Salaf would give so much importance to this mighty fundamental – And that is to boycott Ahlul-Bid'a (People of Innovations) and this is from the most important of affairs, and they would give it the greatest of concern. Their biographies are filled with reports of them boycotting Ahlul-Bid'a, and disgracing them and humiliating them – and were I to write that which has been narrated from them in that regard it would reach a volume, rather volumes."

Source: Ijmaa al-'Ulamaa 'alal-Hajri wat-Tahdheeri min ahlil-Ahwaa

Mujāhid said:

"I do not know which of the two blessings of Allah upon me is greater, that He guided me to Islam or that He saved from [following] these desires(innovations)?!"

Source: Dhamm Al-Kalām wa Ahlihi 786.

Awn bin Abdullaah said:

"Whoever dies upon Islaam and the Sunnah, then he has the glad tidings of all that is good."

Source: Sharh Usool I'tiqaad by Laalkaee

Ibn 'Awn was saying on his deathbed:

"[Cling to] the Sunnah, the Sunnah and beware of Bid'ah." till he died

Source: Sharhus-Sunnah by al-Barbahari

www.ingramcontent.com/pod-product-compliance
Lightning Source LLC
Chambersburg PA
CBHW050253010526
44107CB00003B/307